Wittgenstein, Concept Possession and Philosophy

Wittgenstein, Concept Possession and Philosophy

A Dialogue

H. A. Knott

First published in 2007 by
PALGRAVE MACMILLAN
Houndmills, Basingstoke, Hampshire RG21 6XS and
175 Fifth Avenue, New York, N.Y. 10010
Companies and representatives throughout the world.

PALGRAVE MACMILLAN is the global academic imprint of the Palgrave
Macmillan division of St. Martin's Press, LLC and of Palgrave Macmillan Ltd.
Macmillan® is a registered trademark in the United States, United Kingdom
and other countries. Palgrave is a registered trademark in the European
Union and other countries.

ISBN-13: 978–0–230–50682–4 hardback
ISBN-10: 0–230–50682–8 hardback

This book is printed on paper suitable for recycling and made from fully
managed and sustained forest sources.

A catalogue record for this book is available from the British Library.

Library of Congress Cataloging-in-Publication Data

Knott, H. A. (Hugh A.), 1949–
    Wittgenstein, concept possession, and philosophy : a dialogue / H. A. Knott.
        p. cm.
    Includes bibliographical references (p.) and index.
    ISBN 0–230–50682–8 (cloth)
        1. Wittgenstein, Ludwig, 1889–1951. 2. Conceptualism 3. Plato.
    4. Form (Philosophy) I. Title.

B3376.W564K56 2007
192—dc22   2006049428

10 9 8 7 6 5 4 3 2 1
16 15 14 13 12 11 10 09 08 07

Printed and bound in Great Britain by
Antony Rowe Ltd, Chippenham and Eastbourne

To my mother and to the memory of my father

Ummon's verse:

A sentence which does not reveal its meaning
Attains its end before being spoken.
You press forward with mouth a-chatter
Betraying your not knowing what to do.

(Trans. R. H. Blyth, Zen & Zen Classics)

Contents

Abbreviations of Works by Wittgenstein

BB   *The Blue and Brown Books*, ed. R. Rhees (Oxford: Blackwell, 1969).

BT   'Philosophy', Sections 86–93 of the "Big Typescript" in *Philosophical Occasions 1912–1951*, eds J. C. Klagge and A. Nordmann, trans. C. G. Luckhardt and M. A. E. Aue (Indianapolis & Cambridge: Hackett, 1993).

CE   'Cause and Effect: Intuitive Awareness', in *Philosophical Occasions 1912–1951*, eds J. C. Klagge and A. Nordmann (Indianapolis & Cambridge: Hackett, 1993).

CV   *Culture and Value*, eds G. H. von Wright and H. Nyman, trans. P. Winch (Oxford: Blackwell, 1998).

LW1   *Last Writings on the Philosophy of Psychology*, Volume I, eds G. H. von Wright and H. Nyman, trans. C. G. Luckhardt and M. A. E. Aue (Oxford: Blackwell, 1990).

LW2   *Last Writings on the Philosophy of Psychology*, Volume II, eds G. H. von Wright and H. Nyman, trans. C. G. Luckhardt and M. A. E. Aue (Oxford: Blackwell, 1992).

NFL   'Notes for Lectures on "Private Experience" and "Sense Data" ', in *Philosophical Occasions 1912–1951*, eds J. C. Klagge and A. Nordmann, trans. R. Rhees (Indianapolis & Cambridge: Hackett, 1993).

OC   *On Certainty*, eds G. E. M. Anscombe and G. H. von Wright, trans. D. Paul and G. E. M. Anscombe (Oxford: Blackwell, 1974).

PI   *Philosophical Investigations*, eds G. E. M. Anscombe and R. Rhees, trans. G. E. M. Anscombe (Oxford: Blackwell, 2001).

RFGB 'Remarks on Fraser's *Golden Bough*', in *Philosophical Occasions 1912–1951*, eds J. C. Klagge and A. Nordmann, trans. J. Beversluis (Indianapolis & Cambridge: Hackett, 1993).

RFM   *Remarks on the Foundations of Mathematics*, eds G. H. von Wright, R. Rhees and G. E. M. Anscombe, trans. G. E. M. Anscombe (Oxford: Blackwell, 1978).

ROC   *Remarks on Colour*, ed. G. E. M. Anscombe, trans. L. L. McAlister and M. Schättle (Oxford: Blackwell, 1977).

RPP1   *Remarks on the Philosophy of Psychology*, Volume I, eds G. E. M. Anscombe and G. H. von Wright, trans. G. E. M. Anscombe (Oxford: Blackwell, 1980).

RPP2   *Remarks on the Philosophy of Psychology*, Volume II, eds G. H. von Wright and H. Nyman, trans. C. G. Luckhardt and M. A. E. Aue (Oxford: Blackwell, 1980).

TLP   *Tractatus Logico-Philosophicus*, trans. D. F. Pears and B. F. McGuinness (London: Routledge, 1971).

Z   *Zettel*, eds G. E. M. Anscombe and G. H. von Wright, trans. G. E. M. Anscombe (Oxford: Blackwell, 1981).

Acknowledgements

This book is based on a thesis for the degree of Doctor of Philosophy, which I undertook at the University of Wales, Swansea. I would like to record my indebtedness to the late R. W. 'Dick' Beardsmore without whose support and encouragement I would almost certainly never have embarked upon this work and who supervised the thesis until his untimely death in 1997. As my teacher during my undergraduate years, and supervisor of my M.A. thesis during the 1970s at the University College of North Wales, Bangor, Dick was largely responsible for such understanding as I have of the philosophy of Wittgenstein. I would also like to thank Howard Mounce, who took over the supervision of the thesis following Dick's death, for the invaluable advice and critical comment I have received from him since.

I am indebted to the anonymous reviewer for suggesting many improvements and especially for identifying those elements that were only of self-indulgent interest.

Much of the material in Dialogue 4 was first published in an article 'Before Language and After' in the journal *Philosophical Investigations*. I am grateful to the publishers, Blackwell, for permission to reuse this material here. I am also grateful to Blackwell for permission to quote extracts from Wittgenstein's *Philosophical Investigations*.

Prologue

The radical view of Wittgenstein's achievement in philosophy is that it signalled an end to the age-old dominance of a tradition based on opposing theories: rationalist versus empiricist, idealist versus realist, correspondence versus coherence theories of truth, and many more. This view of Wittgenstein's philosophy is not currently popular; but it is my view and it is the aim of this book to maintain it. It is usual to describe Wittgenstein's prime preoccupation in philosophy as being with language. This is not wrong, but I have preferred to make my approach in terms of *concept possession*; for I think that it is by this avenue that questions central to an understanding of the human form of life can be seen more clearly to cross with questions of the nature of philosophy. Together they force the departure from the former tradition.

This claim about the nature of Wittgenstein's achievement is, of course, also a claim about where philosophy should be going in the future.—And my purpose is indeed to look forward. But it is also a claim about Wittgenstein's relation to the past. And so, while wishing to avoid burdening both the reader and myself with heavyweight scholarly comparisons, it did nevertheless seem apposite to *frame* my discussions with a glimpse down that long perspective to the origins of Western Philosophy.

Among these opposing theories, the dichotomy between rationalism and empiricism is perhaps the most fundamental. The struggle between the two has certainly been a dominant feature in philosophical debate for much of the time since Descartes. But its origins are more ancient. Indeed, if asked to choose just one theory to epitomize—or even caricature—rationalism, most would probably still opt for Plato's Theory of Forms, which still stands out vividly at the gateway to Western philosophy. The reasons for its status are partly historical—for the influence it has had throughout the development of Western culture, both within and beyond philosophy—but no doubt also because of the very simplicity of its outlines and the extremeness of its contrast with empiricism.

The rationalism in the Theory derives from the fact that reason resides in the Forms, which exist as independent intellectual objects *prior* to experience. And what a Form holds within itself is the immutable essence of the nature of a thing. Of this we have direct knowledge; indeed, it is *only* the Forms that we can truly be said to *know*. The world and the objects of sense experience, on the other hand, are what they are only to the extent that they participate in the Forms; and we learn of them and form beliefs about them only to the extent that they *recall* the Forms. This is the theory of learning by Recollection. So the Theory of Forms is a part of a theory of knowledge at the heart of which is a rationalist theory of ideas or concepts: of what they are, of our relation to them and of their relation to the world.

The Theory also contains within it a conception of the nature of the soul and, combined with this, a profound view of the nature of philosophy. The soul is conceived of as co-extensive with the Forms and sharing their immutable essences. But unlike the Forms, the soul is also conceived of as corruptible by contact with the body and the world. Hence, it is through the purifying effect of reflecting upon the Forms away from these influences, which is the way of philosophy, that the soul finally emancipates itself from the body and the world and prepares itself for eternal life after death.

Now a comparison in *outline* between the philosophies of Plato and Wittgenstein is clear. Wittgenstein's philosophy too is an investigation into the nature of human knowledge, with at its heart an account of the nature of concepts, of our relation them and of their relation to the world. It is also true that the possession of concepts through the acquisition of language is, in his philosophy, *constitutive* of our natures as persons or souls. Moreover, Wittgenstein's reflections on the nature of concepts and the life with language are of a piece with his views on the nature and purpose of philosophy.—For Wittgenstein too, philosophy was a path to self-knowledge. And so, even across the great period of time that separates them, there remain these similarities.

But as regards the *content* lying within that outline, the contrast with Plato's vision could hardly be greater; so great in fact that it takes us beyond even the dichotomy between rationalism and empiricism—of which Wittgenstein's philosophy is equally critical. For the conceptual world and the soul, far from being separated from the body, experience and the world, are now seen together with these as aspects of the one thing: the human form of life. It should be impressed here that 'form of life' is not a theoretical construct but is a 'grammatical' device. It is a way of saying that the concepts of language, meaning, concept, reason, person, soul, experience, action and reality are all interdependent.— They are *internally* related to each other, which means that they are only intelligible in relation to one another. The problems of philosophy arise out of a failure to see clearly into these relations; and so its work is no more and no less than their elucidation. This is why there is no longer any room for any 'transcendental' perspective,—and hence why it marks the end of theoretical explanation in philosophy.

It is because of these similarities and contrasts, and because of its historical status, that Plato's Theory of Forms was the obvious choice to provide the long perspective I sought. However, as I have implied, the reader should not expect an in-depth account of Plato's Theory of Forms and its relation to the philosophy of Wittgenstein. This is because the aims and objectives of the book remain contemporary and philosophical rather than of the history of ideas. And so to keep this reference to the past alive throughout but without intruding, I also chose to present my thoughts in the form of a dialogue between Lato and Crates—the *alter egos* of Plato and Socrates, whose names I have fictionalized precisely to keep them a part of the frame but out of the picture.

The choice of dialogue form was also made with the intention of allowing the reader more ease in following the intricacies of the arguments. At times the form is exploited to the full with question and answer and critical interventions; but elsewhere and for a lot of the time it serves simply as an additional way of punctuating the arguments—which I think is reason enough for its choice.

H. A. Knott
Menai Bridge, Anglesey
April 2006

Dialogue 1   Synopsis

1   Introduction

CRATES: Lato, in the nearly two and a half millennia since you began to write down the philosophical thoughts and ideas that you and I evolved together, we have witnessed great transformations in our subject. But throughout much of this period, and until very recently, we have never felt able to conclude that what we established as fundamental in the study of philosophy—notwithstanding the contributions of our predecessors— had been superseded or that a genuinely new chapter had been opened. Indeed, it was with some satisfaction that we heard the words of a philosopher of the early twentieth century proclaim that the whole of philosophy to date had been merely 'a series of footnotes' to our own work.[1]

A philosopher from the previous century had described the progress of philosophy as one in which the true philosophers called across the centuries to each other from mountain tops, while the mediocrities bus- ied themselves on the lower slopes.[2]

LATO:—Which we recall with irony. The man thought that philosophy went into *decline* with us!

CRATES: Yet, the image both appealed to us and contained a truth. For it was through hearing another's words calling back to us that we believe we heard the turning of a new chapter and witnessed a new departure.

As a result of this experience, we agreed that you should cross over to engage with him and investigate more closely the thoughts and ideas that seemed to us, from afar at least, to demand such changes in our thinking. Many such visits followed, Lato, and over the course of these last few months we have devoted much of our time to discussing your meetings with Wittgenstein and his followers—and indeed with some of his opponents too. These discussions have moved over such a range of topics that we have felt ourselves in danger of losing track of where our philosophical travels have taken us. For this reason, we believe we have arrived at the point where we should explore in a rather more systematic way the themes that have most caught our attention and put these on the record. We would also like to think that, arising out of these discussions, we have been able to develop some new thoughts of our own. This too is an important reason for setting these ideas down.

LATO: Before we continue, Crates, there is a further irony in connection with that philosopher of the nineteenth century. He blamed us above all for making a 'tyrant of *reason*'—both in philosophy and in life— for 'producing a permanent *daylight*—the daylight of reason'.[3] This we made in opposition to *instinct* as a cure for its anarchy and darkness.[4] But for him, instinct was key to the noble character of our philosophical predecessors, and our 'cure' a sign of *descent*.[5] He also observed instinct to be at the very origin of *thought* and *philosophical thinking*.[6] Our irony, as the reader will find out, is that this observation—pre-echoing Wittgenstein's more thoroughly reasoned call—anticipated both that which will take us forward to new ground *and* that which will return us to the *ascent* of former times: 'happiness and instinct are one'![7]

CRATES: Lato, the format for our book is straightforward. In this first dialogue, we shall swiftly traverse the main topics and our conclusions. This will give the reader an overview of where we are going; and it will be followed by six further dialogues. These are not a literal record but are composed quite deliberately from the conversations between ourselves that arose out of your recollections of your meetings.

So without further ado, let's get straight on to indicate our main areas of interest and to outline how these discussions will unfold.

LATO: Crates, you have spoken of *themes* in his thinking. I think it would be right to say that there is one theme especially that unifies our various interests. Looking at Wittgenstein as we do across such an expanse of time and across such a history of philosophical thinking, we are most struck by the way he has reoriented our attitude towards the *nature* of philosophy and philosophical problems. Even in our own time we might have said that when we struggle in philosophy we are, from the beginning, struggling with *Forms*—with their content, their nature, our relations to them and their relations to the world.[8] Moreover, we see a clear parallel between our view that philosophy is the purification of our knowledge of the Forms through reflection and Wittgenstein's view that the aim of philosophy is to obtain a clearer reflective understanding of our concepts. For our Theory of Forms is nothing other than what might now be called a theory of concepts. However, there is one major difference: *our* Forms had an independence from the contingencies of life—as did our souls as the vehicles of their reflection—while what we have found most persuasive in Wittgenstein, and what marks him off so decisively from our own former way of thinking, is his perception that the existence of concepts is of necessity a direct function of the *lives and the culture in which they are embedded*. Moreover, we acknowledge that Wittgenstein's account of concepts is in an important sense *not* a theory. These differences are of great importance, as they change much in the way we must conduct ourselves while doing philosophy. It is true that over the course of time we came to loosen the strictness of the division between our knowledge of Forms and our engagement with sense experience.[9] But it remained the case that for *us* philosophy was the purest mode of reflection, the purest mode of detachment from the conditions of life and a preparation for death.[10]

Against the criticisms of both our elders and our contemporaries, we wanted to maintain our conviction that the Forms existed in their own right, because we believed that without such Forms discourse would not be possible.[11] But we confess that we never could demonstrate how knowledge of the Forms was possible nor how they related to particular beings. Since that time, many new kinds of sophistry have flourished— mostly under the name of empiricism and what came to be called 'positivism'—and denied the reality of the Forms, our knowledge of them and the knowledge of the world that they contain. Against these influences, we have admired especially the efforts of Immanuel Kant to reinstate the priority of certain concepts above experience—*space, time, cause, goodness*, and others as well. But he too was not able to avoid anal- ogous difficulties to our own;—difficulties that arise for as long as we treat the individual as responsible *before himself* for his knowledge of concepts and their relations to particular things and, linked with this, for as long as we treat them, either implicitly or explicitly, as existences in their own right.

We believe that Wittgenstein resolved many of our former difficulties through a more thorough examination of the relations between language, concepts and the life that is lived. In this way he was able finally to emancipate our notion of Forms into an understanding of *concepts* that discards what can no longer be supported but which does recognize and retain some of those essential features which we acknowl- edged. As a result of his efforts, we may retain, with respect to our con- cepts, certain notions of priority and necessity. We may also demonstrate a knowledge of them—though one which is neither empirical nor, in some illegitimate and other-worldly way, *transcendental*. Moreover, we may maintain that these concepts, while not existing 'in their own right', nevertheless contain *in their own right* a knowledge of the world, but again a knowledge originating neither from somewhere beyond this world nor by observing it.[12] And finally, and perhaps most importantly, we may at last understand the harmony between our concepts and our souls,—that they are fabricated of one another.

In an important sense our notion of philosophy as *reflection* lives on in Wittgenstein's philosophy, but no longer as a reflection in eternity on the essence of those Forms, rather as a remembrance in our everyday minds of an understanding already given in our concepts, an understanding that neither transcends experience nor is read from it. This may seem to detract from the spirit of our former conception of philosophy. Yet, in other respects, we feel the more liberated that our 'seeing the world aright' might be realized in the midst of life rather than in going apart from it.[13] We held, at that time, that the body was but a hindrance to knowledge; but it is *truth* that purifies, and if the body and its movements are, after all, a part of the vehicle for seeking truth, then return to the body we must.

CRATES: And so truth and the soul are indivisible from *this* life.

LATO: Indeed.

Given this shared placement of Forms or concepts at the heart of our philosophies, what interests us now is to explore what is novel in Wittgenstein's investigations into how our concepts are positioned in our lives, of what our relations to them are—both in our handling of them in daily life and in our handling of them in philosophy—and of what their relations are to the world.

On the other hand, as I have already intimated, this is not the whole of our ambition. Wittgenstein himself has come in for hard criticism. Much of this has been retrograde in our opinion, but some—the best and most positive criticism—has been to the point. Perhaps the most pertinent issued from one of his closest colleagues and more fervent apologists, Rush Rhees. His contributions especially have become a point of departure for our own attempts to move forward Wittgenstein's insights in the directions that are of most interest to us, pre-eminent among which is the exploration of the sense—or *various* sense—in which the possession of concepts is *constitutive* of our lives,—of our lives as *persons*, that is. This is of particular interest because, as Rhees was gracious enough to point out, we have from the first been especially keen, *contra* the sophists, to maintain that the emergence of the human soul—or the 'growth of understanding', as Rhees termed it—is key to the development of discourse and the possession of concepts, and *vice versa*.[14] For us it has always been our view that the development of the soul and the capacity for discourse are *one*.

Shortly we will be summarizing my most relevant discussions with Rhees; but before that, as we agreed, I shall say something more general about the whole approach to philosophy that we have accepted from Wittgenstein. This is the core issue of the discussions represented in the first of the dialogues that follow.

2   Philosophical subject matter and method

We follow Wittgenstein in the view that the understanding that philosophy seeks is essentially *conceptual* in nature; that is, that philosophical enlightenment is founded on commanding a clearer understanding of those concepts that are characteristically at the bottom of philosophical problems. This is not a view that has been arrived at by prejudice or by *a priori* theorizing. It is a view that has evolved as a result of the critical processes—familiar in philosophy—having come to recognize *themselves* as conceptual in nature. And what this recognition amounts to is that the difficulties arise in connection with the *sense* of what we are trying to say or understand rather than in any difficulty that might be resolved by discovering some new *fact* about the world through observation or theory. For reasons that we shall be treating at length, facts are not and cannot be the fundamental determinants of a great many of our concepts—especially those of most interest in philosophy. Their determination lies elsewhere: in *practice*. It is here that we must go to find the illumination we seek.

This does not mean, as we shall see, that adducing facts is irrelevant in philosophy—on the contrary. But where matters of fact *do* arise, they do so in a conceptual setting. What I mean can be explained like this. In a great many cases, concepts *are* determined by reference to facts. Moreover, there is no doubt that philosophical problems can and do often arise out of a failure to acknowledge either the facts that are constitutive of a concept, or what the logical order is of such facts in constituting the concept. Yet, it remains the *logical* significance of the facts that is of relevance, not the facts in themselves.[15]

So it is a distinguishing mark of philosophical problems that they do not require theoretical insights for their resolution, nor do they require the discovery of new facts about the world—either necessary or contingent. The problems arise out of a lack of clarity *within* our understanding of our concepts, and this must be met by a process of reflection upon and elucidation of the concepts at issue. This may *involve* reflection on matters of fact, in the way we have just described, but philosophy is most challenging where it does not,—where it involves reflections *of another kind*. Indeed making clear when and how it does not and making clear the nature of these other modes of reflection are among the central ambitions of this book.

If I may just add a further observation on the conception of logic that we are working with here, we accept and defend the insight already alluded to—and again as it has emerged through this critical process— that the relations between concepts are logical relations and that therefore the investigation into our concepts is a logical investigation. This notion of logic is apt to cause confusion, especially among those not well versed in the development of philosophical terminology; for it has not to do with the formal relations between propositions and arguments. It is not to be compared with the logic of the syllogism, for example. Rather, it is a conception that is bound to notions of the *sense*— or otherwise—of what is said and the *coherence* and *intelligibility* of concepts. It is a conception of logic that has to do with meaning rather than with what is formally valid. This is the context in which we speak of the 'logical significance of facts', that is, as determinants of meaning in specific contexts.

But let's move on. It goes with all of this, and with the idea that our concepts are to be understood as comprising a part of the fabric of our lives, that the notion of a *concept* is interdependent with that of *language*. Furthermore, we take the view that it is only intelligible to speak of language *at all* in the context of a human (or similar) form of life which is in active engagement with its physical and social environment. This is just a restatement of our earlier observation to the effect that the existence of ideas, or concepts, is of necessity a function of the lives and the culture in which they are embedded. We agree with Wittgenstein, therefore, that the philosophical investigation into our concepts is at the same time an investigation into how they are constructed in language *in as much as it forms a part of the normal lives of persons in real situations* and not as we might imagine them constituted in abstraction from their daily reality.

CRATES: We do agree on this, Lato. And yet it will immediately prompt an objection from a certain quarter. The accusation will be that it takes for granted a notion of 'normal' or 'real' life and so already contains assumptions that may be challenged. It will be said that we cannot brush aside scepticism regarding the reality of discourse in this way.

After all, much of the point of philosophizing on these matters—it is generally assumed—is to overcome the sceptical urge, while *we*, in our resort to what we call 'normal' and 'real', may seem merely to be dismissing it.

LATO: An important point, Crates, and one we shall address. Our response is that we do *not* make such an assumption.

First, there is the fact that the reflective examination of our concepts, in the form in which they find their natural expression in daily discourse, is itself an activity arising legitimately directly out of that discourse and is on a par with any other kind of questioning that goes on in our lives.

Second, and in the more self-consciously philosophical context, the investigation of our concepts in their natural setting also arises directly from the recognition of the conceptual nature of these questions *in general*. For such a recognition will of necessity invite an examination of the conceptual relations between *all* the various key conceptions of the life in which there is language, within which the conceptions of daily discourse are also numbered. So there is a subject matter to be addressed here whether or not you hold that assumptions are being made. Or to put it another way, it would be an unwarranted *a priori* prejudice to insist that the sceptical question needs to be addressed *before* an investigation into the concepts having currency in our daily lives can have any validity.

For both of these reasons, philosophical reflection upon our concepts can originate with preoccupations that are *not* driven by scepticism and to which the raising of sceptical questioning will rightly be regarded as an irrelevant intrusion. To the extent that scepticism is not a part of this context, the validity of the investigation is not touched by it. It should be remembered that the importance of philosophical insight may lie in the need for a deeper appreciation of the order in our thinking arising from *within* our daily lives. It need not be rooted in a preoccupation with philosophical problems in the form in which they have been established during the unfolding of the sceptical academic tradition.

The die-hard sceptic will no doubt persist in the assertion that the investigation makes assumptions all the same; for he will also claim that daily discourse too is founded, albeit unconsciously, on such assumptions. Well, we would reject that too; but it raises issues that are beyond the scope of our present enterprise, and so reluctantly we must leave that for another occasion.

CRATES: I support your reaction to my interjection, Lato. There is no doubt that the temptation exists—especially among us philosophers who are trained in this way—to suppose that the relevance of philosophical thinking has to be by reference to those issues that have been established historically as its principal pillars. The challenge of scepticism is one of these.

Here we diverge from Rhees, who clearly held that for Wittgenstein— as it certainly was for himself—combating scepticism and accounting for 'the possibility of discourse' in the face of such scepticism was of the essence. We, on the other hand, shall emphasize the diversity of ways in which the need for philosophical thinking may enter into our lives. And it certainly seems to us that Wittgenstein, of all philosophers, would want us to recognize philosophical questioning as arising quite naturally out of our lives and not *necessarily* as a result of a prior introduction to the works of philosophy.

As it happens, this alternative also follows directly from the better understanding that we seek of the place of language and concepts in our lives. For *one* source of the difficulties we experience with our concepts lies in a disorientation arising from the very intimacy of our relation to language. This is an influence to which *all* language users are exposed and is not something at home only within a well-developed intellectual philosophical tradition.

LATO: This is at the very heart of our own interests.

But returning to matters of method, we agree that philosophical reasoning itself has led us to the settled view of philosophy as essentially an investigation into our *concepts*,—that we seek a clearer reflective understanding of them. Moreover, we accept that the quest for a greater insight into the sense of a concept and into the relations of sense between concepts is a quest for a clearer view of the *logical* relations between concepts. Philosophy is essentially a logical investigation. However, there is another way of expressing this that Wittgenstein himself made much resort to and which has become current in Wittgensteinian discussion. I am thinking of the way in which Wittgenstein spoke of philosophy as an investigation into the 'grammar' of a concept,—that philosophy is a *grammatical* investigation. We shall be making much use of this expression in just this sense ourselves, and it is a way of speaking that is natural enough. For if we accept the close tie between language and concepts, then it should not seem controversial to want to look at our concepts from the point of view of how they direct the handling of our words. So why should we not speak of distinguishing one concept from another as a 'grammatical investigation'? The fact remains, however, that it is a way of speaking that has caused consternation in the philosophical community. Indeed, we ourselves are not entirely happy with its unqualified use.

Our main concern is that it is a phrase that, by placing the emphasis on rules and conventions, may blind us to other aspects of how the grasp of a concept may be constituted. In the first place, it may encourage the idea that using language can be understood as *merely* the operation of a method or system. We have found common cause with Rhees in rejecting such a conception of language.

It is also linked to the problematic idea that resolving philosophical difficulties may be just a matter of untangling confusing grammars. I had a lively debate with Rhees over how restrictive we should be in characterizing philosophy as a grammatical investigation. Does it lead necessarily to a trivialization of philosophical problems? Or can it indeed do justice to those other dimensions of our lives that belong to the possession of concepts and from which difficulties may emerge?

Too much talk of grammar may also detract from an understanding of the way that our possession of our concepts is bound up with our lives as willing *subjects* and with what is natural or spontaneous in the use of language. We shall explore this too.

In conclusion, the conception of philosophy as a grammatical investigation is an important one; but it is one that requires further exploration and shall not be taken for granted.

CRATES: Agreed.

LATO: Before I hand the lead back to you, Crates, I will mention one or two related issues that we shall also be examining in the first of the following dialogues. The first—and keeping hold of the idea that grammatical investigation remains, at the very least, an important aspect of philosophical investigation—has to do with the *form* of an account of the grammar of a concept. The second has to do with the *status* of concepts within human understanding generally. Both these issues have a major bearing on how we treat concepts in philosophy.

With regard to the first, Wittgenstein frequently stated that the job of the philosopher is to *describe* the grammars of concepts. But the description of grammar in philosophy can surely be of no ordinary kind. We shall certainly see that there are some quite obvious senses in which we *are* perfectly well able to describe how and when words are used in the language. But in philosophy such descriptions are bound to have an unusual property, for they must have *logical* consequences, otherwise they will not contribute to resolving a philosophical difficulty. Moreover, these logical consequences must be understood—and understood as logically compelling—*directly* from the descriptions. So it is clear that these are not going to be empirical descriptions as normally understood.

This is a difficult conception to get to grips with and it is connected with a further point, which is that for much of the time in philosophy if we are to avoid the accusation of reductionism—that is, of trying illegitimately to reduce one concept to another, of trying to 'explain' the one concept in terms of another—then the descriptions must already take for granted the *sense* of the concept whose grammar is being described. We certainly do not deny that there are many concepts that can be given reductive definitions using concepts that *are* independent, but on the whole—and as we shall be arguing at length—these are not the ones that cause the most difficulty in philosophy. As a result, there will almost always be some circularity in any descriptions we give; and this, I think, is in conflict with what most people would think of as valid description— which would normally be regarded as *essentially* independent of the thing described.

As a matter of fact, we once also noted this circularity ourselves with disapproval.[16] What we failed to see at that time was that where the aim is *elucidation* and not *explanation* this circularity is not pernicious. For it is precisely these circles that *show* the relationships between concepts. This concept of 'showing', which I first encountered in my earliest discussions with Wittgenstein,[17] remained, in our view, an important conception in his later thinking—though reconstituted in important ways. We also believe that his contemporaries and followers have taken too little notice of this conception as it applies in his later philosophy, which is why we accord it a central position on our own discussions.

The second major point here—and both will be discussed at length— is the status of any given concept as constituting an element in our understanding of the world. I was often assured in discussions with his contemporaries and near contemporaries that it was his view that grammar is *autonomous* and *arbitrary*. These are closely related conceptions and we do not doubt that they capture important truths—which we shall try to explain. But they were often taken to mean—wrongly in our view—that concepts may be compared with an arbitrary set of measures, the construction of which does not itself owe anything to the nature of the world,—of what the world 'is like'. If this were truly the case, it would both diminish the sense in which the possession of our concepts is *constitutive* of our selves as persons and would undermine the notion that, through the elucidation of concepts in philosophy, we may come to a better understanding of what the world is like,—of what *kind* of thing anything is.[18] We believe that this position is confused. The confusion seems to be this: that if concepts are not 'arbitrary' then *a priori* propositions must have some *necessary* content, just because the relations between concepts are *logical* relations. This leads to the objectionable notion of necessary truths about the world. We believe that this analysis is muddled. Here our discussions with Peter Hacker, who has done much to spread a greater understanding of Wittgenstein but with whom we have found disagreement on this topic, are especially prominent.[19] So we have had quite a lot of work to do here to establish our point of view.

I think this covers the main topics of our second dialogue, and so, Crates, perhaps you would now take us forward and introduce our third dialogue with a summary of what we have called 'Rhees' objection'.

3 Rhees' objection: using signs is not speaking

CRATES: Rush Rhees was among Wittgenstein's closest philosophical confidants. After Wittgenstein's death, Rhees became one of his literary executors, and devoted much of his life to the editing and publishing of Wittgenstein's work. Probably no one understood his thought at that time better than Rhees and he became famous for his vehement defence of Wittgenstein. And yet, from the midst of this there emerged some cogent criticisms of Wittgenstein. This became most strikingly evident after Rhees' death, when the making public of his own extensive writings showed the degree to which he took Wittgenstein to task on some fundamental issues.[20]

Wittgenstein was intent on challenging what he saw to be systematic prejudices and confusions in the way we think about language. These prejudices show up in our reflections on the nature of language—on how words refer to objects, for example, or on how the meanings of words are *kept*. They also show up in confusions over the nature of certain things not directly to do with language—or *apparently* not directly to do with language—the nature of mental life, for example.

To break down these prejudices and simplistic conceptions of how words get their meanings, he attended to all sorts of concrete situations in which language is used. These observations were aimed at helping to bring home the very diverse ways in which different words operate. By the same token, they would also illustrate the different ways in which concepts can be embedded in language. They would help to show the different ways in which words can refer to things and what is involved in keeping to the meaning of a word. By these and other means, he also began to illustrate how different the grammars of our concepts can be, and hence how different *kinds* of things can be represented through the use of language.

On the other hand, when viewed in a larger philosophical context, the situations Wittgenstein described in a great many of his language-games were themselves very simplified or even *excessively* simplified caricatures of normal speech and its usual surroundings in life—the language-games of the 'builders' being the most obvious instances.[21] It was here that Rhees' anxieties were first raised. For, in Rhees' view, Wittgenstein was not only trying to make clear certain specific aspects of word use and concept articulation—which is fine—but was also wanting to elucidate in a more comprehensive way what speaking a language *is*,—what it is to have things to *say*. To this end Rhees found Wittgenstein's discussions less adequate.

Rhees was very insistent that this was Wittgenstein's intent.[22] For he saw Wittgenstein's whole effort in this direction as ultimately addressing itself not just to these specific aspects of language but to the overarching problems in philosophy—such as scepticism—that call into question the very nature and reality of discourse. Given Wittgenstein's ultimate aim, then, the simple language-games should be able to stand up as genuine instances of discourse. Unfortunately, Rhees didn't think they did.

This was mainly because he felt that the simplified illustrations of the builders' 'speech' were just too simple to count as true speech. In the 'language-games' that Wittgenstein described, the uses of language depicted look more like methods or techniques merely for *doing something*, that is, for achieving some practical result, than anything we might genuinely call carrying on a conversation, or articulating or exchanging ideas, beliefs, knowledge, and so on. Consequently, philosophical arguments reliant on these language-games to illustrate the nature of speech cannot, on their own, open the door wide enough to allow the bigger questions about the nature of discourse to be addressed. Hence they do not provide the bulwark against scepticism that Rhees was looking for. He therefore set off to provide a much broader and more holistic view of the place of language in our lives. On this account, language is seen not merely as a method or practice but as being at the heart of our very constitution as *persons*. And this can only be revealed by placing the emphasis on the circumstances in which a person can be said to 'have something to say', as he put it.[23] This is not a simple matter, but shows up in our lives in hugely many ways,—ways which must therefore be reflected in our manner of doing philosophy.

LATO: But we do not deny that the application of language in very practical situations and with practical *consequences* is integral to the understanding and use of language and so must be accounted for fully, do we Crates?

Dialogue 1 Synopsis 13

CRATES: Indeed we do not. But it does mean that for such application to be a part of *speaking*, it must be an intimate and full part of the life of a *person*. It must lie in his engagement with his world, with himself and the people about him; it must lie in the way that language is threaded throughout his life and not just in the practical circumstances of some specific situation. And so we have to look at these more pervasive and constitutive features of persons if we are to achieve an understanding of language and speaking. Only in this larger context can we understand what it is to 'have something to say'. Rhees thought that Wittgenstein's rather too narrow focus on language as 'a way of *working*' tended to cut him off from the larger picture. As a result he could not answer what Rhees asserted to be the principal philosophical questions regarding the nature of discourse, the relation of discourse to reality, and indeed the nature of reality itself.[24]

This is of especial interest to us. Alone among his contemporaries, Rhees acknowledged the parallel between his anxieties over Wittgenstein's discussions here and our own rejection of the sophists' attitude towards language; that is, that they were unable to account for how—as we have already adverted to—the 'growth of understanding' is key to the development of discourse.

Whether Rhees was entirely fair to Wittgenstein on this point is another matter. Without denying that Rhees was the more wide ranging in his treatment of discourse in its relation to life as a whole, Wittgenstein's own discussions certainly did not restrict themselves to comparisons with the simple language-games. And when he did focus on these comparisons, it is arguable that his intent was not so much to account for the nature of speaking as such but to rebut certain very specific confusions about language. In these discussions Wittgenstein was responding quite explicitly to his own youthful views,[25] and so—to our minds at any rate—there can be little doubt that he was rather more concerned here with the nature of logic and logical necessity than with giving a general account of what it is to speak a language. And of course, an account of the nature of rule-following is key to any such discussion of logic. For these reasons we are more inclined than Rhees to be generous to Wittgenstein and to regard his use of the simple language-games as a part of *this* discussion. We are not convinced that they were intended to bear the whole weight of a general account of speaking and discourse.

LATO: Yes, indeed.—Though I think we should also show at least some sympathy towards Rhees in his predicament. There is no doubt that Wittgenstein did *not* develop an account of speaking in the depth that

Rhees did; and there is equally no doubt that Rhees was right that such a development is required to meet the broader philosophical aims. So his critique at least served the purpose of kick-starting the discussion in this direction. He may also have been right to be anxious that, in the absence of this further development, there was a danger of the simple language-games being given an emphasis they do not warrant. Such a treatment has been rife in philosophy since Wittgenstein, which rather vindicates Rhees' position.

CRATES: We might also add that, regardless of whether he was factually correct about Wittgenstein's intentions, Rhees would certainly have agreed that such criticisms are not of such strength as would force a retreat from Wittgenstein's philosophy. On the contrary, his criticisms were themselves Wittgensteinian in origin and they called us to *advance* from where Wittgenstein left off, not to regress to some earlier philosophical position.

LATO: So how is all this relevant to the question we set ourselves at the outset, namely: what comprises the possession of a concept and how are concepts seated in our lives?

CRATES: Well, the same principles apply to *concepts* as they do to *speaking*. That is, a concept is not possessed merely in the mastery of a technique for using words; for, like speaking, this possession too is a function of the part it plays in the life of the individual *as a whole*. So our understanding of what it is to possess concepts will develop together with our understanding of what speaking is and of how speaking differs from merely applying a technique or using words as a means of achieving certain ends. A better understanding of what speaking is will be found to go together with a clearer appreciation of the various ways in which concepts can be established in our lives. This will also teach us of the logical differences between these concepts, and hence also of the nature of the phenomena that are articulated by means of them. Of particular interest, we will see how the possession of certain concepts to do with the nature of human life is integrated into the various phenomena of human life. Here, the very possession of the concept is *constitutive* (or partly constitutive) of a whole dimension of life; it is part of the *structure* of this complex.

The development of these issues will arise naturally from our discussions of Rhees' reactions to Wittgenstein, and they will take us a long way from any merely operative account of language. But before we can make progress here, we will at the same time need to work our way in from another direction. An appreciation of how language and concepts are positioned in our lives will have to be resistant to certain theories of how we as individuals hold on to language and its concepts, and of how our grasp of word uses originate and concepts are formed. In extending Rhees' observations on the nature of speaking, we will already be drawing away from certain behaviouristic accounts of language and speaking. But we will also be intent on resisting some rather more persistent and universally held beliefs about language of a quite different kind.

LATO: Many of which—we might add—we must accept a significant degree of responsibility for.

CRATES: Quite so. The first among the latter are *mentalistic* beliefs or theories, which tie the possession of concepts both to dualistic conceptions of the nature of mental life and to confused notions of mental privacy and private ostensive definition. In the second place, and related to this, are *rationalistic* theories that suppose language and concepts to be founded on some prior process of reasoning, where a capacity to conceptualize is supposed to *anticipate* the linguistic formulation of concepts and thoughts. Indeed such processes are often supposed to underlie human action *in general*.

Resisting these ways of thinking will be an underlying feature of our whole enterprise; and the dismissal of such theories will be achieved by drawing attention to the logical links between the concepts of linguistic use and those of behaviour and action. When seen clearly, these links will show that these concepts do *not* take for granted a more fundamental conception of reason—of logical thought—or concept-formation.— They will show that reason is born in the *development* of the capacity for speech, not the other way about.

LATO: May I add a clarification here, Crates? We are intent on rejecting both behaviouristic and mentalistic or rationalistic accounts of language and concepts. What we are rejecting here are, on the one hand, accounts of language that are dependent on a conception of behaviour that is divorced from the mental (in the fully fledged sense, which includes *all* the concepts of a person), for otherwise language could indeed be accounted for merely as the employment of a technique,— which is a confusion. Equally, we reject accounts of language and concepts that are dependent on a conception of the mental that is purely 'internal'—that is *divorced* from the behavioural—as otherwise language could be accounted for in terms of processes confined to a mentally private world,—which is also a confusion.

The view we wish to maintain, then, is that behavioural and psychological concepts are themselves logically intertwined but not reducible to one another, and that linguistic concepts are then intertwined with the two. So we have a trio of interdependent but irreducible sets of concepts: the linguistic, the behavioural and the psychological.

From one direction, then, the attack on mentalism and rationalism is based on the recognition of the logical links between linguistic and behavioural concepts; while from the other, the rejection of behaviourism is based on the existence of logical links between the concepts of linguistic use and more widely ramified concepts of a person, which include psychological concepts.[26] This is because the whole suite of concepts is logically linked. Once this is recognized, it will be seen that there is no way back either for behaviourism or for mentalism and rationalism.

CRATES: Absolutely not.

On this point of acknowledging the links between the concepts of speaking (and language generally) and psychological concepts, there is a further *caveat*. We shall be arguing that reason does not anticipate the use of language but emerges with it. But of course, an infant already demonstrates complex behaviour and mental capacities *prior* to the acquisition of language. This is characteristic of what Wittgenstein called our 'form of life'. So we cannot say that the *whole* emerges together. In fact we might even assert that the concepts of linguistic use and concept-formation do presuppose intelligence of at least *some* kind. We do not have to deny pre-linguistic intelligence; we simply have to be absolutely clear to distinguish any such modes of intelligence that language *presupposes* from those which can only emerge *together with* the linguistic capacity.

It will be important to be clear about this firstly to avoid the accusation of according language too much weight in the development of human life. But it will also be vital to recognize from the outset that much of what we have to say will be aimed at understanding the very complex conceptual links between the post-linguistic and pre-linguistic dimensions of the human form of life, and at assigning the correct weight to each.

LATO: Before moving on, Crates, this reminds me that we shall need to explain in more detail this important notion of a 'form of life', which, as you suggest, begins to take on special relevance here. Wittgenstein's use of the phrase was only very seldom, but as a concept it is surely integral to his philosophy. Its function is to direct the attention to the *whole*, even when considering quite specific aspects of human life. The human form of life comprises those patterns in our ways of acting, feeling and reacting in speech that make up its most fundamental components.

Hence, the rôle of this concept in philosophy is to say that the concepts of human life—of action and intention, of belief and knowledge, of feeling and expressing, and so on—have to be understood in relation to one another and as constituting this whole. Again we should emphasize that 'form of life' is not an explanatory or theoretical concept in philosophy, but one that directs attention in a particular way to the order among our concepts—in this case the galaxy of concepts of human life itself.

I have raised this now because of its bearing on Rhees' complaint. For his demand to understand language in the larger context of the development of the human *person* was precisely to invoke the demand for its holistic treatment. Language is an integral part of the human form of life. It is not merely some skilful activity exercised by it.

CRATES: I quite agree. There is another reason why we should give it a thorough examination. The very sparseness of Wittgenstein's explicit references to 'forms of life' has resulted in some widely differing interpretations of its meaning and its significance in his philosophy. So we will be expected to justify our interpretation against some of the more well-established versions of it.

4 Philosophy-as-theory and conceptual confusion

LATO: I wish to make a general point now, Crates, having to do with theorizing in philosophy and the nature of conceptual confusion. When it is supposed that the proper response to a philosophical problem is to seek a theory to explain the phenomenon or state of affairs that is found puzzling, a particular view of the starting point for philosophical inquiry is already assumed, namely that the original problem has arisen out of some ignorance of what the world is like. A theory is therefore needed to direct us towards some new facts that will answer our difficulty. Now this is a position that we rejected when putting forward the case for treating philosophy as essentially a *conceptual* and not a *factual* investigation. Do you not agree?

CRATES: I do.

LATO: But of course, adopting this position does not in itself render a person invulnerable to confusion. For instance, the inclination to adopt a rationalistic view of the origin of language and concepts may not manifest itself *only* in the person already committed to the theory-forming conception of philosophy. It may also arise in one committed to our own more recently adopted approach, but who goes astray in his conceptual investigation by misadventure. In the present example, it would take the form of a tendency to place the capacity for reason as logically *prior* to the capacity for speech,—the difference with our own conclusion being that we would regard such an analysis as confused.

CRATES: I agree again.

LATO: And of course the commitment to philosophy-as-theory is itself the *product* of conceptual confusion. So my point is that confusion over the priority of rational over linguistic capacity may occur either in the presence of the philosophy-as-theory conception or without it.

I really just want to make the point that there are various possibilities here, and that it is important to remember that rejecting philosophy-as-theory does not insure us against those very confusions which, in another context, would form the basis for such illegitimate theorizing. So it is not just the temptation to *theorize* about language in these ways that we would hope to exorcize, but also the inclination to *order* concepts in a particular way. This may cling to us regardless of our final view.

CRATES: I take your point, Lato.

5   The language-game and the concept of the language-game

In fact, you have brought us to another matter on which we agreed to say something at this point: a device of analysis which we make much use of throughout our discussions.

LATO: Perhaps Wittgenstein's most well-known analytical tool is the 'language-game'. There is no doubt that he used this phrase in various senses—we won't go into all of them now. There is also no doubt that this very phrase 'language-game' was one root of Rhees' misgivings. For, especially in the case of the simple builders' language-games, it evidently lends itself to the idea that language lies little nearer the core of life than any other skill that we may pick up along the course of our lives. As a result it can have the effect of disengaging language from the constitution of our souls. But leaving that aside for the moment, in other respects we still regard it as a useful tool, as long as it is applied in the right context and its limitations understood.

Wittgenstein's most explicit statement of how he meant to use the phrase 'language-game' was where he said simply that the term is 'meant to bring into prominence the fact that the *speaking* of language is part of an activity or form of life'.[27] Again this should be treated as a conceptual insight, not as part of a theory of language. And the insight is, first, that specific language uses are logically related to broader features of human activity. So, for example, the concept of an *order* goes together with (is logically related to) other concepts of human interaction; and he gives plenty of other examples too, such as asking, thanking, cursing, greeting, and so on.[28] But arising out of this is the further insight that these language-games comprise *suites* of interrelated linguistic activities, concepts and actions. Take *intention* as an example. We have the interrelated concepts of the *expression, formulation* and *description* of intentions. These uses of language do not occur in a linguistic vacuum but within the context of our daily activities—such as our behavioural expressions of intention or our observations and responses to the behaviour of others. An account of intention will therefore comprise an account of the logical relations between these various concepts and our conceptions of the modes of behaviour or activity into which they are woven.[29] Similarly, *within* the language-game of expressing intentions, we will also recognize logical relations between *temporal* and *behavioural* concepts. This is because expressing an intention brings together behavioural and temporal concepts in a particular way. So the idea of a language-game goes with the idea of widely ramified links between concepts.

It is not the purpose of the concept of a language-game to identify and mark out discrete entities. The service that this notion provides is really only to remind us that the concept of language is the concept of something that is a part of the activities and modes of life that make up our form of life. This is an important insight in its own right. And it directs us in philosophy as to the scope of the investigation that we need to make to respond to any one problem. As an analytical tool it is not a theoretical concept but simply a device for teasing out different suites of concepts and looking at how they relate to each other and to the activities into which their employment is integrated. And of course, what *constitutes* a suite of concepts will vary according to our interests at the time.

CRATES: Fine, but what is the specific issue we now wish to raise about the nature of language-games?

LATO: Someone playing a particular language-game—if I may express it that way—will be employing a suite of concepts. The example of intention is a case in point, where behavioural, temporal and explicitly intentional concepts are brought together in a particular way. Now the philosopher interested in this language-game will certainly want to see how these concepts are related to each other *within* the language-game of expressing intention—and thus how the grammar of expressing intention differs from the grammars of other kinds of expressions such as hope, expectation or prediction. However, there is another interest that the philosopher may have here; one which is not just in how the concepts are used by the intending agent within the language-game. For he may wish to step up a conceptual level and stand back to look at how these linguistic practices relate to the activities of which they form a part. He will want to look at the contexts in which we *attribute* intentions, and he will want to look at the rôle of the language-game of expressing intentions in someone employing these concepts in the course of his life. So, in this case, we are interested in the employment of the concept of intention as an essential component of human life, and in how the formation of the concepts of intention and the use of intentional language go to make up this dimension of our lives.

Again, this is not an empirical investigation but one that looks at the logical relations between the concepts of human behaviour and the concepts both *of* and *within* the linguistic practices associated with those forms of behaviour. For this reason we could call it an investigation into the concept *of* the language-game of expressing intentions to contrast it with the investigation into the concepts employed *in* expressing intentions.

This latter distinction is a general one that informs our discussions of various language-games and concepts throughout our dialogues. We also believe that it is an important distinction. There is no need for us to expand at length in this first dialogue on *why* it is important—which will unfold as we go along. Suffice it to say that we believe that the failure to make this distinction has been problematic in philosophy. In particular it is implicated in the considerable muddle that has arisen over whether or not philosophy can 'get outside' language. For example, it is often wondered whether it is legitimate to criticize or justify language-games by looking at their dependence on forms of behaviour or on external features of reality, and so on. For in viewing a language-game from this different conceptual level, it may look as if we are attempting a 'transcendental' account of the 'possibility' of the concepts embedded in it from some point beyond normal discourse—which emphatically we are not.

CRATES: I agree, Lato. The philosopher's perspective upon these language-games is not unique. Having the concept of any given language-game is a normal part of everyone's conceptual armoury, as each has his own conceptual perspective on the linguistic practices of his fellow human beings and the relations of these practices to the surrounding behaviour and reality. I concur that this is not a 'transcendental' view of those practices; it is a normal part of discourse. The concept *of* a language-game is itself the component of a language-game in its own right.

Philosophy consists largely in trying to see more clearly our conceptions *of* the myriad language-games just as much as it is to elucidate the concepts *within* those language-games. We do not only ask how the concept *knowledge* stands in relation to other related concepts, such as belief or certainty; we also ask what is going on in the life of a person claiming knowledge or what are the circumstances in which a person may claim to know something. And this amounts to asking for the conceptual links between the various concepts appropriate to the *description* of those circumstances.

6   Instinctive behaviour, speaking and concept-formation

But let's return to the main issue and to the subject of our fourth dialogue. We were saying that the rejection of both mentalistic and rationalistic theories of language-use and concept-formation requires that we make clear the conceptual connections between language and concept-formation, on the one hand, and behaviour and action, on the other. This is generally referred to as demonstrating the *groundlessness* of language, the essence of which is to show that there is conceptual confusion in wanting to provide a justification for our use of language and our concepts,—justifications we are wont to give either by an appeal to reason or by reference to subjective experience or internal mental events of some kind. This notion of groundlessness can also be expressed from the other direction by emphasizing the *spontaneous* or *instinctive* nature of language.

LATO: Can I just stop you for one moment there, Crates, because I would like to make a preliminary clarification of this notion of instinct, which can be ambiguous. When we speak of instinct in animals, we generally have in mind certain quite specific forms of behaviour that occur naturally and are not *learned*. The retrieving instinct in certain breeds of dog would be an example, or the nest-building of a bird. However, we also speak of instinct where we simply wish to say that the action, in the human case at least, is *not dependent on thought*. The difference between the two becomes clear when we observe that in the second case we may be describing an action that was originally learned, but has *become* instinctive in this sense. Here we will speak of the action having become 'second nature' (we may also apply a similar concept to animals, where it would mean that a learned behaviour had simply become fluent). Now in philosophy we are generally concerned with instinct in this second 'thoughtless' sense, but with a special restriction. For when we use it in philosophy to express the groundlessness of language, we mean that whereas it may originally have been learned it could not *conceivably* have been dependent on thought. This is a grammatical statement, which says that it would make *no sense* to speak of it as being founded on or dependent on thought. Are you in agreement with this, Crates?

CRATES: Yes indeed, and thank you for the clarification. So let me now introduce a further distinction between two situations in the use of language in which we may speak of its instinctive nature, and where our principal concern will be with your latter, 'groundless' sense of instinct. These two situations will play important parts throughout our discussions.

The concept of language is the concept of something depending on and growing out of instinctive reactions. This observation, which again is a conceptual and not a factual point, applies in two directions: first, to language-use *as such* and second to *concept-formation*. Let me explain this distinction.

By 'language-use *as such*,' I mean first the fundamental capacity to carry on with the use of a word in the sense that has been established for it. This is closely related to the capacity to act in accordance with a rule and belongs with the extent to which the use of language *can* be compared with the application of a practical technique; though we may also include here the capacity to *talk*, to make sense and converse,—in other words, our capacity to take language into our life and for it to have that rôle in our life. This is the first dimension within which we can examine the relations between concepts to do with language and those of instinctive behaviour. And as regards the distinction you have just made, human beings evidently do have an innate capacity to behave in a rule-governed way, but the main point is that the capacity maintains action according to a rule *without* grounds, which is fundamental to the use of language—but which is not to deny that in other contexts we may also act *with* grounds.

When I speak of the rôle of instinct in *concept-formation*, on the other hand, I mean something different again. There are hugely many modes or dimensions to our lives. There are endless different aspects to the way in which the 'form' of our life is manifested,—in the expression of beliefs, perceptions, hopes, expectations and intentions, for example, or in the way we recognize other human beings as other than merely animated objects, and so on. The list is virtually limitless. And it is in the way that language attaches itself to this complex of responses and reactions—which makes up the instinctive base of our lives—that the corresponding concepts of belief, expectation, hope, intention, person, and so on, are determined.

Again, with respect to your distinction, this host of basic responses that make up the fundamental structure of our form of life may be largely innate—though much will also have been learned; but the important point here is the way these combine as ungrounded modes of behaviour with ungrounded linguistic reactions to comprise concept-formation. We are interested in the ungrounded nature of the way that specific foundational concepts are formed from the midst of our life and are woven into its structure or form.

So our aim will be to display the conceptual connections between language, concept-formation, the phenomena that are constitutive of our lives (e.g., intention, hope, belief, and so on) and action, but in a way that always keeps in mind that this complex is without a rational source or justification beyond itself. This is why we shall maintain the emphasis on instinct and instinctive reactions.

So in these two regards, we can say that the concept of instinct is important both in understanding the concept of speech as behaviour and also for understanding concept-formation and conceptual content. Again, we must emphasize that it is *not* that we maintain a *theory* of instinctive reactions as explaining language; neither should we attribute such a theory to Wittgenstein—though some have done, as we shall see.

LATO: Yes, indeed.

Crates, before we move on, can we just say a little more about this distinction between the two situations in which we shall speak of the instinctive nature of language and about how we are going to treat these in our discussions. As you say, the first has to do with how, roughly speaking, our grasp of the use of a word is *maintained*. This, as you rightly say, then leads on to the wider question of how speaking should be regarded as a primal manifestation of our form of life. The second has more to do with the meaningful *content* of the concepts that we are acquiring. Here, our interest is with how instinctively or spontaneously grasped word uses, woven together with other characteristic modes of our form of life, are *primitive* to the language-games in which they occur, and so go to determine what the words mean and hence the content of the different concepts. So far so good.

CRATES: Agreed.

LATO: Now of the first, I said that we want to understand *how* the grasp of word uses and meanings is maintained. In a way this is an unfortunate phraseology, as it makes it look as if we were interested in the factual conditions that make language 'possible',—which is already pulling us back towards treating it as a factual matter requiring a theoretical response. But the question remains a conceptual one, for what we really want to understand are the *logical* relations between the concept of language-use (and its maintenance) and other concepts of personal understanding. The objective here will be to establish those links between language and action which are *not* dependent on any notion of an internal justification, rationalization or verification. Indeed we want to establish that these latter concepts cannot be coherently employed in this context.

This view came out very clearly in Wittgenstein's discussions of following a linguistic rule. In its *negative* aspect, it emerged in that series of remarks, often referred to as his 'private language argument',[30] the object of which was to establish the confusion in the notion of private ostensive definition. It was an attack on a certain deeply entrenched view of how words refer to sensations.[31]

The *positive* statement of the instinctive nature of rule-following, on the other hand, was expressed, for example, in his remark 'I obey the rule *blindly*'.[32] Here he meant that my ability to follow a rule is not, except in cases we shall discuss later, grounded on a 'seeing'—a private insight which 'justifies' it—but on a pure 'doing'. Understanding a rule—and, by implication, understanding a concept—is directly linked to the notion of spontaneous or instinctive *use*.—Though, of course, it is not identical with it.

CRATES: Yes, your last proviso is important. For we are not advocating a behaviourist explanation of understanding a language. This will become more clear when we look at the spontaneous nature of speech and of 'having something to say', because, as already observed, an examination of 'having something to say' will force us to make more clear the links between language and concepts of the person, mind and consciousness.

But I have interrupted you Lato. We want to emphasize the distinction between the groundlessness of rule-following as such and this second situation: the rôle of specific instinctive ungrounded behaviours and linguistic reactions in concept-formation. The latter is a very important topic for us; in fact it has taken up more of our time than any other. You were going to say a little more in summary of our discussions of this topic.

LATO: Wittgenstein's thoughts on the relationship between language, following rules and instinct have been thoroughly documented. I also had plenty of opportunity to discuss these topics with him. On the other hand, the relationship between instinctive behaviour and the formation of specific concepts was a topic that sadly we rather neglected. This

scantier treatment left the field wide open for imaginative interpretations of his views—some supportive, others sceptical. Indeed this is a
prime area where—counter to his own avowed intent—he himself has
been accused of metaphysical theorizing.

CRATES: And no doubt we too will be accused of such things!

LATO: No doubt at all! But the fact remains that there are many unex-
plored paths here, and so our purpose will therefore be to try to open up
at least some of them. This will be partly by means of our own efforts;
but we shall always acknowledge and remain true to the opening up of
this area which is thanks both to him and to others too, such as Rhees
and Lars Hertzberg.

We will have two main challenges. The first will be to make our
responses initially to those who have taken issue with Wittgenstein's
remarks on instinct and concept-formation—who we believe have
generally been misguided—and then, and equally importantly, to the
one or two who have made the opposite mistake and perhaps not been
sufficiently guarded in their enthusiasm.

The second will be to examine, in some detail, a selection of concepts
that are situated in our lives in ways that are much less straightforward
than first appearances and age-old philosophical prejudice might
suggest. These are concepts whose primitive linguistic roots are related
intimately and in complex ways to fundamental and instinctive features
of our form of life. It will be vital to unravel and to display the many
sides to this relationship. The difference it makes that language is *not*
merely the exercise of a technique but is a manifestation of what is most
intimate to our humanity—that we 'have things to say', for example—
will be especially prominent in these discussions.

In this fourth dialogue the formation of the concepts of belief and
time will be examined briefly, though the more detailed discussions of
the possession of certain specific concepts will be dealt with in the fifth,
which will concentrate on psychological concepts, such as *intending* and
seeing, and will focus especially on the rôle of our own subjectivity in the
formation of these concepts. These discussions are at the core of what
we believe to be our own special contribution to this topic. We hope
that the reader will be surprised at our revelations, which will show the
relationship between these concepts and our lives in unusual perspectives:
how they are constituted in our lives, and of how our lives—and our
souls indeed—are constituted through them.

The fifth dialogue will conclude with a series of discussions of how
certain peculiarities in the way these concepts are possessed—and
certain other features of the way we experience that possession—are

implicated in the problems we experience reflecting on them in philosophy. This links, once again, the twin themes of our dialogues.

7 An instinct for metaphysics

And so to the final topic, Lato, which follows on directly from this. The dialogues in this book begin with questions relating to the *status* of philosophical understanding—questions about the content of our concepts and our philosophical understanding of them, about whether and how this differs from factual knowledge, about the nature of necessity, and so on. And as we go along, we also look at how aspects of the way certain specific concepts are embedded in our lives bear on how we are able to reflect on them in philosophy. In particular we look at the difficulties arising out of the very intimacy of that possession and out of our subjective relations to language. But in the sixth dialogue, we approach the nature of philosophy from some different directions, the way to these also having been cleared by the intervening discussions. Our particular interest here will be to examine how the metaphysical urges that are at the bottom of much philosophizing may themselves be instinctive in nature—in both of the senses you described earlier—that is, as being the product of certain apparently innate tendencies while not being the *product* of thought. In this regard, we shall explore the extent to which the operation of these urges may itself be compared with concept-formation. Let me explain this a little further.

Philosophical problems and difficulties, and the prejudices in our thinking that are at their source, originate very frequently—like our concepts—in instinctive reactions, primitive reactions. To this extent they are no more *founded* on reason (false or otherwise) than language is, and so are best not regarded as *mistakes*,—though this is not to deny either that there are irrational processes at work or that unreason and mistakes of reasoning are often involved. For example, we commonly experience as compelling the idea or impression that we can give ourselves a private ostensive definition of a word referring to a sensation; or, in a similar vein, we feel we can never really know whether other human beings have minds. These reactions seem to be prompted *directly* by our self-conscious perceptions or our perceptions of other people, and once established have wide ramifications and lead off in many directions. So the processes here resemble closely the processes associated with the formation of our most fundamental concepts. Our discussions here are supported by further comparisons with two other forms of instinctive, ungrounded uses of language: superstitious reactions and 'secondary' uses of language—such as the use of 'dull' (removed from its 'primary' use) to describe a pain.

What we try to establish above all in this dialogue is how deeply entrenched in our lives are these metaphysical urges—as deeply entrenched as language itself and its concepts.

LATO: And so in our final and briefest dialogue, our Epilogue, we come full circle and summarize our discussions. We conclude with some last thoughts on the vision for philosophy we have carried with us and which we believe we share with Wittgenstein: the reflection upon and elucidation of the nature of our selves and our situation in the world.

Dialogue 2   Facts, Concepts and Philosophy

1   Introduction

CRATES: It is a principal aim of our book to examine the way that concepts are seated in our lives,—that is, to try to understand better what it is to *have* concepts. But since it is also a fundamental presupposition of our investigation that its very *method* is by the elucidation of concepts, the outcome of the investigation is almost certain to have a bearing on its own methods.—Our understanding of what concepts *are* ought to be relevant to the *conduct* of our conceptual examination of the nature of concepts.

In anticipation of this, it would be helpful if we were to begin by examining certain aspects of the nature of conceptual investigation and of how concepts operate within such an investigation. In this way we may hope that our reader will be able to grasp more readily, as we progress, the relevance of the unfolding insights into the nature of concepts to our understanding of the methods being used to illuminate them. Thus the understanding of the two—of the nature of concepts and of the nature of philosophical reflection—may develop in parallel with one another.

Since we ourselves have already followed this course from beginning to end, the methods we now employ are already informed by the outcome of our own investigations. This has insured us against our methods being undermined by the fruits of the dialogues that follow; and so the reader will already be benefiting, albeit unwittingly, from the results of this circularity. But so far as our immediate discussion of the nature of philosophical subject matter and method is concerned, we will confine ourselves to those aspects—arising out of your discussions with Wittgenstein—that are helpful towards this parallel understanding but which do not anticipate too much what we may hope to reveal in subsequent dialogues. This will enable us to avoid entering those discussions prematurely.

2 Conceptual and factual investigation

LATO: Crates, we stated in the previous dialogue that we follow Wittgenstein in the view that a philosophical investigation is essentially a *conceptual* investigation. For the problems it has to deal with are problems arising out of how we *conceive* of things, while the 'solutions' lie in tracing out the internal features of, and the connections between, the concepts that are at the root of the problems. However, we also said that one of the major new elements in Wittgenstein's thinking is that the existence of concepts is of necessity a function of the lives and the culture in which they are embedded. A direct effect of this shift from our previous way of thinking, if I may greatly condense matters for the moment, has been the realization that the formation and employment of concepts are much more mixed up in the 'hurly-burly' of life—to use Wittgenstein's phrase—than we once recognized.[1] The difficulties that we get into with our concepts, and which give rise to philosophical perplexity, arise largely from our failure to see their outlines clearly within this hurly-burly or to extract them from it, for the purpose of reflection and analysis, without distortion.

CRATES: In our own more extreme moods, we would have regarded such explanation with disdain, since for us it was not the concepts, or Forms, that needed to be extracted from the hurly-burly but *our selves*, so that we might reflect on the Forms in contemplative isolation.

LATO: Indeed. So it was perhaps for that reason that we were not able to recognize—as Wittgenstein came to recognize—the various forces at work that make this 'seeing' of our concepts, and the correct means of extracting them, so difficult.

One of these forces—one that is so well concealed in the flow of life and discourse—is the difficulty of distinguishing between concepts and statements of fact, and the confusions over the difference between conceptual and factual investigations that this gives rise to. And so a helpful way of entering this whole arena and bringing out some of the essential features of the philosophical enterprise—plus how it differs from science and other modes of discourse—will be to examine, from some quite different points of view, the relationship between concepts and statements of fact. We might start with what are, at first sight, some apparent conflicts within Wittgenstein's adherence to this distinction.

Wittgenstein's approach to philosophical method was founded on a clear-cut distinction between factual and conceptual investigations. Indeed he identified the prime manifestation of philosophical confusion—what he called '*metaphysics*'—in the confusion of these two: we treat philosophical problems as if they demanded a factual investigation of phenomena; we interpret what should properly be regarded as logical insights into our concepts and their relations as if they were statements of necessary fact about the world. He was quite emphatic about this:

> Philosophical investigations: conceptual investigations. The essential thing about metaphysics: that the difference between factual and conceptual investigations is not clear to it. A metaphysical question is always in appearance a factual one, although the problem is a conceptual one. (RPP1 949, cf. Z 458)

We employ concepts in the representation of facts. Therefore, an investigation into our concepts must be distinct from an investigation of the world *by means of* those concepts. The difference seems obvious enough. Philosophy, it would seem, ought not to be interested in facts. And yet what is perplexing in his account quickly enters. For when we examine his method more closely—and the other claims he made for it— we find a re-emergence of an interest in facts. In the first place, the philosophical account of how a concept is represented in or expressed through language—what he called the 'grammar' of a concept—was said by him to be by *description*, suggesting a comparison with factual investigation. In the second place, Wittgenstein frequently entreated philosophers to remind themselves of *general facts of nature*—facts which we normally overlook just because of their great generality.[2] On one occasion I recall him saying:

> What we are supplying are really remarks on the natural history of human beings; we are not contributing curiosities however, but observations which no one has doubted, but which have escaped remark only because they are always before our eyes. (PI 415)

Clearly there is more than one issue at stake here; but at first sight—as I am sure you will agree—a rather confusing picture emerges.

CRATES: A first reaction to this—at least where the description of this 'grammar' is concerned—might be simply to point out that this is not quite the confusion of fact and concept that you started with. I mean, the issues that surround accounting for the workings of our *concepts* don't have to be the same as those that surround our approach to the understanding of worldly *phenomena*. When Wittgenstein spoke of confusing factual and conceptual investigations he was surely speaking of the investigation of such phenomena as comprising the factual dimension. There evidently remains a difference between describing the world and giving an account of the grammar of a concept. Having established this distinction, the question of whether investigating our concepts is in at least *some* sense descriptive is another matter, and so there need be nothing especially puzzling or contradictory about all this. This is a view that might be taken. From this angle, only his remarks about our interest in 'general facts of nature' seem resolutely at odds with the earlier remark.

LATO: Well, in the first place, I think we will see that how we approach the account of a *concept* and how we approach the account of a *phenomenon* are in fact closely entwined—though this will only really emerge clearly in later discussions.

Second, I don't think that the issue of how we can describe grammar can be glossed over quite so lightly. Your statement that investigating our concepts may be descriptive 'in at least some sense' underestimates the difficulties that are concealed here. I think we'll find that the philosophical 'description' of grammar—especially as it relates to the concepts that are of most interest to philosophers—fails in important respects to conform with what we normally count as description.—It certainly fails in these particular respects to conform with what we think of in philosophy as *empirical* description. Indeed it departs from it at precisely the point at which it is required to fulfil its rôle in philosophy. For this reason alone, we need to consider whether it may be misleading to speak of description here *at all*. But this is a very complex area and there will be a variety of situations to account for.

This is also relevant to our equivocation over the wisdom of the *unqualified* use of the term 'grammar' in philosophy, or of speaking of the philosophical investigation of our concepts as essentially a 'grammatical investigation'. So these are issues that need more working over and which Wittgenstein may not have addressed in every particular.

The propriety of philosophy's interest in 'general facts of nature', on the other hand, will, I believe, be easier to resolve in Wittgenstein's favour.

CRATES: Then I suggest that we begin by addressing the trickier issue while it remains fresh in our minds.

3   Describing grammar

LATO: Notwithstanding my *caveat* regarding the use of this term 'grammar', we may start by questioning how far the philosopher's representation of the grammar of a concept may be favourably compared with factual description in general. Throughout the major part of my discussions with Wittgenstein, he never doubted that grammar can be *described*; indeed he often stated that it was the principal job of the philosopher to describe grammar or linguistic rules. If I may quote, these are some typical examples I recall from discussions on several occasions:

> Grammar does not tell us how language must be constructed in order to fulfil its purpose, in order to have such-and-such an effect on human beings. It only describes and in no way explains the use of signs. (PI 496)

> There must not be anything hypothetical in our considerations. We must do away with all *explanation*, and description alone must take its place. And this description gets it light, that is to say its purpose, from the philosophical problems. These are, of course, not empirical problems; they are solved, rather, by looking into the workings of our language, ... (PI 109)

> (We want to replace wild conjectures and explanations by quiet weighing of linguistic facts.) (Z 447)

> Philosophy may in no way interfere with the actual use of language; it can in the end only describe it. (PI 124)

> In giving explanations I already have to use language full-blown (not some sort of preparatory, provisional one); this by itself shews that I can adduce only exterior facts about language. (PI 120)

> Is grammar, *as I use the word*, only the description of the actual handling of language? So that its propositions could actually be understood as the propositions of science?

> That could be called the descriptive science of speaking, in contrast to that of thinking. (BT, p. 163)

> When we say 'Certain propositions must be excluded from doubt', it sounds as if I ought to put these propositions – for example, that I am called L.W. – into a logic-book. For if it belongs to the description of a language-game, it belongs to logic. (OC 628)

> And everything descriptive of a language-game is part of logic. (OC 56)

Only, as I recall, at our very last meeting did he seem troubled that grammar—or logic—might not be describable after all:

> Am I not getting closer and closer to saying that in the end logic cannot be described? You must look at the practice of language, then you will see it. (OC 501)

This is at first sight a strange and puzzling remark. There are many striking aspects to these statements, some of which we can pass over for the moment because we will surely be coming back to them; but for our present purposes, there are two themes in particular we may identify and focus our attention upon. These are very closely related and may overlap in many respects, but we shall treat them consecutively, as this will help us lead off in different directions from each towards other issues.

The first is where the description of 'linguistic facts' has to do with how words are used in connection with one another *within our speech*; that is, where we are concerned with describing the uses of expressions and propositions just in relation to each other.

The second is where the description is of the *language-game,*— meaning 'language and the actions into which it is woven'.[3] That is to say, we would be interested here in the wider context in which language is embedded: the relations between speech, what we *do* and the environment generally in which language is used. This will also lead on to the discussion of 'general facts of nature', which we have already adverted to.

In both cases we will be interested in *if* and *how* such descriptions are possible. We will show that in both cases—and for the same reasons— the nature of what we are referring to here as description is problematic,— or at least stands in need of qualification.

We will also be interested in whether such descriptions can be conceived of as contributions to *logic*, that is, to our understanding of what is *systematic* and *necessary* in the grammar of our concepts. These are of the essence of grammar. And we will be interested in how the notion of *describing* grammar engages with the idea that the elucidation of our concepts in philosophy should also develop our *understanding* of the concepts—which, we will maintain, is also essential to grammar in this philosophical sense.

CRATES: Then let's take them in that order and begin with the situation where we are interested in the description of grammatical relations *within* language. We may start with a further distinction.

There is one very obvious respect in which language *can* be described. I am thinking of the situation where our intent is merely to describe *external* facts about language: how a word occurs in propositions or sentences, how it occurs in connection with other expressions, and so on. Here we might also imagine the kind description to be found in the empirical study of linguistics, for example, or in the description that a palaeographer might give of an unknown script. Perhaps this is what

Wittgenstein was referring to as the 'descriptive science of speaking'. At any rate, this easily qualifies as factual description, because it simply describes *from an external point of view* the relations between expressions. But I think it is equally obvious that, insofar as such an account may be said to describe the grammar of a concept, it will do so only in the extent to which it does *not* have to engage with our *understanding* of the concept. Hence, it will only deal with what is most superficial in the way a concept is represented in language, and for this reason will not meet the needs of philosophy.

LATO: No, I agree. There is no doubt, as I think we shall be able to demonstrate, that philosophy must reach into our understanding of our concepts if it is to satisfy our real needs. But returning to the kind of account you first described, this had already been clearly identified by Wittgenstein himself as the description of what he called 'surface grammar':

> In the use of words one might distinguish 'surface grammar' from 'depth grammar'. What immediately impresses itself upon us about the use of a word is the way it is used in the construction of the sentence, the part of its use—one might say—that can be taken in by the ear. (PI 664)

Surface grammar was not of interest to Wittgenstein, even though it surely corresponds to what is meant by 'grammar' in common parlance, namely the empirical properties of language, the different parts of speech, the different forms of sentences, and so on. But in his *philosophy*— as I have already intimated—'grammar' is virtually synonymous with 'logic'. This is not the formal logic of propositions and syllogisms, but the logic of *concepts*; and it is this he referred to as *depth* grammar.

Logic in this sense has to do with what is systematic and necessary in our concepts. But it also has to do with what is *meant*. It has to do with being able to distinguish between sense and nonsense in the employment of a concept: with what it makes sense to say and with what can be ruled out as senseless. Thus we are taken directly to the whole business of the explication of meaning or of making meaning more clear. This is why there has to be a connection between, on the one hand, logic conceived of as the determinant of the configuration of the *system* of concepts and, on the other, our *understanding* of our concepts. So this notion of depth grammar opens up a field in which we are interested both in *meaning* and in what *constrains* meaning (logic). We are interested in what is *expressed* in the system and in the *configuration* of the system. It is in the effort to explain how an account of the grammar of a concept is to satisfy all of these aspects that the special difficulties arise over its description.

CRATES: From what you have said so far, Lato, we have identified two components of depth grammar, the first of which would seem to be amenable to description—with a little bit of effort—while the second appears to sit less comfortably with this notion.

The first treats the description of depth grammar as the description of a system. Where we speak of the *system* of concepts, it would be odd—would it not?—to speak of a system that *cannot* be described. Just now I supported the describable nature of *surface* grammar on the grounds that we may approach it from an 'external point of view'; and so surely in the present case too, where we have a system of concepts in various inclusive and exclusive relations, this is just an objective fact and so ought to have outwardly describable aspects. Hence, what you refer to as the 'configuration' of our system of concepts will surely manifest itself in one way or another in outward linguistic facts.

The second and more problematic component has to do with the fact that, as we are describing a *linguistic* system, 'describing the system' cannot be reduced merely to describing the outwardly visible configuration of the concepts. In the first place, it must also include that certain configurations are necessary while others are ruled out. This is what you have already identified as constitutive of the *logic* of the concept. But giving an account of this logic cannot be just a matter of describing linguistic usage—which is a contingent matter. Neither can it be merely to say that these relations are *just as a matter of fact* treated as necessary, because a sceptic might say that perhaps they shouldn't be treated as necessary. Rather the description must *convince* us of these necessities. Giving an account of the system, then, will be a matter both of affirming the necessary links between concepts and of determining that necessity—without which it will not be a proper description of logic. So, whereas we may say that the logic of the concept must be objective, demonstrating this necessity must be at least as much a matter of *reason* as of *description*.

And when we make the further connection between logic and *meaning*, the clash with any normal notion of 'description' seems even more severe. We are immediately discomforted by the idea of describing meaning. This is because our engagement with meaning has less to do with what we may *observe* than with our *understanding*. Meaning is something we *participate in*. This participation constitutes one sense in which we may speak of the 'internality' of our relation to meaning,—which we then contrast with 'externality'. And yet externality, with its implication of observation, is surely essential to description. So unless we are prepared to forge a quite different conception of description—which we do not yet exclude—talk of describing relations of meaning would seem to be ruled out.

So it seems evident, on the one hand, that our relation to the depth grammar of our concepts has both external and internal components; while, on the other hand, these two components do not seem equally amenable to description. This is puzzling. So let us refine our terms of reference a little. We must first identify these external and internal elements more precisely, and then to ask once more what their relationship is and how description may engage with them both.

LATO: Agreed. And perhaps we should also note at this point that what is important here is not so much how far we may reasonably stretch 'description' to cover the kind of account we give of grammar in philosophy. It is rather that we should seek out and make clear any *logical* differences between this and more familiar contexts in which we speak of description. It is the confusions that arise out of the failure to observe these logical differences that are important, rather than the use of term 'description' as such—though of course, if we confirm that there are such important differences, we may yet recommend that, in philosophy at least, we should avoid using the term in this context on pain of inviting further confusion.

CRATES: Quite.

LATO: I suggest we should next examine more closely some aspects of the understanding we seek in philosophy and say a little more on the nature of 'depth grammar'.

If philosophical confusions are conceptual in nature but are not merely accidental mistakes with words—they are not merely linguistic errors—then they arise from *within* our understanding of our concepts. Let's think of some examples. When we use words such as 'mind', 'truth' and 'time' in normal circumstances, we are not constantly hindered in our employment of them. Neither are we burdened by the thought, during normal discourse, either that we do not understand what we mean by them, or that we do not understand the sense of what we are saying. And yet when we reflect on these and other concepts in philosophy, all of a sudden we are at sea. It now seems as if we don't really understand them after all!

Wittgenstein reminded me of this over and over again. It explains what we mean by saying that the problems arise from *within* our understanding of our concepts; and so it is within this sphere that the problems of philosophy must ultimately be addressed. A philosophical investigation should therefore lead to an enhanced understanding of a concept by bringing us to a more lively reflective awareness of its sense and the force of its connections with other concepts. This comprises a major part of the elucidation of the depth grammar of a concept; and it is achieved by consciously tracing out our understanding of the concept through the wider reaches of its relations to other concepts and within a larger field of meaning than is demanded in everyday circumstances.

CRATES: You speak of achieving a 'more lively awareness' of the sense of our concepts and of the 'force' of their interconnections; and you say that this is achieved by 'tracing out' our understanding of our concepts through their connections of sense, and so on. This process is evidently one in which we are *taken through* the connections of meaning and sense, rather than a process in which we observe and have things described to us. It is, as I have noted, a participatory and reasoning process, not an observational one. This is fine and it makes a little clearer the internal component of our relation to depth grammar. But now, how are these internal and external components related?

LATO: When we say that in philosophy we are aiming to get a better and clearer understanding of a concept—its sense or meaning—we are, as I have said, speaking of a *reflective* understanding. But the result is *not* an ability to employ the concept more effectively in normal (i.e., non-reflective) circumstances. The enlightened philosopher is not one who can use 'time', 'mind', 'truth', and so on, more correctly in daily discourse! Rather, we seek a greater sensitivity to the connections of sense between concepts when preoccupied self-consciously with them or when confronted by the need to consider how they might be projected into novel situations. It is a matter, as Wittgenstein used to say, of 'knowing one's way about' with them in this reflective context.[4] This certainly involves a genuine transformation and enhancement of our *understanding* of our concepts. In philosophy we aim at enriching this understanding.

But now, just because this process *is* reflective, it also allows the introduction of another process, namely the demarcation of the boundaries of these concepts in a more self-conscious and explicit way. So to answer your query, it is here that the elucidation of the sense of the concepts emerges into that process in which the *geography* of the system or network of concepts is made more explicit. The enhanced reflective understanding of a concept necessarily brings with it a clearer grasp of the constraints acting on it—the *logic* of the concept. This is an essential feature of the process and is not merely peripheral. Now, does this clearer demarcation of the concept lend itself to description? One product of reflective philosophizing will be a mapping of the *configuration* of our system of concepts, as I referred to it earlier. This will take the form of descriptions to the effect—for instance—that this set of concepts is more closely related to these than to those, or that in this or that circumstance this concept does not apply but another one does, or that the application of this concept will as a matter of fact exclude that one, and so on. In this way the boundaries of the concepts are demarcated. But insofar as this description goes beyond being a purely exterior statement of these relations—and it does—it will also contain the assertion of the *necessity* of this configuration. And 'necessity' in this context means that the concepts would either lose or change their sense if the configuration were different. So we will have drawn on our understanding of the concepts to produce an objective account of their configuration.

To repeat, this outcome will depend very much on the elucidation of the sense of the individual concepts. For it will only be by working through the possibilities of sense—which will of necessity mean working through our understanding of them in various contexts—that we can identify the logical constraints that determine the configuration of the whole. This is essential to what is meant by elucidating the *logic* of the concepts. So on the one hand there is, as you point out, an appeal to *reason*—as far as our understanding of the concepts is concerned—while on the other hand the conclusions as to what is necessary in them may then be treated as matters of fact and entered into the description of the system.

So it is true that this demarcation of our concepts cannot be grounded merely on observation—as it could in the case of surface grammar—for it must be informed, in one way or another, by our *understanding* of the concepts we are engaging with. But the demarcation is nevertheless legitimately descriptive in form. The philosophical elucidation of depth grammar will consist of a new understanding of our concepts but one that develops within the framework of the effort explicitly to mark out the relations between them. Conscious reflection of this kind and the growth of our understanding therefore complement one another. They are not contrasting or conflicting perspectives.

Perhaps I should add here that reflection of this kind is not exclusive to philosophy; it is a normal part of discourse. Indeed it is an essential part of our conception of the *objective* nature of language. The objectivity of language does not derive from our being able to observe the use of language from outside the parameters of normal discourse, whatever that might mean. It makes no sense to try to construct such a transcendental or 'Archimedean' vantage point; neither does its objectivity depend on this. Rather it is derived from the fact that it is an absolutely normal part of daily discourse to *talk* about language and our use of it. We talk about words and their uses, we distinguish sense from nonsense, we talk about the relations between concepts. This is one important context in which we may sensibly speak of the objectivity of language. It is a habitual part of the use of language.

Compare this with an imaginary culture that does not reflect on its uses of language. Imagine, for example, that these people are bemused if asked to explain meanings or the relations between their concepts, or if asked whether this or that makes sense. Here we really would have the right to say that they did not make their use of language objective to themselves as we do—which is not to deny that we *as observers* could treat it as an objective part of their lives, just as we do with the primitive systems of signs used by animals and birds.

CRATES: What you have accounted for so far, Lato, is how we arrive at the conclusion that a concept is constrained in this way or that in relation to another concept, and in such a way that you can then use these necessary relations to build a picture of the system. This picture can then be described. I agree that this accounts satisfactorily for *one* context in which we may legitimately speak of describing the depth grammar of a concept—and which also acknowledges that there are other non-descriptive processes at work, namely an appeal to reason and understanding. So far so good. But I think we also have to address another context, which rather cuts across this one, in which description generally *is* thought of as being applicable to that very component which *from the participatory point of view* we have just assumed is excluded as a possibility and is non-descriptive. I have already suggested that, for the foregoing reasons, the very idea of describing meaning (as opposed to describing a system) may not be an appetizing one. But having said this, there is a context which at least holds the *promise* of making this intelligible after all, namely in the description of a linguistic *rule*. The description of such a rule would, quite evidently, be an account of the meaning of a word or concept. For if I give someone the rule for the use of a word, then I will expect them to be able to use it *in its meaning*. So our next task must be to examine the possibility of such rule-description, and in particular to distinguish those contexts where it *does* make sense to speak in this way from those where it does *not*.

LATO: As is well known, Wittgenstein's discussions of language were awash with a preoccupation with the nature of rules and rule-governed behaviour. On the one hand, these discussions were immediately relevant to his interest in logic and necessity; however, they were equally relevant to his investigations into the nature of meaning and the grasp and formation of concepts—the grasp of meaning being compared with the grasp of a rule and the formation of a concept with the formation of a rule. After all, the grasp of the meaning of a word must carry with it a grasp of the rightness or wrongness of its use in a given context, which must mean that it is governed by a rule—even if not entirely rigidly. Hence this must be a legitimate route to investigating meaning.

But of course a rule is nothing if it is not objective, and we can think of plenty of rules in ordinary life that are eminently describable—the rules of a game, for example. So this concept of a rule—we may hope—should provide us with another context in which, by showing the relation between *following* a rule and the possibility of *describing* it, we can make clear a connection between our internal and our external relations to language. We will not be arguing that learning to speak amounts to no more than learning a system of rules—and neither did Wittgenstein, far from it in fact. But we do maintain that the fact of being rule-governed is a necessary feature of language, of our possession of concepts and of learning to speak. So we'll examine what it means to describe a rule in various contexts—and what it means to follow one—and then use this to assess in what senses and in what circumstances depth grammar *qua* meaning may be described from within this perspective.

For clarity's sake we might start with some examples of both *non*-linguistic and some very simple *linguistic* rule-governed activities. This should enable us to pick out the more salient features.

If I report a game some people are playing, I will describe what they *do*. From this description I may be able to construct the rules that they are following. Of some of the actions that I describe—for example, that when the ball lands out of the court the player is deducted a point—I may conclude that these are among the rules of the game. Here, we will have no difficulty in acknowledging that the rules, or 'grammar', of the game are being *described*. It is also clear—I hope you will agree—that the description is *external* in the sense of its being *independent* of the game.—You do not have to have mastered the game in any way to understand the description of its rules. There is no circularity.

We could also extend the example—perhaps along the lines of the simple language-games that Wittgenstein described to me early on—to cover the situation where a *function* is assigned to the 'words' or signals that are used within the course of the game.[5] For example, we may observe that the person is only deducted the point if a judge calls the ball 'out'. Similarly, there may be a complex system of signs used by a referee to start and stop the game, to keep score, and so on. Again the description is *external*: the observer does not already have to be a participant in the rule-governed behaviour of the game, and its systems of signs, to observe and describe what is going on and to construct the rules governing these signs. The terms of the description are understood independently of the game. There is nothing in the game that has to be 'understood' prior to understanding the description of it; for so far there is nothing more to it than describing a system of actions.

CRATES: Lato, what you have described so far seems very clear and straightforward. However, I think that there are some qualifications required even with these simple examples.

The first is this. You describe a series of actions on a court and utterances made by a referee. But I think it is ambiguous in what sense they are following rules, which must surely affect the conclusions you draw. If they simply *act* as you describe—and I include the 'signs' in this—then we may if we like call this a game and may compare it with, say, the social behaviour of some animals. And if we also wish to say it is governed by rules, this would just mean that there is this observable pattern or structure in the game. In this case, I can agree that the description is 'independent' in the way you describe. But if they *are* genuinely following rules, are we not then committed to *their* having a conception of the rule and of whether their actions are in conformity with it? You state that the player is deducted a point, but is this enough to establish that there is a rule here? Can we avoid the supposition that these people speak among themselves? It seems we must be tacitly assuming a larger linguistic context, even if the action in question is not in itself linguistic (this is obviously assumed where the action *is* linguistic in character).

So it will be important to your description that it cannot be merely the description of *actions*, but will have two further properties. First, it will also have to contain a description of those aspects of their behaviour that show that they are actually *following rules* and not just behaving with pattern and regularity. Second, is there not a sense in which the observer himself has to *follow* the rules governing the signs, and so is not entirely independent? In other words, he *does* have to have a prior understanding of it.

LATO: It is certainly true that acting in accord with a rule is not the same as merely repeating an action, and so to describe a repeated action is not in itself to describe a person following a rule—though we could argue that it does at least capture the substance of the rule itself even if it does not amount to the *description of someone following it.* But I take your point. We would certainly also have to identify the behaviour as belonging to a situation where there were other features showing that they treated the actions as being in accord or otherwise with the rule.

It remains a matter of controversy whether a creature having no language could ever be said to be following a rule—even if it did show some sort of 'self-corrective' behaviour—or whether a genuine linguistic context must be presupposed. I agree with you, in fact, that our inclination should be towards the latter stipulation, if only because there is a clear difference between any such 'primitive' rule-following and the situation where the agent *does* have a conception of his behaviour as being governed by rules; that is, where the issue can arise for the agent as to whether the action is in accord with the rule or whether a sign is being used rightly or wrongly.

So I concede that describing rule-governed behaviour can never be as straightforward as describing a regular activity and that this does appear to create a difficulty for me. But I know that you have another related point to make, so perhaps you would make that first before I try to settle this problem.

CRATES: Yes. The second need for qualification arises out of related observations. These again require that the description appeals beyond any *one* instance of an action purporting to be the application of the rule.

What I have in mind is that a claim to have described the rule correctly surely requires that we are able to recognize future applications of it. So the issue is: what constitutes 'recognising future applications of the rule'? This might appear at first sight to be simply a matter of forming the correct empirical hypothesis as to which future actions are in accord with the rule.[6] And if—returning to your example of the game— we are thinking just of non-linguistic physical *acts* with no greater linguistic context than the one you provided, then this may well be true. But the situation doesn't seem to be so straightforward where the 'acts' we are considering either involve the agent having a conception of what constitutes being in accord with the rule or are linguistic acts themselves.

Think, first of all, of the rules, or grammar, governing the 'words' or signs used by the referee. Again our first inclination might be to say that the correct description is the one that enables us to predict future applications of it, and that this again is a matter of forming a hypothesis and testing it. But the issues are not the same, and I think that the main difference stems from the fact that when we are describing a linguistic rule—or when linguistic rules are involved at all in the execution of the rule, that is, when a *conception* of the rule is involved—that rule stands in a different kind of relation to the description than would a rule in any purely non-linguistic context (if we can conceive of such a rule, that is—which we doubt). For we are using one set of linguistic rules to capture another. And the problem, or so it seems to me, is that we cannot tell in advance that the linguistic rules embedded in what we wish to describe can be analysed in the terms we are using to describe it. We may appear to describe it correctly in the first instance, only to find in future cases that it goes off in another direction not predicted by our description. If I may take an analogy, I might try to 'describe' the rule of chess to a novice by means of illustrations using the rules of draughts. And I may find that some moves in chess *can* be so described. But it won't be long before we find moves that have no equivalent in (or cannot be constructed from) moves in draughts, so that from this perspective (which is the only one we have in the analogy) the chess moves become incomprehensible and the attempt at description falls apart.

The conclusion would seem to be that to be confident in our description of a linguistic rule, we can never come entirely untutored to the situation but need to be able to take for granted a considerable amount of shared understanding of the whole system of rules within the given context. So we are already brought back to the fact that we must be *participants*. Doesn't this straightaway undermine the independence of the description, and so its very status as a description?

LATO: No, because I think this confuses the independence of the *description* with the independence of the *observer*. In fact, if you remember, this is the very reason why we are now considering the description of meaning in terms of the description of rules and not from the point of view of our participation in language, which—as we have argued—is not a descriptive process.

CRATES: Well, perhaps you were also falling into this confusion when you said that there was nothing in the game that had to be understood before understanding a description of it. I think this would only apply where the capacity to use 'signs' is so primitive that there are no good grounds for saying that this is genuinely a rule-governed activity. In this case, if the individual did go off in another direction with it, we would say that this was a different action and not a different interpretation of a rule.

LATO: Yes, I will agree with that. So the situation we are now dealing with is one where there is a genuinely rule-governed action that the observer does need to be able to follow. But I still wish to maintain the distinction between the independence of the description and of the observer, even in a great many of the cases where the observer *does* have to be a participant in the application of the rule.

I will certainly agree that, as a part of the framework for such a rule description, it is necessary that the rule does not fall outside the scope of those rules governing the terms of the description we wish to use. The situation must also be one in which we are able to take this for granted—which is why, as you say, we must be a participant. But this does not undermine the independence of the description in principle. I agree that there are situations where the independence of the description does break down—we shall come to these and the reasons for this shortly—but let's begin with an example where the independence *does* hold true.

Within the course of a conversation I may pause to give an explanation of the name of some animal: the 'fallow deer', for example. I will describe its defining features: how it differs from other kinds of deer, that it is spotted, that the male has horns of such and such shape, that it is of a certain size, that its call sounds like this, and so on. If it satisfies all these features, it's a fallow deer. So the description of the grammar of 'fallow deer' is of the form: 'fallow deer' is a name used to refer to a creature having these features.

Now in giving such a description we are of course appealing to a larger linguistic context, namely, the one containing all the terms of the definition. We also take it for granted that the concept *fallow deer* doesn't contain any elements that cannot be captured using these terms. We could perhaps express the point by saying that the concept *fallow deer* could be predicted from the meanings of the terms already available to us. It does not introduce any grammatical novelties in these respects.

However, none of *these* terms takes for granted the concept *fallow deer*. And so for this reason, the description, definition, or account of the rule for 'fallow deer' is *independent*, and in just the same way as were the descriptions in the example of the game. For this reason, it is surely perfectly legitimate to call this a *description* of the rule for the use of the word.

So far so good, I hope you will agree.

CRATES: I do.

LATO: Crates, your concern was that the grammar of the concept being described may contain novelties that cannot be captured in the terms of the description, and that this may not be visible to the person describing it. If this is the case, it could manifest itself in various ways.

For example, she'll find that she is just unable to follow subsequent uses of the word; her attempts to describe its uses will keep going wrong. The result is confusion. The situation is resolved, however, where the person— quite independently of the context in which the description of its grammar arises—*already* has an understanding of its use; she already has a practical grasp of its grammar. Her description will then be informed by the understanding she already has of it and she will be immediately conscious of whether the description is or is not adequate.

The answer to your concern, then, is that although this is true—that the person doing the describing must already have an understanding of the rule being described—it does not affect the independence of the description, which is between the *contents* of the concepts. The fact remains that the concepts employed in the description do not assume the grammar of the concept being described.

CRATES: Fine, I am in agreement. But now what about the case where the independence *does* break down?

LATO: There are vast numbers of words or concepts whose grammars might be described in the way I have indicated and with just this kind of independence. Certainly, if *all* grammars were accessible in this way, the job of describing them in philosophy would hardly tax us. The trouble is that this model only works with the very concepts that are of least interest and importance in philosophy. For the concepts that give us the most problems in philosophy are, almost without exception, those concepts that are much more deeply embedded in our system of concepts. It is for this reason that they cannot be approached with the same kind of independence. We might illustrate this by delving down into the deeper conceptual layers of this same concept *fallow deer*.

To have a concept such as *fallow deer* cannot mean merely to be able to label or name an object or to distinguish it verbally from another. That can only account for the most superficial aspects of its possession. Understanding the concept means being able to distinguish relations of *sense*,—being able to talk sense and make sense with the concept as it occurs in discourse generally. This means that whenever the concept is employed, it will take for granted an extensive structure of underlying depth grammatical forms—the deeper system of concepts that bind the whole together.

For example, below this superficial layer, the concept *fallow deer* already rests upon the more general concepts *animal* and *species*. If we are talking sense with the concept, its use will immediately bring these and other concepts into play. Furthermore, underpinning the grammars of all of these concepts—*fallow deer, animal, species*—is the grammar of the concept *physical object*. If they are to fulfil their rôle within the individual's conceptual armoury, this latter concept must already be understood. It defines the larger 'logical space' that they occupy.

CRATES: So, let me try to anticipate the next step in the argument. What we will find, as we reach into these deeper layers of our concepts—'deeper' because they are more deeply pervasive of the system of concepts—is that it will become increasingly difficult to give the kind of account that we were able to give in the case of 'fallow deer'. For it will become impossible not to take for granted the very concepts whose grammars we are trying to describe. For it surely can mean nothing to try to give an account of 'physical object' except by means of concepts whose grammars already partake of the grammar of 'physical object'. Whatever we try to say in elucidation of the concept will always employ other concepts that are logically dependent on it; they will already express at least part of the sense expressed by the concept itself. We can never properly put ourselves at a distance from it. There will always be some circularity. So the independence that we recognized in the other cases is not repeated. Whatever we may offer up as a description of the rule governing these sorts of concepts, or whatever we may claim as to the *logic* of the concept, we cannot escape this non-independence.

LATO: Yes, and as a rule it is just these deeper conceptual layers that are the subjects of our elucidations in philosophy.

Incidentally, this interrelatedness explains what is meant by philosophy being concerned largely with *internal relations* between concepts. It refers to dependent relations of sense between concepts. The concept *fallow deer*—at least in its superficial aspect—is at best only weakly internally related to other concepts. It could be dispensed with without repercussions upon our conceptual system. But this could *not* be said of *physical object* or *time*. For these concepts have no superficial aspect. They are structural to the system of deeper internal relations that underpins such concepts as *fallow deer*.

Note, Crates, that we should not confuse this sense of 'internality'—which is a property of relations of sense—from the internality we spoke of in connection with the participatory character of our understanding of our concepts, which has to do with a person's relations to language. That would be to succumb to the same confusion I warned of earlier between the independence of the *description* contrasted with that of the *observer*.

The conclusion must be that to the extent that the depth grammar of the concept in question is already constitutive of the grammars of the terms used to 'describe' it, what we are offering as an account of the concept will not to that extent constitute independent description at all.

It can make little sense to speak of describing a rule where the rule is also among those governing the terms of description. In such cases the nature of our account will have moved from being an *independent description* to a *circular elucidation*.

CRATES: I wonder whether we can be quite so categorical in our conclusion, Lato? The concept of description is surely determined not only in the detail of the relations between the description itself and its object, but also in its function. The circular elucidation does in important respects function as a description. The recipient comes away with a clearer view of this area of conceptual grammar. Why not call this a description no matter how it is constituted? Do you not agree?

LATO: I believe, in the first place, that we are justified in claiming that the kind of account that we give of the grammar of a concept in philosophy is, by departing from the independence we would normally expect, at odds with our normal conception of description—and certainly with our conception of *empirical* description.

I do not doubt that 'description' *may* be used in a looser sense to include conceptual circularities of this sort. For example, if I am asked to describe a person or a people, I will likely include discussion of their thoughts and beliefs in the description; and this may involve me in conceptual circularities of one sort or another. So you might well conclude from this that we are hair-splitting in our discussion over whether circular elucidations count as descriptions or not. But—and this, as I have already stated, is the *most* important factor—there *is* a conceptual issue at stake here, inasmuch as circular elucidation and 'normal' description are of logically different kinds. Moreover, this conceptual difference has important consequences for how we account for philosophical understanding and philosophical method—as I think we have already established. It also has consequences for our understanding of how we get ourselves into difficulties in philosophy, which is how we started off this whole discussion of concepts and factual discourse— which has not been forgotten and will be returned to. For these reasons it is legitimate to emphasize this conceptual difference, even to the extent of eschewing the use of the word 'description' to refer to the kind of account we give of meaning and depth grammar in philosophy.

To remind ourselves: we have distinguished the different components of a conceptual elucidation as comprising, on the one hand, a development of our *understanding* of a concept in a reflective context and, on the other, a requirement to give an *objective* account of it. The latter itself comprises various components. It will, in the first place, require an explicit statement of the position of the concept in the system of concepts and of how it is constrained in its internal relations and its relations to other concepts. This is not problematic in the case of the concepts we are presently discussing. However, it will also require giving an account or elucidation of the *meaning* of the concept,—its *content*. This is straightforward in the case of concepts such as *fallow deer* and hugely many like it, where we can reach for terms with independent meaning. But it is precisely where we run into difficulties with the concepts we have to manage in philosophy.

To illustrate these points again, consider the following example statement:

> People sometimes compare the grammars of the concepts *time* and *space* in the following way. They say 'space is multidirectional, whereas time has only one direction'. This is meant to be a way of saying that it makes no sense to speak of time 'going backwards',— time can only go forwards, or some such thing. In fact it seems to me that this doesn't go far enough; for if it makes no sense to say that time can go backwards, it makes little sense to say it goes forwards either! In fact, the best we can say is that, contrary to popular superstition, the concept *direction* is not a part of the concept *time*. On the other hand 'space is multi-directional' or even 'space has direction' are valid grammatical remarks (though perhaps rather trivial ones) which in the right context can contribute to elucidation of the concepts *space* and *direction*.

This little collection of grammatical statements contains many of the elements that I have said can legitimately be a part of the description of the grammars of these concepts. For example, it says that the concept of time is not internally related to the concept of direction, while the concept of space is so related. This is a description of this fragment of the system of concepts. Likewise, the statement that it makes no sense to say that time can go backwards, and therefore that it makes no sense to say it can go forwards either, is a statement describing the constraints acting on these concepts.

Fine. But if we now turn to how the meaning of the concept *space* may be 'described' in terms of *direction*, it is clear that, as a grammatical remark, it is circular because *direction* is already a spatial concept. The concepts are internally related. So I conclude that it can only be confusing to call this a description of the grammar of *space*: I have not described the grammar of *space* in terms of *direction*—at least not if that is based on the model established in the case of *fallow deer*. And so this is surely not what we would normally accept as a description, even if the illumination that we derive from such elucidations does play an important rôle in informing what *does* legitimately belong to description, namely that it enables us to confirm, while describing the system of concepts, that a given concept is constrained in relation to some other concept in one way or another.

CRATES: I agree that this has to be our conclusion.

LATO: Interestingly, Crates, this circularity is not something observed only lately in philosophy. Indeed we were only too aware of it ourselves,[7] even to the extent—because at that time we were still convinced that philosophy should *explain* phenomena—of taking it to be a failure of philosophic method. And yet, in spite of having discussed the general issues here on numerous occasions with Wittgenstein, for me it remains a matter of conjecture how far he had already taken these difficulties into account when he spoke of 'describing grammar'. It is not impossible, I suppose, that—along the lines you have described—he viewed the concept of description as broad enough to include accounts that contain circular elucidations and regarded it as only a leftover of positivism and empiricism to think of description *essentially* as empirical. But I am not convinced; for in our final discussions he certainly appeared to be increasingly aware that this circularity created difficulties he might not have given sufficient attention to previously. During a discussion of colour concepts, for example, he raised the question of whether sighted and colour-blind people can have the same conception of colour-blindness and asked what measure of communication can exist between those who do and those who do not have a given concept.[8] He went on:

> And to whom can I describe all the things *we* normal people can learn? Understanding the description itself already presupposes that he has learned something. (ROC 121)

> How can I describe to someone how we use the word 'tomorrow'? I can *teach* it to a child; but this does not mean I'm describing its use to him.
> But can I describe the practice of people who have a concept, e.g. 'reddish-green', that we don't possess?—in any case I certainly can't *teach* this practice to anyone. (ROC 122)

> Can I then only say: 'These people call *this* (brown, for example) reddish green'? Wouldn't it then be just another word for something that I have a word for? If they really have a different concept than I do, this must be shown by the fact that I can't quite figure out their use of words. (ROC 123)

But I have kept on saying that it's conceivable for our concepts to be different than they are. Was that all nonsense? (ROC 124)

CRATES: It is interesting that he did not make a distinction in kind between the case of a temporal concept, *tomorrow*, where we are thwarted in any description of its use by circularity, and the other kind of case where the description fails because the concept, *reddish-green*, falls outside the scope of our own concepts. This may suggest that he had not thought through these differences.

But the most interesting feature of these remarks is how much the sentiment is in keeping with that contemporaneous remark you quoted earlier to the effect that logic cannot be described, we have to *look* at the use of language and we will see it.[9]

Is there not a correspondence here with the distinction between 'saying' and 'showing', which you have often related to me as having had its origins in Wittgenstein's earlier discussions in the *Tractatus* but which surely still has a place in his later thinking? For the primary fruit of the elucidation is not the external description of the location of a concept within the system, nor even the description of its use, but the heightened transparency in our appreciation of its meaning. This transparency corresponds, I believe, to what Wittgenstein called 'seeing' logic in the use of language.

At risk of pre-empting later discussions, Lato, I hope you will agree to our saying something more at this juncture about the nature of this 'seeing'. For, superficially at least, it smacks of something observational and subjective, which would appear to create a further challenge to our account of conceptual elucidation.

4   Grammar and showing

My particular reason for concern, in this regard, is that this extends the qualms I expressed earlier regarding the *participatory* nature of our understanding of our concepts—which seems to undermine the objectivity of linguistic understanding. On that occasion you were able to evade global scepticism over the reality of language by deriving a concept of linguistic objectivity from the independent perspective that some concepts have over others—your example being the definition of 'fallow deer'.[10] Within such a perspective, factual statements can be made as to whether the use of a term is correct or not. But of course this doesn't have any bearing on the apparently subjective nature of the *process* of understanding, which would always appear to depend ultimately on what *seems* to make sense. And if, in the case of the concepts we have to deal with in philosophy, our reflections on our concepts are necessarily circular—with the result that we cannot form the same independent perspective and so must depend on what shows itself in the circular elucidations—are we not now also committed to an account of this *showing* as a subjective phenomenon? Let me explain this some more before you respond.

We have agreed that our need to investigate our concepts is one that arises out of a perplexity emerging from *within* our understanding of them; so that whenever we reach some disagreement over or are perplexed by the scope of a concept, we resolve this by appeal to *other* contexts where we *are* in agreement over its application. We then use this to illuminate the original problem. But this appeal will always depend on what we *accept* as making sense in those cases to which we make our appeal. It is this act of acceptance—which is just another way of expressing the participatory nature of our understanding—that seems to drag us back into subjectivity. For this acceptance is not a matter of acknowledging a *fact* by appeal to agreed and independent terms of definition, as it was in the case of 'fallow deer'; rather it is a matter of making a *judgement* that this is how we understand the employment of the concept in the circumstances to which we are appealing. So this is my difficulty: that 'solving' philosophical problems depends on persuasion and an appeal to our *convictions*.—The 'seeing' of what is shown must surely be a subjective judgement.

And if I remember correctly, Wittgenstein himself said that philosophy is a matter of persuasion.[11]

LATO: Crates, we resolve a difficulty in philosophy by guiding ourselves through various employments of the concepts in question, some of which we *do* accept while others are rejected as senseless. We then hope that these interventions will reorientate our understanding of the concept in the situation giving us difficulty. We develop our more lucid appreciation of the concept at issue by appealing to instances of its employment that we do not find problematic. This—as you have stated— is a matter of accepting an understanding of what makes sense in one context as determining what we should accept as making sense in another.

There is also an important difference between this and the case of 'fallow deer', which I think we need to make clearer in this context. We agree that in the case of disagreement over 'fallow deer', and the like, we can appeal to independent concepts to define 'fallow deer'. We also agree that this option is lacking in the cases we deal with in philosophy, where the *same* concept occurs in both the context that puzzles us and the context we appeal to in order to settle the issue. On the other hand, in *both* cases the appeal depends on an *acceptance* at one level or another— for example, in the acceptance of the use of the terms to define 'fallow deer'. So there is scope for sceptical challenge throughout. Hence, it is not simply that in the one case there is an issue of acceptance and subjectivity while in the other there is not. Yet, there does remain a difference between the two cases in respect of this acceptance, inasmuch as in the case of 'fallow deer' we are appealing to a set of concepts that are independent and *not in fact at issue*; while in the other kind of case— *time*, for example—the contexts we appeal to in seeking agreement on the use of the concept are *not* independent of the ones we find puzzling and so are a part of the problem. It is because of this—because of the circular nature of the appeal and because there is no higher court of appeal— that the apparently subjective nature of the appeal seems the more pernicious and inescapable. Hence, in this case, we seem to be all the more thrown back upon our own judgement.—The slippery slope into subjectivity seems the slipperier in this instance!—which, incidentally, is why it bothers us so much in philosophy. Fine. I agree. But I do not think we are now driven to your conclusion regarding subjectivity in quite the way you suggest.

The first issue we need to attend to, and which I think is confusing matters here, is what has been referred to as the ultimate *groundlessness* of the use of language; that is, that it makes no sense to speak of an *ultimate* justification for our concepts or linguistic rules. Of course, where concepts are defined or can be given a definition, we may speak of the justification for their use. But in the case of the concepts that we deal with in philosophy, these are fundamental to our ways of thinking and are already part of the framework for *any* justification. This again is a manifestation of the circularity we have discussed; for we can hardly speak of a 'justification' where it assumes the very thing at issue. And yet, none of this means that the foundation of language is subjective, as language is in any case *not* founded on any judgement—either socially or 'before ourselves', as it were. In the end it is, as Wittgenstein remarked, primarily and essentially a matter of what we *do*;[12]—it does not issue from *thought*.

CRATES: I certainly agree that, as a general observation, the use of language is groundless; that is, it is not supported by *judgement*—and so not by subjective judgement either. Similarly, if we are to speak of the objectivity of language *as such*—that is, not in the restricted sense, described above, of giving an independent account of one part of language from another—then this is not in any case the objectivity of something based on *certain* judgement but on its simply being *a fact of life*. It is like the singing of birds; '[i]t is there—like our life'.[13] Likewise, to speak of the 'objectivity' of language should not be taken as a meta-physical or transcendental statement of its objectivity; rather it would be a *grammatical* statement linking the concept of language internally with those of the objective circumstances of human life. On so much, we can agree.

But this doesn't address the situation *within* philosophy,—which is what is at issue. For it belongs to philosophy's paradoxical nature pre-cisely that it *does* try to project judgements into this groundless base of language. When developing a philosophical argument, we are required, in an important and correct sense, to halt normal discourse to force into the open *judgements* as to whether this or that is a sensible employment of a concept. This cannot be avoided. It is also clear that we are forced to do this right down at the level at which we should otherwise say that its use is groundless, that is, at the level of 'bedrock'.[14] This is the paradox, for it now looks as if we were having to make judgements that we can-not justify. And this of course is characteristic of what is subjective, and so stands in need of explanation. Merely pointing out that language *as such* is ultimately groundless does not in itself get us out of this bind.

LATO: I believe your paradox arises firstly because you are working with too narrow a conception of the way that *judgement* enters into philosophical discussion.

I also think there is a confusion here similar to the one I identified before, namely a confusion between the position we find ourselves in in having to make these judgements and the *nature* of the truths that they are intended to convey.

Taking the first of these, it is true that in philosophy we seek an *explicit* acceptance of what it makes sense to say in the use of a concept, and that this is something that would otherwise lie unspoken in normal discourse. And yet in spite of this, the acceptance surely does *not* take the form of *discrete* subjective judgements,—and certainly not such judgements as we might construe on the model of the subjective judge-ments of visual perception, for example, or of arbitrary impressions as what makes sense. We should not compare the latter with the judge-ments that enter into genuine and reflective philosophical elucidations.

Neither should that other familiar token of subjectivity be allowed to enter here: 'agreeing to differ' on the judgements as to what is a sensible application of a concept. There is no question of our agreeing to a *relativistic* conception of these judgements—quite the contrary. For the context of any process of philosophical elucidation is the overwhelming broad body of agreement in discourse. You anticipated this, as it happens, when you drew attention to the fact that we resolve disagreements by appealing to contexts in which there *is* agreement over the employment of a concept. For whatever we find acceptable in philosophy is sought to be consistent with discourse *as a whole*—or at least to those tranches of discourse with which we wish it to be consistent—the acceptance of the intelligibility of which is implicit in discourse and could not be otherwise. This acceptance is not in the ordinary sense *judgemental*. In philosophy we appeal to the grammars of these concepts in the arena in which everyone *is* of one mind and where, if we were not in implicit agreement, there would be no speech. We then seek to extend this understanding through intermediate cases into the areas of controversy. Our understanding as to what is intelligible in the employment of a concept is engaged in every sort of way with this background. So, notwithstanding the fact that the process depends very much on the capacity for the individual to draw upon his own use of these concepts, I think it would be wrong—or at least confusing—to call it subjective, or certainly so to suggest that it is dependent on subjective judgement.

This brings me to the second point. In philosophy we are dealing with a situation where the individual is challenged over his understanding of the most fundamental concepts. Moreover, when we are dealing with concepts so structural to our thinking, there is no a higher court of appeal if conflict or uncertainty arise—as you rightly point out. But the recognition of this does not entail that we are forced into subjective reflections and judgements as to what seems to us at the time to make sense. For if we are confused or challenged, the only response we *can* make is to resort to the more familiar contexts in which the concepts are employed and then to reiterate what is accepted in those contexts. When challenged over the meanings or grammars that are so fundamental and pervasive of discourse, the concepts must, as it were, open our mouths and speak 'for themselves'.[15] Because we cannot give language a foundation—because we cannot justify our use of language before ourselves—we really can only be 'puppets' of the language, which must then speak out on our behalf. The most we can do is to bring together examples of the ways in which a concept is determined and its sense expressed. This is in the nature of philosophical reflection.

CRATES: And of course this is also the *showing*—or at least the 'seeing' of what is shown—that Wittgenstein referred to.[16]

It is interesting that the difficulty of describing grammar only seemed to occur latterly to Wittgenstein, because it draws us to an aspect of his view of the nature of language which—as you relate—Rush Rhees was especially critical of and which we shall be discussing in detail in the next dialogue.[17] As I understand it, Rhees argued that Wittgenstein—at times at least—had too much the view of language as the operation of a *system* or the application of a *technique*,—over impressed perhaps by his own comparisons between language and games. The view of language as a technique—thinking of it in functional terms as a 'way of doing things'—lends itself to treating the use of a word as an object that can be exhaustively described 'externally', as we have put it. On this account, descriptions of grammar would grade seamlessly into factual descriptions of the surrounding circumstances of the use of words, in just the same way that we may pass from the description of the actual use of a hammer to a wider description of the activity of building within which that use occurs. How a word is used is regarded as just one fact among others and on the same level. Wittgenstein's apparent lack of concern, until so late in his thinking, that there might be anything problematic in describing grammar on this model certainly seems to be consistent with this alleged trend in his thinking.

LATO: Our own view, as I think we can now agree, is that there remain important differences between empirical description in general and the kind of 'description' or account we give of language that is intended to reveal the depth grammar of a concept. We agree that the account will contain an important descriptive element in the way it outlines the configuration of the *system*. But our conviction of what is *necessary* in the grammar of a concept, which is essential to the account, depends rather more on *reason* than on description as such.

Similarly, when we elucidate the *meaning* of a concept, we do not doubt the existence of contexts where we may describe the rule governing the use of a word—namely where that word is defined using terms that are independent in meaning. But in the case of the concepts we have to deal with in philosophy, these are usually so structural to our thinking that there is no higher order set of concepts from which they might be viewed. Hence the explanation of their meaning is of necessity circular. Our real need is a greater reflective *understanding* of the concept. This can only be achieved by reflecting more clearly the connections of sense between our concepts. These departures from what we normally think of as description can only be obscured by bringing them under this same heading; and so for this reason it would be wise and would cause least confusion if we were to restrict talk of describing grammar to those specific contexts where its application is more straightforward.[18]

At this point we might turn our attention for a moment to one way in which the issue of the 'describability' of grammar may get muddled up with other issues. A follower of Wittgenstein, Kathleen Emmett,[19] berated the 'transcendentalist' philosophers who held that linguistic rules—except in their most superficial aspects—are ineffable;[20] that is, they cannot be described and represent non-empirical necessities.[21] She held that it's just an empirical fact that we have the linguistic rules that we do have and that these must therefore be describable.[22]

The problem with presenting the dichotomy in this way is that it ties together the issues of *describability* and *necessity*; for it appears that if grammatical rules are not empirical then they must be both indescribable and necessary, so that if they turn out not to be necessary after all, then they must be describable after all. But I think that Emmett fails to distinguish *empirical* fact from *contingent* fact. What she should have said is that it is a contingent fact that we have the concepts that we do have; hence the existence of concepts with these grammars is a contingent fact and not a necessary one (the more general issue of necessity we shall return to later in this dialogue). But, as should be clear from the foregoing discussion, this is not at all to say that our grasp of their properties is a matter of *sense* experience: of observation and description. Our relation to the grammars of our concepts is not essentially an empirical relation but is, as we have argued, a participatory one. I do not learn a language by describing what you are doing; still less by forming a 'theory' of what you are doing. Rather, I try to say things and to follow what *you* are saying.

5   General facts of nature, concepts and philosophical investigation

CRATES: Lato, at the beginning of the third section of this dialogue, you said that there were two themes you wished to extract from Wittgenstein's remarks on describing language. We have dealt with the first of these, where our concern was with describing the relations *within* our speech,—the relations *between* the uses of different expressions. The second theme, on the other hand, has rather more to do with describing the use of language in relation to the *circumstances* of its use. Here our interest is in 'language and the actions into which it is woven'. You then said that this would lead to a discussion of the rôle of 'general facts of nature' in philosophy. Let's now turn to these topics.

LATO: A complicating factor in all these discussions is that quite certainly there are many cases where concepts *are* determined by reference to facts. Indeed we have already discussed an example of this, 'fallow deer', which we defined by describing a suite of *facts* about the animal. Another example might be that of a disease, which may be defined on the basis of the description of an array of symptoms and causes.

In this sort of case it is easy to see how facts are a part of the *constitution* of the concept;—they are internal to it, they are a functional part of its grammar. Understanding these constituent facts is, therefore, internal to the understanding of the concept, and citing them will belong to an account of its grammar. This falls within the category of defining a concept using an independent set of concepts, for it is through the gathering together of facts described by means of these other concepts that the new concept is formed.

Now there are certainly plenty of instances in philosophy where the concepts of interest are themselves at least *partly* constituted by reference to facts,—so that the revelation of these facts will play an important rôle in their elucidation. But it is *also* true that such revelations will not in themselves be adequate to illuminating the most fundamental problems of philosophy. This is partly for reasons that we have already given at length, namely that the problem concepts in philosophy are generally not those that can be exhaustively analysed by means of such definitions but are among those that can only be elucidated by circular accounts.— Philosophy is in its element when occupied with concepts that are rooted essentially in our *practices*.[23] Nevertheless, it remains the case that facts do play at least some part—and sometimes an important part—in the constitution of most or perhaps all of these concepts. Moreover, the failure to observe this is the cause of a great deal of the confusion in philosophy.

Do you agree so far, Crates?

CRATES: Yes, I do, Lato, and the specific case we have in mind is the one I have just reminded you of, namely where the facts in question are those that we describe when we describe 'language and the actions into which it is woven'. In other words, it is the situation where the concept determined by reference to these facts is the concept *of* the language-game in question. This may—at first sight, at least—seem an odd or obscure kind of concept to concern ourselves with, but we will soon show that this is an extremely familiar and important situation in philosophy—and indeed in discourse generally.

LATO: Quite right. So let's begin with an example in this category. What you call 'having the concept *of* the language-game' is perhaps most familiar, and indeed most important in philosophy, in connection with what are generally called 'psychological concepts', that is, any concepts to do with the mental life.

We can begin our account of these concepts by distinguishing at the outset the different levels that they can occupy in our lives. Taking the concept of intention as our prime example, if we now examine how the concept is constituted, we will find that in its most essential aspects it is *not* determined by reference to any facts and neither is it explicable by reference to any facts. A child acquires this concept as he begins to express intentions through first person future tense uses of verbs such as 'I am going to do …' or 'I will do …'. In fact he acquires the concept initially without necessarily using the *words* 'intention' or 'intend' at all; only later are these words used to express intentions. But the important point is that these uses are not based on reference to facts; neither could it be explained to someone how to express intentions in these ways by pointing out any facts. The concept *thus far* is learned through practice. It also follows from this that to the extent that philosophy elucidates the concept thus far determined, it will also not be by reference to facts but rather by showing the logical relations between this and related concepts—*action, time, person* and so on. This we might refer to as the 'first level' of analysis of the concept.

But of course, the use of the concept is not confined to first person expressions of intention; for we also have a language-game of attributing intentions to others. This language-game certainly takes for granted the concept as determined through first person uses, but it has the additional feature of determining a concept *of* the expression of intention. And a major element in the determination of this additional concept is evidently factual. For facts relating to aspects of behaviour, and the fact of things that are said, are a part of the determination of the concept,—and which may then be employed as criteria for attributing intentions: 'From what he says and the way he has been acting, he clearly intends to do such and such'. So here we have a concept of the expression of intention as a mode of linguistic behaviour with various typical outward characteristics set in the larger context of human activity.

CRATES: As it happens, the divide between fact-based and non fact-based employments of the concept of intention does not mirror exactly the distinction between first and third person uses, as we shall discuss later in the fourth dialogue. We shall show that even third person attributions of psychological concepts also have a significant non fact-based component. But for present purposes, this detail need not concern us.

LATO: No, I agree. So, what this concept *of* a language-game does is place the first person or non fact-based linguistic uses in a behavioural and environmental context. This is what we shall call a 'second-level' concept, because it views the first person possession and application of the concept as an *item*, or fact, which it takes together with other behavioural and environmental facts. Returning to Wittgenstein's definition of a language-game as 'language and the actions into which it is woven', then, we can say that it is a concept *of* the language-game in this sense.

CRATES: And this, of course, is a language-game in its own right.

LATO: Quite. Within the scope of these sorts of concepts, then, we adopt a view of the language-game *as such*; we view it as a functioning part of a wider circumstance in human life. And so, through the way that intentionality is constituted through the integration of expressive uses of language, a *phenomenon* is created in human life—one which comprises both linguistic and non-linguistic elements. Neither is intention the lone example; there are many other phenomena in human life which are constituted through such linguistic extensions: hope, expectation, belief, indeed the whole range of psychological phenomena.[24] So we may conclude, firstly, that it is typical of these concepts that they have both a primary expressive use and a second level of use in which that expressive employment is conceived of as constituting a part of the larger psychological phenomenon.

CRATES: So the description of the language-game, where this is the description of 'language and the actions into which it is woven' is, in the kind of situation we have been discussing, an account of the concept of that language-game and so also of the phenomenon that is constituted through the formation of that language-game,—in this case the expression of intention. And it is an account that is genuinely descriptive—in the sense we have accounted for previously—inasmuch as it describes facts about the circumstances in which we attribute intentions, and inasmuch as it employs concepts that are not themselves taken for granted in the concept we are elucidating. These facts are the *general facts of nature*—in this case general facts about human life—that form a part of the basis of the concept. But we must also note that this second-level concept in addition *assumes* the first-level concept, which is also employed in its account; and so to this extent the elucidation remains circular. So the concept of the language-game is heterogeneous in this respect, and its elucidation will contain both non-independent, circular elements and independent, descriptive elements. We shall come back to this point as we summarize this section.

LATO: Yes, and we might add that there are further variations on this theme. This second-level investigation may itself be pitched at different levels. For example, the second-level investigation of intention, being an investigation into the way that language enters into the formation of the phenomenon of intention, may equally be treated at a different level as belonging to an elucidation of the nature of *language*. By examining different modes in the use of language, and marking out the different grammars lying in our conceptions of different language-games, we say something about the variety in what counts as a grammar. By looking at how language enters into and is partly constitutive of phenomena such as intention, hope, or belief, we illuminate the concept *language*.

CRATES: Before you continue, Lato, there is a *caveat* we should add. The failure to appreciate that grammars may be established and investigated at these different conceptual levels may give rise to confusion over *which* elements in the investigation are factual and which are purely conceptual. These different levels are evidently a bit of a tangle and likely to cause confusion in philosophy. There are also other influences that can confuse the situation further.

In the first place, in philosophy it is commonplace to utter propositions that resemble statements of fact but which on examination turn out to be grammatical in nature. This is a source of confusion in its own right. The proposition 'Every rod has a length', for instance, evidently looks like a statement of fact. But propositions of this type can readily be distinguished from ordinary statements of fact by trying to imagine the opposite. For example, it can mean nothing to say, 'Not every rod has a length'.

LATO: Wittgenstein spoke of this:

> Of course, here 'I can't imagine the opposite of this' doesn't mean: my powers of imagination are unequal to the task. These words are a defence against something whose form makes it look like an empirical proposition, but which is really a grammatical one. (PI 251)

We must certainly remain on our guard as to whether a proposition is a statement of fact or simply a non-factual grammatical remark in disguise.

CRATES: If I may develop my point a little further, Lato, a misleading impression of factuality may be magnified—as I have said—by confusion over the conceptual level of the investigation. This can be illustrated with some other remarks of Wittgenstein's that you have related to me, starting with a description of two different settings in which we may describe a visual experience:

> I look at an animal and am asked: 'What do you see?' I answer: 'A rabbit'.—I see a landscape; suddenly a rabbit runs past. I exclaim 'A rabbit!'

He then commented:

> Both things, both the report and the exclamation, are expressions of perception and of visual experience. But the exclamation is so in a different sense from the report: it is forced from us.—It is related to the experience as a cry is to pain. (PI, p. 168)

Wittgenstein was not trying to distinguish two concepts of visual experience but two concepts of the verbal *expression* of visual experience, making this a second-level investigation. He was interested in two language-games: one in which the expression takes the form of an *exclamation*; the other in which it takes the form of a *report*. And they are *second-level* because the concept of visual experience, having itself been taken for granted, is then combined with two factual linguistic circumstances—'responding to a question' and 'being forced from us'— to form the two distinct concepts of the expression of visual experience.

Confusion over the rôle of these facts in the investigation may then arise in the following way. In trying to explain the difference between reports and exclamations of visual experience, it may look as if Wittgenstein were giving a *causal* explanation: if the use of 'rabbit' is forced from us, then the result is an exclamation of visual experience rather than a report. At the same time, it also looks like an explanation of the *nature* of this kind of expression of visual experience. So it appears that we now have a different kind of philosophical investigation,—not a *grammatical* one, but one belonging to a *theoretical* account of this dimension of human life; for the statement that the exclamation is forced from us looks in this instance like a general fact of nature being used to support a theory. And this is characteristic of second-level investigations,—that they can give the impression of being given from 'outside the language-game', of explaining the theoretical *possibility* of a language-game—in this case, the expression of visual experience—on the basis of a phenomenon lying outside the language-game. But this is an illusion of the nature of second-level investigation, and it is typical of metaphysical explanation.

Such ways of interpreting this kind of investigation are common enough in philosophy, even, by all accounts, among Wittgenstein's apologists. You have quoted to me Elizabeth Wolgast as saying (and I think this a very typical example): 'In *On Certainty*, Wittgenstein wrestled with the question *how there can be* such certainties, a task which a Kantian might call transcendental'.[25] But it is surely a confusion to think that we have ever *transcended* grammatical investigation,—as if we were now in the realms of a transcendental investigation *as opposed to* a grammatical investigation;—as if we could observe and theorize upon the conditions of the phenomenon in question from a point of view lying beyond the language-game or indeed beyond the concepts of daily discourse altogether.

Wittgenstein's comments on these utterances may take the outward form of an external account of the circumstances of their use; and general facts of nature are certainly referred to. Yet they are a part of what remains an internal account of the grammar of these concepts, but at this second level. His general observations about the nature and cir- cumstances of the use of the phrase 'A rabbit!' are indeed grammatical remarks: the statement that the exclamation is forced from us says that the concept of an exclamation *contains* the concept of being forced. So we may indeed say that the difference between these two concepts can be explained by saying that the fact that some utterances are forced from us while others are not is integrated into two contrasting concepts, *report* and *exclamation*. This is exactly the way we spoke earlier. But this does not mean that they are distinguished by a general fact of nature,—as if this might be something we discover later about them. For whereas 'some utterances are forced from us, while others are not' is a general fact of nature in the ordinary sense, 'exclamations are forced from us' is not and neither is 'reports are not forced from us'.—They are grammatical remarks.

What we *might* say is that this general fact of nature shows the *logical* possibility of the two concepts of the verbal expression of visual experi- ence, where this would be just another way of saying that it may be logically integrated into the formation of the two concepts. But 'logical possibility' in this sense is not 'transcendental possibility'.

LATO: With these points in mind, Crates, we can summarize this distinction between first and second-level conceptual investigations, especially as this applies to psychological concepts—which are the ones of chief interest to us—and to the rôle of facts within these concepts.

At the first level, a concept is typically employed expressively, for example, to express an intention—though it might equally apply to hope, or belief or whatever. It is not excluded that such a concept might contain facts, but generally and fundamentally such concepts are based in *practice*. At the second level, the concept is *of* this linguistic expres- sion, of its analogous natural expression and of its circumstances; and together these constitute the concept of the phenomena within human life of intention, hope, belief, and so on. This we have called the concept *of* the language-game. This second-level concept in an obvious sense *contains* the first-level concept—it is embedded in it—but typically it will also comprise general facts about the circumstances of the use of the first-level concept. An aspect of the second-level investigation, therefore, will be to describe these facts and how they are integrated into the concept. Hence the elucidation of the concept of the language-game may be circular in respect of the embedded concept, but not circular in respect of the facts integrated into it.

At this point it will be important to remember that these facts are relevant for their *logical* status; they are *constitutive* of the concept. They are not facts that explain the language-game, and so are not part of a transcendental account of the possibility of the language-game or of the phenomenon of which the linguistic expressions are a component.

In conclusion, then, it is not inconsistent to suggest on one occasion that philosophy is a conceptual as opposed to a factual investigation, while insisting on another that general facts of nature may indeed be relevant to a philosophical investigation. Whereas the concepts of special interest in philosophy are generally based on *practice* and not *facts*, in certain instances facts may have logical significance within them.

6   Facts, concepts and necessity

Crates, we have examined how facts may have logical significance when integrated into a concept. This appeal to logic was also important to our argument earlier in this dialogue, where we agreed that describing grammar—or at least, depth grammar—is different from describing natural phenomena insofar as it takes for granted an *understanding* of the concepts whose grammar is being described. For the appeal to our understanding of a concept is also an appeal to what is *necessary* (logical) in its constitution, which can only be grasped through that understanding. For this reason, another difficulty for the purely descriptive conception of accounting for the grammar of a concept is the failure to bring home what is *necessary* in it. This problem fascinated Wittgenstein:

> Is grammar, *as I use the word*, only the description of the actual handling of the language//languages//? So that its propositions could actually be understood as the propositions of a natural science?
>
> That could be called the descriptive science of speaking, in contrast to that of thinking.
>
> Indeed, the rules *of chess* could be taken as propositions from the natural history of man. (As the games of animals are described in books on natural history.) (BT, p. 163)

I should like to be able to describe how it comes about that mathematics appears to us now as the natural history of the domain of numbers, now again as a collection of rules. (RFM, p. 230)

What you say seems to amount to this, that logic belongs to the natural history of man. And that is not combinable with the hardness of the logical 'must'.

But the logical 'must' is a component part of the propositions of logic, and these are not propositions of human natural history. If what a proposition of logic said was: Human beings agree with one another in such and such ways (and that would be the form of the natural-historical proposition), then its contradictory would say that there is here a *lack* of agreement. Not, that there is an agreement of another kind. (RFM, pp. 352–353)

If a proposition is to be a proposition of logic, then it cannot be merely a statement of natural history. If the account of the language-game is to have logical force, then the grasp of the 'must' must lie outside the simple statement of fact that the words are used in such and such a way. 'Logic' is certainly a phenomenon of human life,—it is an aspect of a human activity. That we have a concept of logic playing such a special rôle in our concept of discourse is a part of our natural history. But propositions offered just from a natural historical point of view cannot be propositions of logic, which must be expressive *of*, and therefore must appeal *to*, the 'must'. Without this there is no internal connection between the account we are giving and the philosophical problems we are trying to understand. For the understanding that is required in philosophy is the understanding of why there is *confusion* if we try to speak in one way rather than another, not just that we *do not* speak in that way. Philosophy is a logical and not merely an anthropological investigation.

CRATES: Yes, indeed. And yet even among Wittgensteinian philosophers there has been equivocation over this point and a nervousness of speaking of 'necessity' *at all*. This has arisen largely, I suspect, because once we have started to speak of necessity, it is difficult to see how we can then avoid the undesirable consequence of sliding towards the idea of necessities inherent in the world. These reservations arise most obviously in connection with general facts of nature that have been integrated into a concept. But they are surely misunderstandings;[26] for this necessity relates *not* to the propositions themselves as statements of fact, but follows from the statements being given logical significance within the language-game.—Given the constitution of the concept, these facts are necessary components of it: if someone has measles, then *of necessity* we are talking of these observable symptoms and not others. The facts are necessary in as much as they are constitutive of the concept,—which is not to deny that they are in themselves anything other than contingent. The facts could have been otherwise, and if so would simply have gone to determine different concepts.

LATO: Quite so. Interestingly, this temptation to treat grammatical necessities as if they were worldly ones also has its converse in the temptation to dismiss logic and to deny necessity. Let me explain.

In the case of any fact that is integrated into a concept, we may also imagine circumstances where that fact is stated *without* drawing attention to its logical rôle. Hence, for example, we may remark on some symptom exhibited by a patient without having in mind that it also belongs to the definition of a disease. In fact, we might even discuss the *fact* of his having measles and then go on to discuss aspects of his symptoms again without making it explicit that these symptoms are definitive of the disease.

Now a rather similar situation may arise and implicate itself in what I have just adverted to in the origins of philosophical confusion. Take the example of scepticism. It is a fact that in the ordinary course of events doubts are directed towards some states of affairs and not others. And it may be further observed that *as a matter of fact* this is always the case where doubts are raised;—wherever there is a doubt, there is always *something* that is not doubted. In other words, it is an observable fact that in practice a doubt is accompanied by other things that are not doubted. In this instance, then, we have been able to state certain facts about the general circumstances in which doubting occurs *without* drawing attention to the *logical* significance of these facts within our concept of doubting.

Now one consequence of this possibility is that it can lead to a superficial approach to the philosophical problem of scepticism—and *mutatis mutandis* to other philosophical problems—as it might appear that the observable fact is sufficient in itself to 'solving' this problem. For it might be argued—in certain quarters at least—that global scepticism is shown to be just false on the grounds that it simply fails to acknowledge the fact that the doubting of any one fact is always accompanied by the acceptance of other facts that are not doubted. It is not that we *cannot* doubt beyond this point—which now just looks like an *a priori* prejudice— it is just that we *do not*, and that is enough. The temptation then is to generalize from this to the idea that we can do philosophy without drawing upon *any* conception of necessity.

But this would be a confusion, for it fails to acknowledge that the fact that doubting comes to an end is part of what *determines* our concept (of the language-game) of doubting. It is a part of its logical constitution. Moreover, unless the force of this logical connection is acknowledged—its *necessity*—the force of the idea of the possibility of global scepticism will not have been met. And if we were to express 'doubts' in ways that differed radically from the usual ones, we would have to say that this is now a different concept,—it is no longer what we call *doubting*.[27] Observing the limit we place upon doubting is a contribution to our understanding of its logic,[28] but only to the extent that we recognize that this follows from our concept of doubting. Recalling Wittgenstein's remark 'And everything descriptive of a language-game is part of logic',[29] no proposition can belong to logic unless it appeals to a conception of necessity.

It is not that we are driven by some external, or worldly, necessity to stop doubting at a certain point, or to stop at one point rather than another. In a certain sense it just is a fact that we stop doubting at a certain point. But there is a circularity here which is essential; for the fact that we do stop is, as D. Z. Phillips pointed out, '*what characterizes our thinking*'.[30] And if normally we did 'doubt' beyond this point, then—as I have just intimated—it would just not be the same language-game and 'doubting' would mean something different. So it is of the *logical* character of our thinking that there is a limit to doubt; and the only contingency is that we have this concept and not another. The fact that we stop doubting at a certain point is, in this sense, the same fact as that we have this concept rather than another.

So we have nothing to fear from this concept of necessity as it is used in relation to certain 'facts'; we only have to locate it and the facts in the right place within the determination of concepts.

CRATES: I agree with most of what you say here, Lato, but I think there is one aspect that has been overlooked, because I am not convinced that the analogy with the definition of measles works in every way you would like. This has to do with the use of the phrase 'the logical significance' of the facts about the circumstances of doubt. For unlike these other instances where facts are integrated into concepts, the description you gave of the circumstances of doubt itself *employed* the concept of doubt. So there is this further circularity here—the nature of which we have already discussed at length—which makes the status of the description less clear.

To resolve this I think we need to say that the temptation you referred to, which interprets the philosophical problem as factual rather than logical, arises *not* from the failure to recognize that these 'facts' about the circumstances of doubt are integral to the concept, but from a rather more profound failure to recognize the underlying logical structure, or grammar, of the concept of doubting. The observations regarding the circumstances of doubting are only *general* observations about the nature of doubting to the extent that they are reflections of this logical structure. This, I think, is why the parallel with 'measles' is not so clear. For it certainly cannot have been the case that we formed the concept of doubt on the basis of observations to the effect that people only doubt a thing against the background of the myriad of things they do not doubt.—It evidently cannot make sense to suppose that such facts were used to determine the concept, as the concept of doubt is already employed in the description of the facts. What we do in philosophy to combat the sceptic in this sort of case is to *appeal to his understanding of the concept* of doubt, which will mean getting him to accept that the intelligibility of doubting in any particular circumstance (i.e., the possibility of recognizing it as a genuine doubt) depends on the doubter accepting many other things without any question of doubt. So by a judicious use of examples and descriptions of the circumstances in which people doubt—all *employing* the concept of doubt—the sceptic's final acknowledgement of the limits of doubt must be made to flow from his own understanding of the concept. In the case of measles, on the other hand, it would at most be a matter of getting him to accept something stipulated.

This is another example of elucidating the concept of the language-game,—one in which we view the concept *doubt* in relation to the circumstances in human life in which we doubt, and where our view of those circumstances (that wherever there are doubts there is plenty that is not doubted) is partly conditioned by the concept *doubt* itself, which is prior to the concept of the language-game. So, whereas in the particular case we can identify *as a matter of fact* what the doubter doubts and what he doesn't doubt, the necessity that there are such facts follows from the concept *doubt* rather than the other way about.

This has to do, again, with our distinction between concepts at the first and at the second level. For collating facts in the determination of a concept at the second level depends on the related concept already being established at the first level. We have a concept *of* the expression of intention because we have already an established employment of the concept of intention *to* express intention.

LATO: I agree with your analysis, Crates; this is a rather different case from measles. But, if you remember, my point was that in both situations we can alight on certain facts without observing their logical surroundings,—their *conceptual* connections. I agree that the logical circumstances are different in this case; they are more integral to the facts themselves. But it remains the case that the failure to acknowledge the logical surroundings amounts to a failure to observe the necessities that are essential to resolving the philosophical difficulties that may arise with the concept. Would you not agree?

CRATES: I do. Lato, you have argued persuasively that we should not shy away from speaking of *necessity* in connection with the logic of our concepts as long as we remain clear in our minds that this does not imply any worldly necessity. But I think there is another interesting question here as to whether certain concepts may *themselves* be regarded as necessary.—I mean *necessary* in the sense that we could not conceivably do without them. This is something of a diversion from our main topic, but I believe it is of some interest and relevance. Let me explain.

It may be said of a great many concepts—perhaps even the overwhelming majority—that their inclusion in the lexicon of concepts is *optional*. That is, we might imagine linguistic cultures in which either these concepts are lacking or variants take their place and occupy similar positions in their lives. Such variants may be observed either where they are determined by reference to facts *or* where they are determined through practice. It is probably true that the concepts we can most easily imagine dispensing with, or to which we might easily imagine alternatives, are those defined by reference to facts. For we do not normally have much trouble imagining the facts being different from what we are used to and so can easily imagine different suites of facts being brought together to determine different concepts.[31] On the other hand, it isn't so much more difficult to imagine variations among those of our concepts that are determined essentially through *practice*. For example, if we imagine a different perceptual mode and its associated behaviours—say, something akin to the echo-location of bats—then we could fairly easily imagine how different perceptual concepts might emerge in a practical way.

However, I think this situation could be contrasted with the case of certain other concepts where, if persons possess concepts *at all*, it would be difficult to imagine *those concepts* either lacking or in a radically different form. These comprise, I would suggest, most of the concepts that typically give rise to the problems of philosophy; indeed it is partly because of their special properties that puzzlement over them has endured across millennia. I am thinking especially of those concepts that are taken for granted even in the very commencement of speech: *language, meaning, concept, and sense,* and of all those related to them such as *belief, truth, knowledge, necessity,* and so on. These concepts—as we have discussed already—are structural to the whole of our thinking.— They are the branch on which we sit. If we are speaking *at all* then we have the concept of speaking.[32]—It is not an optional concept for a speaker. Hence, a kind of necessity attaches to these concepts that we do not find elsewhere.

LATO: Yes. And it is an unusual kind of necessity—if we can call it that— which I am sure we will have occasion to refer to again. As for its status as a mode of necessity, this is difficult to gauge. Perhaps it would be better described as a necessity of *self-reference* rather than a *logical* necessity. Certainly it is not a *worldly* necessity!

7   Concepts, generality and the world

Finally in this dialogue, Crates, we need to explore another area where difficulties over the relationship between facts and concepts have given rise to misunderstandings. By Wittgenstein's time, it had become a commonplace—inherited from the positivist tradition—to view con- cepts as essentially content-less vessels that do not in themselves embody anything we might call a *knowledge* or *understanding* of the world. Only through the falsifiable proposition can we capture 'what the world is like'. And so, except insofar as our concepts are defined by reference to facts, concepts are merely the arbitrary system of measures from which propositions are fashioned. The elucidations of our concepts are merely tautological or 'analytic', their only function being the straightening out of confusions over how terms are defined.

This also relates to another matter that follows on directly from the problem of *necessity* as we have just been discussing it. There we were interested in necessity as it becomes involved in confusions about the way that facts enter into concepts. But there are also parallel issues about necessity that arise in connection with concepts that are determined essentially through *practice*. So we shall be returning to this topic in this section.

This strict dichotomy on the matter of conceptual content was used by many of Wittgenstein's followers to defend a non-revisionist concep- tion of philosophy; that is, the view that there can be no such thing as our querying our concepts (inside or outside philosophy)—the argument being that as the concepts have no corrigible content there is nothing of substance to revise. But it was also used by his critics, who turned it the other way about and complained that he was committed to a negative conception of philosophy: as concepts have no corrigible content, a philosophy based on the elucidation of concepts cannot illuminate the *nature* of things. Either way, it would seem that the conception of philosophy as essentially a conceptual inquiry is the conception of a barren enterprise!

CRATES: We, on the other hand, are opposed to both of these positions. We would also wish to defend Wittgenstein as an opponent of them too; but from what you have been saying, Lato, he may not have entirely shaken off the positivistic leanings that were evident in his earlier thinking and so may not be invulnerable to such criticism.

LATO: I think it is a matter of debate how much positivism there remained in his thinking even towards the end,—that this was one of the 'egg-shells' of his earlier way of thinking, as he himself put it, that still clung to him.[33] But the view that concepts are *in their own right* part of our understanding of 'what the world is like' (independently of whether or not they contain facts) can, I believe, be shown to be more characteristic of the thrust of his philosophy than these positivistic remnants. The strict analytic/empirical dichotomy arises because we are dominated by this one model—the positivist model—of what constitutes an understanding 'what the world is like', namely that which is expressed in statements of empirical fact. But Wittgenstein always eschewed obsession with any one model.

Let's remind ourselves of one of the essential differences between concepts and facts. Wittgenstein argued at length that when we look at the foundations of language, bedrock lies in the *practice* of language;[34] that is, in the *application* of a linguistic rule unaided by the acknowledgement of any fact. As the possibility of facts being integrated into concepts depends ultimately on the facts *themselves* being formulated according to linguistic rules,[35] we would clearly have an infinite regress if the concepts had to be founded ultimately on facts. Facts take for granted the concepts by means of which they are expressed. Hence the establishment of linguistic practices is more fundamental to—and so in an important sense more characteristic of—the formation of concepts than the determination of concepts based on facts. What is at stake, therefore, in the matter of whether or not concepts, in their most fundamental aspects, have content—and hence also whether an investigation to elucidate that content carries substance—is how the formation of a linguistic practice may itself be regarded as constitutive of our understanding of 'what the world is like'. But how can we show this?

CRATES: One point of entry into the question of whether concepts based in practice have genuine content might be to re-examine certain aspects of the propositions we use to elucidate these concepts in philosophy.

Starting again with the positivist's view, we have seen that he states that propositions can be classed either as analytic or empirical. Moreover, it is the function of the analytic propositions to describe the relations between concepts. But these propositions are true by definition; they are tautologies and tautologies have no substance. They simply describe the order within the language, and so in effect are the propositions we referred to earlier as describing only the external manifestations of the grammars of our concepts. And because it is taken for granted that the concepts themselves have no content, the analytic propositions do not seek to illuminate anything beyond this order. They have nothing to do with what the world is like, which is reserved for factual discourse.

In response to this simple dichotomy, there have been various attempts to find a middle way between analytic emptiness and empirical/ factual substance. The notion of *a priori*/synthetic propositions was introduced for just this purpose by Immanuel Kant. And at first sight it appears to work in our favour as follows. To say that propositions are *a priori* is to say that they belong to the realm of logic or understanding and not observation. To say that they are synthetic is to say precisely that they have content: they say something about the world. Now, this step appears to be taking us in the right direction. For if it is the function of such propositions to elucidate what is given in our concepts, then what is synthetic in them derives from the significant content of the concepts,—or, as we might say, from what is synthetic in the *concepts*. So our final position would be something like this: the propositions are *a priori* in as much as they elucidate something already given in a concept, but synthetic in as much as the concepts are determined through engagement with the world.

LATO: Yes, that would be fine if it properly reflected the nature and status of *a priori*/synthetic propositions; but I think there are problems here.

In the first place, the status of *a priori*/synthetic propositions is itself problematic in the way they present themselves as expressing *necessary* truths about the world. They were not originally thought of as elucidating concepts, since logical propositions were still thought of as analytic; hence their necessity was always thought of as being of the world. But of course, we have already argued against the idea that our concepts contain such worldly necessities; or at least, we have argued this in the case where and in the extent to which concepts are constituted by reference to facts—where we may be confused by the attainment of logical status by certain facts into thinking that they are necessary facts. So a part of our present task will be to maintain this position with respect to the concepts determined essentially through practice.

This brings me to my main problem, which is related to this and is that *a priori*/synthetic propositions themselves have inescapably the form of factual propositions and so belong to a mode of *factual* discourse. For Kant, these propositions were intended to describe some necessary feature of experience, and were arrived at not by reason or logic nor by observation but by the 'understanding'—whatever that may be. Now it may well be that what he supposed to be captured in his *a priori* propositions would, if examined more closely, turn out to be conceptual in character after all; and that the necessity derives from this, not from the world. But that is not our present concern, which is that whatever it was that interested Kant was *factual* in kind, whereas our interest is precisely in that which lies in our concepts that is *not* expressed in statements of fact, but in the *practice* that underlies all statements of fact; so that the very point at issue here is whether we can account for the sense in which concepts may be expressive of the nature of reality in ways that *cannot* be expressed in statement of fact. Whatever may be 'true' in a concept of this type is not a 'fact'. Truth functional *a priori*/synthetic propositions just do not bring us close enough to the understanding we seek of how concepts—or at least those of importance in philosophy—possess content; in fact they take us straight off in the wrong direction. On the other hand, what we are interested in may indeed be characterized as an interest in the synthetic nature of concept-formation.

A point to note here is that, in the case of the concepts that are determined by integrating facts into themselves, the formation of the concept does not itself constitute a synthesis, as this was achieved in the determination of the original facts. So the concept-formation here merely makes a rule out of selected existing facts. But in the case of the concepts determined in practice, we wish to argue that this process itself is synthetic. So it is the demonstration of the synthetic nature of this process that is our current task.

And as regards the elucidation of these concepts, we are back with our earlier observations that grammatical propositions do not *describe* grammar in these cases—except in their outwardly formal aspects—but work by elucidating the sense of the concepts that is determined in practice; so that it is not that grammatical propositions are themselves synthetic, but that they help to illuminate what is synthetic in the formation of the concepts.

And just one more word on the analytic; there is a clear sense in which grammatical propositions are related to analytic propositions, and may indeed exhibit analytic features at times. This has already been implied in the way we have spoken of the circular nature of these propositions and of the elucidation of internal connections. But one thing that is clear—and will become clearer—is that the grammatical proposition searches out wide ranging and often deep seated and not so obvious connections of meaning; it is not, or only in a limited way, interested in equivalences of meaning.

CRATES: If I may try to pull these issues together, Lato, and begin with a summary; to remove ourselves from the horns of the dilemma—either that philosophy is condemned to analytic emptiness or that it requires some higher order factual investigation, making it more in the nature of a science—we need to show, first, how concept-formation *as such* represents, in some substantial sense, a grasp of 'what the world is like'. We need to show how it is synthetic. When we speak of 'concept-formation' here, we are referring to the practical dimension of the grasp of our most fundamental concepts, which cannot be substituted for by the grasp of any fact—general or particular. *A priori*/synthetic propositions do not help in this regard, because they are themselves factual in nature and recreate difficulties with *necessity*. So let's take another tack.

We might begin with a negative by saying that concepts would *not* tell us what the world is like if they were 'arbitrary'. We could put it like this: if our concepts were arbitrary, then for any change in the world our concepts would *not* have to change; the only exception being where they embody facts that have changed. On this view, *any* genuine change in the world would be reportable as *fact*, and any changes to our concepts would be driven by the recognition of these new facts, which might then be taken up into a new or revised concept—new facts about the nature or cause of a disease, for example. By contrast, if concepts are to be recognized as not arbitrary in their *practical* dimension, then this will be by observing how we may be forced to change our concepts in ways that cannot be accounted for merely in terms of the recognition of a need to integrate new facts into a language-game.

We might illustrate this with the now rather hackneyed but still live example from physics: two modes of description, two concepts, *particle* and *wave*, are effective up to a point in the description of sub-atomic phenomena but are ultimately recognized as being conceptually incompatible. We cannot consistently describe the observed phenomena by using either mode; neither can the concepts be integrated. This dilemma cannot be resolved by adducing new facts. Rather its solution will be driven from within the *practice* of science and mathematics to generate a new mode of description. In this way, a new concept, a new grammatical *form*, will come directly into being. In forming this new concept we will have created a new way of understanding the world, but not new facts—though of course new facts will now be expressible by means of it. We now see the world under the aspect of this new form,—from within a new *formal* relation to it. In this and related ways the world prompts us to the formation of new concepts. Moreover, the generation of the new concept is 'spontaneous', which means that it is *not* founded on the prior observation of some fact. You often quote Wittgenstein's remark:

> Something new (spontaneous, 'specific') is always a language-game. (PI, p. 191)

LATO: And that, of course, is a grammatical remark.—It would make *no sense* to say that the new concept, in this present case, is founded on the observation of a fact.

I think what you say, Crates, is exactly correct. But I believe we need to hold back a little at this point and broaden our discussion of the arbitrariness (or otherwise) of our language and concepts. Otherwise there will be complaints that we are rushing ahead without taking into account other contemporary discussions of this topic.

This supposed arbitrariness is closely linked with what has also been called the 'autonomy' of grammar. These twin conceptions have been argued for at length by Wittgenstein's followers. We need to learn from these and most especially to ensure that our own interests here are not getting muddled up with other issues. I discussed this question on two occasions and at length with the Wittgensteinian scholar, Peter Hacker, together with his colleague, G. P. Baker, on one of these occasions.[36] Hacker's views have been influential and so deserve our attention.

Hacker derived from Wittgenstein two 'doctrines', as he calls them: the first doctrine is of the 'autonomy of language' and the second is of the 'autonomy of grammar'. The autonomy of language relates to the anti-foundationalist view that it makes no sense to speak of *justifying* our use of language as such and in general. This view is of course a constant and approved theme in our own discussions, so I will not explain it further now. The second, which is related to this, is directed against the idea that our grammar, our system of concepts, is based on the structure of the world and in such a way that the question may then be raised as to whether the concepts we have *correctly* capture this structure.[37] This notion of the 'correctness' of our concepts has an even more extreme and deplorable form in the idea that our grammars reflect *necessary* truths about the world.[38]

Against these conceptions, Baker and Hacker argued that there is 'no such thing as justifying grammar by reference to reality. For grammar determines the bounds of sense, what it makes sense to say'.[39] We construct our concepts according to rules of our own making (though not necessarily freely or according to whim—they are not arbitrary in that sense).[40] The only challenge we may raise against them would be on the grounds of their utility,[41] *not* their correctness. Grammar doesn't conflict with reality,[42] and if the grammar of a concept *does* change, then this simply determines a new concept, a new logical space; it does not compete for a logical space;[43] it does not compete with others on the correctness of its representation of some aspect of reality. So the correctness or otherwise of our concepts cannot be asserted, still less that they are *necessary* reflections of the nature of reality.[44] Indeed we may divide up reality in any number of alternative ways.[45]

CRATES: So far, Lato, I think we agree with Hacker,—or at least, inasmuch as the concept of correctness he is attacking is to be understood along the lines of a *justification*, a comparison of our concepts with reality. This is entirely consistent with our own arguments; for we could not give an account of this reality except by taking for granted the very grammars that we were trying to justify. From this all the rest follows.

LATO: Yes, indeed. Hacker was arguing against a transcendental conception of correctness: it makes no sense to 'get outside' our concepts to verify their correspondence with reality. With this we concur. But where we do not agree is that all that is left to say of the relation between our concepts and reality is their *utility*; or at least, we take the view that this utility comprises an important test of this relation in its own right.

To be fair, at the end of our conversations Hacker introduced important qualifications to these notions of the arbitrariness and autonomy of grammar. Notwithstanding his foregoing arguments, he allowed that there are significant regards in which grammar is *not* arbitrary. He was intrigued by Wittgenstein's response to the idea that nature may *not* play a part in the formation of our concepts:[46]

> Yes, but has nature nothing to say here? Indeed she has—but she makes herself audible in another way.
> 'You'll surely run up against existence and non-existence somewhere!' But that means against *facts*, not concepts. (Z 364)

Taking up Wittgenstein's suggestion, Baker and Hacker drew attention to several respects in which grammar is not arbitrary, one of which is of particular relevance and interest to us. In the first place, facts of experience may 'prompt' us to change our concepts. For example, if we found material objects behaving in unpredictable ways, this would force us to change our concepts of counting and calculating; similarly, in a *liquid* world the inhabitants may not form arithmetical concepts at all.[47] If the world were different in such ways, we would have different concepts. This is of particular interest because Baker and Hacker's examples were not of concepts modified by having different *facts* integrated into them, but of a different world leading to the establishment of different *practices*. So this is very much in line with our own thinking. It also recalls a remark of Wittgenstein's to the effect that we can get rid of the idea that our concepts are 'absolutely the correct ones' by imagining certain facts of nature to be different, which would enable us to imagine the formation of different concepts,[48] which evidently implies that our concepts are to this extent a function of what the world is like.

CRATES: If I may stop you there, Lato, the reader may well ask at this point whether Baker, Hacker and Wittgenstein—and ourselves for that matter—are not sliding back towards the very transcendental viewpoint that we have eschewed. So we should explain why this is not the case, while not forgetting that there certainly are limits to how far we may distance ourselves from a language-game.

Earlier we explained the idea of having the concept *of* a language-game. This means to have a conception of the circumstances in which we possess a given concept. And so by imagining different circumstances, we may imagine different linguistic practices appropriate to those circumstances. This is a perfectly normal exercise of our concepts. In this way, as we also argued earlier, the accusation is avoided of stepping beyond the conceptual circle to view the relation between our concepts and the world from the 'outside'. On the other hand, the linguistic practices and circumstances we *are* able to describe must fall within the scope of our existing concepts; so we are only describing variations within our range of concepts—at most we are only fashioning new concepts out of existing grammars, which also shows that such descriptions of the language-game are not in any sense a justification for it.

LATO: Correct. But at this point Baker and Hacker shied away from developing this line of thought as we believe it deserves. As I have said, they allowed that 'to this extent experience *prompts* us [in the formation of concepts], although it does not make our grammars true'.[49] But what is this 'prompting'? Is there nothing more to be said other than that it determines what we will find *useful*? We will have to prove that our concepts have corrigible content. For that, we need to show that the demonstration of the utility of a concept is *actually* corrective. Again, if what is at issue is the correspondence between the factual content of our concepts and reality, then we will have no difficulty with the idea of testing the correctness of the concepts. For example, if we discover that the facts on which a concept has been founded are in fact false, then this undermines the concept and we will abandon it as false. So if we find that the symptoms of measles are in fact caused by a number of different and unrelated physiological events, we do not just say that the word 'measles' is now useless, we say that in fact there is no such thing as measles. We now need to show that there is an equivalent process of rejection in relation to concepts established essentially through practice.

CRATES: I must say, Lato, that I find this puzzling. From one point of view I do not see why it should be up to us to show that the utility of a concept is not a function of the nature of the world but merely of our measures. After all, if we find that some tool is useless, it is because it doesn't deal effectively with its intended object; and that of course will be a function of the nature of the object. But on the other hand, the formation of concepts has been called arbitrary on the grounds that the ways in which we construct the world through our concepts are *unlimited*—akin to the way that the graduations on a ruler are arbitrary. If that is the case—which we do not doubt—then doesn't this already do away with the notion of correctness with regard to our concepts?

LATO: I think not. It doesn't follow from the fact that there are unlimited ways of dividing up the world that the ways we do adopt do not reflect the nature of the world. For it also doesn't follow that *any* conceptual construction will do. To take your analogy, there may be no limit to the number of ways we divide up the world for the purpose of measuring it; and yet if we found we could never obtain consistent results from taking measurements, this would evidently tells us something of its nature. If no worldly constraints acted on the formation of our concepts, then there would be no such thing as running into difficulty or inconsistency in the projection of our concepts into situations, and the only inconsistency would be *internal* to language. We go out into the world and we make rules out of the ways in which we engage practically with it. The phenomena we engage with are integrated into and indeed become *part of* the language. Wittgenstein spoke of this as the use of samples, and he insisted that '[i]t is most natural ....to reckon the samples among the instruments of the language'.[50] *That* our concepts are not arbitrary—the extent to which they are not arbitrary—therefore shows in the fact that discord and confusion in our attempts to form and *apply* concepts cannot be ruled out. The failure to make consistent use of samples is one possible manifestation of this. Certainly, if we are unable to make consistent use of certain words, the propositions in which they occur will be useless, that is, *senseless*.[51] But this does not only reflect on the propositions; it reflects on our understanding of 'what the world is like'.

CRATES: So, what we are saying is that the modification of our concepts to make them more useful may also be viewed as an adjustment of them to the world. Similarly, a failure to make them useful would show a failure of adjustment to the world.

LATO: Following from this, Crates, a related point is suggested in this remark by Wittgenstein:

> ....We don't perceive that we see space perspectivally or that the visual image is in some sense blurred near its edge. We don't notice this, and can never notice it, because it is the mode of perception. We never think about it, and it is impossible, because **the form of our world has no contrary**. (BT, p. 191) (my emphasis)

The relevance of this is that if we say that the *practice-based* formation of our concepts is one aspect of our understanding of what the world is like, it might be objected that this cannot be right because—unlike statements of *fact*—we cannot in this case imagine the opposite of what our world is like. Our concepts cannot contain genuine content, because otherwise we ought to be able to imagine this contrary world; so that if we did try to imagine it we would not be doing violence to the world, as it were, we would simply be violating our system of definitions. But this is not correct. For our world is as it is; and unlike the contrast between possible facts *within* the world, the only contrary to the most *general* form of our world is *another* kind of world. And to imagine *this*, we would first have to create a different set of concepts *within which* to imagine possible states of affairs within it. And of course we cannot do this starting just from those we already have. So the fact that we cannot imagine the contrary is, in this instance, a sign that we are at the highest generality in our understanding of the world in which we live.—It is not a sign that we are no longer dealing with the content of that understanding, which would then have to reside solely in the world of facts.

CRATES: To command a clear view of a concept, then, is to command a clear view of a phenomenon in its most fundamental aspect, namely at the level at which we construct it and integrate it into—'rule it into'—our language in the form of a concept. To explore the grammar of a concept is to explore our intelligible relations to a phenomenon at the greatest level of generality, which is to explore the *nature* of the phenomenon in its most general aspects.

LATO: Hence any question of 'what the world is like' on this level has to be a matter of logic and not fact; otherwise it would not be a question about the *essential* nature of the phenomenon.

Let's say something more of Wittgenstein's talk of the 'form' of our world, and begin by saying something more about the rôle of logic in all of this—again with the aim of banishing any suggestion of worldly necessity. The logical nature of a conceptual inquiry means that the content lying within our concepts remains in an important sense *prior* to fact (except, of course, those facts that may have been integrated into the concept). This lends itself to the supposition that philosophy is an investigation into necessary features of the world,—that the world has a necessary or logical structure that is mirrored in language. This impression is again encouraged by the idea—which we have already criticized—of *a priori truths*, where the idea is that the concepts (as such and in general) are founded on factual truths which may be represented by means of *a priori*/synthetic factual propositions—their *a priori* necessity being all that distinguishes them from empirical truths. But such a point of view is not supported by the idea that a conceptual investigation may be 'about the world', at least not in the way that we have tried to explain this. For the *necessity* of a logical insight lies within the terms of reference of our concepts and not with reference to the world. Clarifications of our concepts express necessity because they express what makes them the concepts they are; this is what is meant by the 'essential nature of the phenomenon'. But it does not follow from this that the understanding of the world that lies in the grasp of a concept is the grasp of a worldly necessity. The form of the world is no more necessary than any facts about it.

One way of expressing our more positive view of conceptual content would be to say that concepts are *not* arbitrary to the extent that they represent a grasp of the *form* of the world. But this way of speaking presents immediate dangers and is likely to attract adverse comment. For one thing, it seems to hark back to an earlier period in Wittgenstein's thinking, which turned on the idea of the world as possessing a *logical* structure, or form, from which states of affairs or facts are constructed.[52] It also resounds of our own former conception of the 'Forms'. But perhaps the greatest danger here is of our seeming to be suggesting some kind of *ontological* distinction between the *form* of the world, on the one hand, and the *facts* (general or particular) that are constructed from it, on the other. This is the road back to that old-fashioned idea of metaphysics as calling for special theoretical explanation of this higher realm.

Against this we say that the distinction we are aiming at here is one arising naturally out of our reflections on the nature of our linguistic engagement with the world, and we say that the transition from speaking of *fact* to speaking of *form* is essentially to do with the generality of the level at which we engage with it. Moreover, there is no reason to suppose that this distinction brings with it a transition from content to an absence of content. It is certainly true that we may view the world at this greater level of generality within a multitude of perspectives—there is no logical limit to the number of concepts we may form, for the form of the world is not comprised of essences that *must* determine any one concept in particular. But again, this multiplicity does not conflict with our conception of the form of the world.

To clarify this, let's ignore the world for the moment and approach from the point of view of how this distinction operates relative to the circumstances that make language 'possible'—or in which it makes sense to speak of language at all. First, it is clear that discourse requires that we have formal relations to the world. Without this we can have no means of making statements of fact, or any other kind of utterance for that matter. There would be no such thing as *saying anything* if there were nothing corresponding to a grasp of the form of the world as distinct from making actual statements of fact. When we speak of 'the form of the world', then, we are as yet presupposing nothing about the world. A distinction between *form* and *fact* is an inherent feature of conceptualizing the world *at all*; it is a distinction that belongs to the grammar of 'talking about the world'. Our concepts are our formal relations to the world. And remember, all these observations are *grammatical* in nature: we are making a logical, internal link between the notion of the form of the world and the notion of what is understood of the world through the formation of concepts.

CRATES: If I may try to summarize, Lato, the distinction between fact and form represents, on the one hand, a transition in the *generality* of the level at which we understand the world. Philosophy, we may say, studies the world at the greater level of generality. The notion of the form of the world in this context is not a metaphysical or transcendental concept, but has to be understood in terms of a necessary distinction within language between the conceptual and the factual. There is, therefore, a link with an important underlying theme in the view of language that we are developing. For the distinction between form and fact is a necessary distinction within our concept of language, just because our intelligent engagement with the world reaches bedrock in *practice* and not in the realization of a fact—that too being a grammatical remark. So if we want to understand what is meant by 'the form of the world', we have to understand what is meant by the *formation* of concepts through practice.

LATO: There is another interesting and important point here, Crates, which has to do with the comparison between the sense in which scientific statements are about the world, in contrast to the sense in which the utterances of philosophy are about the world. Superficially, it might look as though we are saying that science investigates the world by producing factual statements about it, while philosophy investigates the world by producing conceptual statements about it. But it would be very misleading to explain the distinction between the two in this way. Indeed it is another source of the confused impression that philosophy makes *necessary* statements about the world. For in elucidating a concept, philosophy does not *itself* have anything to say about the world; rather it aims to elucidate what the concept already says about it. The outcome of the investigation is that we see the world more clearly because we now see the grammar of the concept more clearly.

It is our *concepts* that are about the world, not our *statements about our concepts*. *A priori* and empirical propositions are, in this sense, not on the same plane. For insofar as statements of fact are about the world, they complement *the concepts themselves*, not *a priori* grammatical propositions. The latter only illuminate the nature of the world because they illuminate what is already given in our concepts. It would be a confusion to think that whereas science finds out new facts about the world, philosophy also finds out new facts about the world only at the *a priori*, conceptual level. Neither does it follow from our concepts being 'about the world', that it is the job of philosophy to correct our concepts and change them if necessary. Philosophy has no privileged access to the world. And if—as explained previously in relation to the example of concepts in physics—a change to a concept *is* demanded, then this arises not out of philosophy but directly out of our linguistic engagement with the world and is effected through the formation of a new concept. It may be part of the task of philosophy to warn of difficulties in our concepts and to help avoid the logical traps that appear when we are self-consciously engaged in managing them; but the formation of new concepts itself remains 'spontaneous',—that is, unanticipated by any rational or philosophical process. Concepts are formed in practice and are corrigible in practice.

CRATES: Lato, what we have been saying of the content of our concepts, and of how the grasp of concepts at the practical level is also constitutive of our understanding of the nature of reality, may also be demonstrated by reference to the way we might speak of a child who is developing her understanding of such concepts. Here it becomes clear that her grasp of the concept is not the grasp merely of the utility of a symbol. Let me give an example.

If I am learning to compare the lengths of objects by measuring with a ruler and am learning how to describe the lengths of objects, and so on, I am learning the concept *length*. But we may also express this by saying that I know, or am getting to understand, what length *is*. It is informative to express the point in this way just because it reminds us that to have a concept is not merely to operate with a sign or to have command over a technique; rather, the concept pervades our intelligent relations to the world. My understanding of the concept shows not only in the methods I use to measure and compare, but is distributed throughout my ways of speaking, throughout the *sense* I make of things by means of language. It is not difficult to imagine the breakdown of a person's grasp of the concept *length* and the loss of understanding and general intellectual collapse in the person's life that would manifest it. It would not be adequate in these circumstances to say that the person had merely lost the use of a word. Neither could it be accounted for as the loss of knowledge of any fact that might be referred to in the application of the concept. No, she no longer understands *what length is*, and in an important sense she is losing her grip on reality, on 'what the world is like'.

Likewise, if a child is getting hold of the concept *cause*, this cannot be shown merely by an ability to make simple judgements of the relation of one event to another. Rather, it is something that has to work its way into the whole of her thinking and is manifested in the myriad ways in which she is able to make connections between things that are said and things that are done. If, on the other hand, the child failed to become fluent in all these connections, again it would not be adequate to say that this was simply a failure to grasp how to use a word (indeed, she might fail to grasp the use of the word even if her grasp of the concept showed in others things that she said). Here again we would have the right to say that there was a failure at the conceptual level to grasp the nature of the reality in which she lived. Beyond the reportage of facts, a person shows she has a grip on reality *in being able to talk sense*.

So the idea that our concepts—those grasped practically and not just those determined by reference to facts—may themselves constitute a part of our understanding of 'what the world is like' is shown in the fact that we treat the formation of our concepts as a part of the development of this understanding. The formation of concepts is itself a major component in the way we synthesize our world. This could hardly be characterized as simply a matter of whether we have yet learned to do anything *useful* with these words, as if it were merely a matter of getting or failing to get a *result* of some kind.

8 Conclusion

LATO: Crates, our objective is to make clearer how our concepts are seated in our lives. In this present dialogue, we began by pointing out that how we set about this task is *itself* a function of how they are so seated, since our investigation is itself conceptual and so is dependent on our understanding of the nature and working of concepts. For this reason we followed immediately with an examination of some the difficulties inherent in accounting for our concepts which arise from the way they are so seated.

A constant theme of this discussion has been the confusion over the relationship between facts and concepts—and between factual and conceptual investigations—and how this affects our thinking on these issues. These confusions can take quite different forms, and so in the first part of the dialogue we made an issue of the differences and similarities between an account of the grammar of a concept and *description* in general. We tried to show that the process of elucidating our concepts and their grammars is, for good reasons, best not thought of as descriptive in kind—or at least that it differs from 'normal' description in significant ways—principally because it involves circular uses of the terms of the account. Here the elucidation relies on something that is 'shown' rather than described, a notion that originated in Wittgenstein's earlier phase of philosophical thinking but which re-emerged in his later work, with certain important modifications.

We also noted that, in spite of certain fundamental differences between conceptual and factual investigations, there are also situations in which the account of a concept does entail reference to facts. These situations arise where facts are *incorporated* into the concept. They *can* occur in relatively straightforward instances, for example, where symptoms are referred to in the definition of a disease. But they can also arise in the special and rather more complex situation where the concept in question is *of* the language-game; that is, where it is the concept of a particular use of language in specific material circumstances. This is of especial interest in philosophy in the case of psychological concepts, such as *intention*, where the concept of the language-game is in effect the concept of a phenomenon within human life constituted partly through first person linguistic expressions of intention but also incorporating facts relating to the circumstances of the linguistic acts. Confusion over the rôle of facts in these sorts of situations can also cause trouble, especially if the failure to identify the correct 'conceptual level' of the investigation leads to the impression of an attempt to give a transcendental account of a concept from beyond established discourse.

Finally, we have tried to explain how the nature and the content of our elucidations of our concepts are determined by the nature of the relation between concepts and reality. All the while we have upheld the *logical* nature of conceptual investigation. But the recognition of this property has in the past led first to a shying away from the idea that concepts themselves constitute an intrinsic part of our understanding of the nature of reality, and second to a gravitation towards the idea that only factual investigations yield insight into the nature of reality. This reticence has also flourished because the notion that concepts possess *content*, coupled with the observation that the elucidation of a concept is of its *necessary* relations, appears to entail the idea of the world as possessing *a priori* necessary properties. We have denied this link, while maintaining that conceptual investigations do indeed yield insight into the nature of reality, because they make more manifest what is synthetic in the formation of our concepts. So again we have found the misguided preoccupation with facts darkening our understanding of the nature of our concepts, their relation to reality and our relations to them.

CRATES: Lato, at the very end of our discussion, I referred to the circumstances in which we may acknowledge that a child is getting to grips with a concept. I said that a child's grasp of certain deeply embedded concepts is something distributed *throughout* his ways of speaking and thinking, and implied that this cannot be reduced to simplistic notions of his capacity to operate with signs. We then concluded that this provides a context in which our view of concept possession as comprising at least a part of our understanding of 'what the world is like' makes itself manifest. It should be evident from this that the circumstances in which a child may truly be said to possess a concept, and the distinction between this and mere operational ability, are pivotal to our understanding of how our concepts are seated in our lives and of the nature of their relation to reality. This will be the subject of our next dialogue.

Dialogue 3 Concepts, Speaking and Persons

1 Introduction

LATO: In the last fifteen years of his life, Wittgenstein counted among his closest and most trusted philosophical colleagues, Rush Rhees. From the mid-1940s, Wittgenstein spent much time in Rhees' company at Swansea in Wales, where Rhees lectured at the University. Wittgenstein later appointed Rhees to be one of his literary executors, who then devoted much of the rest of his life to the task of editing and publishing Wittgenstein's posthumous works. No one was better placed to interpret Wittgenstein to the world and to make the constructive criticisms of his philosophy that would establish a fruitful tradition in the development of Wittgensteinian thinking. My own encounters with Rhees—almost as much as my encounters with Wittgenstein—have been essential to my understanding of Wittgenstein's philosophy.

In the present dialogue, we intend to apply ourselves especially to certain criticisms of Wittgenstein's account of the nature of human discourse that Rhees felt were needed to meet the challenge of the deeper and more universal problems of philosophy,—above all the problem of scepticism.[1] Our own rather more narrow interest in Rhees' criticisms is that it takes us to the next stage of our investigation into the nature of the possession of concepts.

CRATES: You explained in the fourth section of the previous dialogue that Rhees detected in Wittgenstein's thinking, at times at least, an inclination to think of the use of language—or *speaking* a language—as essentially the exercise of a 'technique', where he meant by this a way of *doing* something. Our interest at the time was to suggest that such a tendency went with the idea that in philosophy it may be sufficient, for the purpose of giving an account of the grammar of a concept, to describe, from an *external* point of view, its relations to other concepts. And our riposte was that the elucidation of the grammar of a concept in philosophy trades on an understanding of the concept itself. This is because our difficulty arises *within* our understanding of the concept. Hence, the requirement in philosophy is that we see more clearly, explicitly and *internally* the connections of sense between our concepts. This falls outside the realm of purely external observation of how various expressions are normally used in connection with one another.

In the present dialogue we shall revisit Rhees' objection from a somewhat different point of view; indeed from the point of view that he himself developed most thoroughly.

LATO: Perhaps we should note here, Crates, that we do not necessarily endorse Rhees' estimation of Wittgenstein's failings on this point. We support Wittgenstein's insistence that learning a language requires training and *does* involve learning techniques for the use of words. However we do endorse, for the most part, Rhees' account of the concept of speaking, which he developed in reaction to the idea of language as *just* the application of a technique—whatever its source may be. We shall refer to this again along the way.

CRATES: Rhees' thoughts on this subject were subsequently followed up by Raimond Gaita,[2] and so we shall draw on both of these sources. The essence of Rhees' position is that the concept of a person and the concept of language—or of *speaking* a language—are mutually constitutive. We may therefore approach the one by means of the other: we may understand the nature of persons better by seeing how life is transformed and extended in the use of language; likewise, we may understand the nature of language better by seeing how it partakes of and extends the qualities that are definitive of our selves as persons. It is the second of these alternatives that we shall focus upon for the present. Expressed in the jargon of the grammatical investigation, we need to see how far the concept of language is constituted in its relations with the concept of a person.

The need to move on from the notion of speaking a language as merely the exercise of a technique is not so difficult to grasp. For the exercise of a technique—in the sense in which we are using it—is just a mode of action; and whereas the concepts of language, speaking and *action* are undoubtedly internally related in a multitude of ways, the constitutive links between the concepts of speaking and of a person are not reducible to the links between each and the concept of action.

Rhees' principal tool for introducing this element into the discussion of the nature of language lay in the way he distinguished between operating a system of signals and *having something to say*.—Only a *person* can 'say' anything. Coming to have things to say is of the very nature of the coming into being of our selves as persons. So if we have not investigated how speaking is a manifestation of person-hood, then we will have overlooked something quite fundamental to the nature of language.

The relevance of this to our present interests lies in the fact that it is only when a person can properly be said to be *speaking* that he can properly be said to possess concepts. So this larger context must be understood if we are to understand the nature of this possession.

LATO: We may begin by looking at how Rhees worked his way towards this position starting from Wittgenstein's discussions of language-games.

2   Wittgenstein's builders

Wittgenstein wanted to break up certain very common assumptions or prejudices about how language works. One of his favourite tools for doing this was through the invention of very simple 'language-games' intended to illustrate the varied ways in which words acquire a rôle in our lives and connect up with reality. The best known of these are his descriptions of the simple, builders' language-games.[3]

The beauty and effectiveness of these language-games lies in the fact that in spite of their simplicity they are able to illustrate the great variety in the ways that words can operate within our lives. On the other hand, it is precisely this capacity that has tempted many to suppose that they contain all the essential elements required for a comprehensive general account of language. Such an account would then treat the speaking of a language as essentially a technique for carrying out certain operations with signs—though, of course, within a much more complicated setting than illustrated in the builders' language-games themselves. In other words, the difference between the builders' language-games and a full account of language will be quantitative rather than qualitative, and speaking a language conceived as just a very complicated technique for achieving certain ends.

The prominent position of these language-games at the opening of his discussions has no doubt encouraged this interpretation. But whether this position truly reflects Wittgenstein's intentions for them is less certain. It is true that such an interpretation does at least appear to agree with some of his more generally expressed views about language. It is also true that Rhees understood them in this light—and so we might be inclined to take Rhees' word for it. He then based his criticisms of Wittgenstein on this understanding. On the other hand, we have also suggested that in certain important but limited respects, the use of language *can* be compared with the employment of a technique or practical method; so we might also say that Rhees should have done more to acknowledge this.

So we have here a potentially major issue in Wittgensteinian scholarship. However, it is not our interest here to try to settle just how far Wittgenstein might have been aware of the limitations of the language-games as models. The exegetical issue is not so important for our purposes. The real value of the arguments that Rhees derived from his interpretation is that they led on in a convenient way to the richer conception of the nature of language that he wished to develop. Moreover, there is also no doubt that this richer conception was derived from nowhere other than his discussions with Wittgenstein. It is absolutely rooted in the understanding of language that originated in Wittgenstein's thinking. So it is fitting that we should try, with Rhees' help, to advance Wittgenstein's insights, beginning with what he himself might well have regarded as yet another example of 'egg-shells of the old material'.[4] With this in mind we will take Rhees' interpretation at face value and move forward from there.

Do you agree, Crates?

CRATES: I do. So let's go back to the beginning.

As I understand it, Lato, Rhees held that Wittgenstein should be regarded from the outset as wanting to give an account of what it is to *speak* a language.[5] He made a start on this by showing, *contra* Augustine, the variety of things we do with language and the variety of ways in which we connect it up among ourselves and with the world about us.[6] He began by imagining very simple language-games used by builders on a building site, the builders having no other language than the one they use on the site; and he insisted that this might be the *whole* of their language. This is where Rhees' difficulties started; for if the language-games are to illustrate speaking, they must themselves be *bona fide* examples of speaking a language. Rhees' feeling was that they are not, and he argued that the language-games are so impoverished that what would make them illustrative of speaking is no longer in view. What were supposed by Wittgenstein to be examples of language are nothing but a system of signals.[7]

LATO: Yes, Rhees developed this distinction between speaking and merely using a system of signals along two avenues, which he wove closely together. The first, which he described as his 'chief difficulty', is that there is no room for the distinction between sense and nonsense.[8] The second is that the games cannot show what it is to have 'something to say', or to recognize others as having things to say, in short, what it is to *converse*.[9] What Wittgenstein described is just a routine: if the use of one of the signals were out of place, or if an unaccustomed signal were used, then this might cause confusion, but the confusion would not be the confusion or uncertainty over the sense of a remark, it would simply be confusion in the face of a departure from what was normally done.[10] This is not sufficient to attract the range of concepts that belong to treating an utterance as having or lacking sense. Neither does it add up to the individuals making sensible conversation. Without these they are not speaking and cannot properly be said to be using language.

The impossibility of reducing the finding of sense in a remark to following the purely functional consequences of the use of a word is shown principally by drawing attention to the difference it makes that the 'words' are not used in just one situation but are employed elsewhere. Rhees said:

> The meaning that they have within this game is not to be seen simply in what we do with them or how we react to them in this game. ... And their remarks could have no bearing on one another unless the expressions they used were used in other connexions as well. (Rhees, 1970c, p. 79)

Rhees was careful to avoid confusing the *meaning* that the words have in a given situation with the *function* they have there,—even in a language-game where they do also function in a practical way, or are a part of achieving some 'common enterprise'.[11]

Unless the utterances have a use elsewhere they are not 'words' at all;— it is not as a *word* that an utterance can have a function unless it has a *meaning* established in a different kind of context. Gaita concurred with Rhees on this point:

> We *do* things with words—we have *words* to do things with—only because we do more with them than achieve our purposes. (Gaita, 1991, p. 108)

Distinguishing the sense—or otherwise—of what is said, or even trying to make sense *at all*, belongs to the life that is 'penetrated by speech'.[12] And the principal manifestation of a life 'penetrated by speech', and so of words being used 'elsewhere', is seen in the way that words are used in *conversation*. Conversation may of course occur either within or independently of concrete situations; but the important point surely is that there is a conversational *dimension*, of which it is essential that, beyond merely achieving our purposes, we have 'something to say' to one another. In language we articulate our thoughts and ideas, and an essential feature of that lies in the striving to make and to recognize sense and in 'the connectedness of what we say to one another'.[13] The growth of conversation is of a piece with learning 'what it makes sense to say' and with looking for the sense *in* and trying to make sensible connections *between* remarks;[14] it is in conversation that the distinction between sense and nonsense has its home.

It is essential to this account that the notions of having something to say and of distinguishing sense from nonsense are seen to go hand in hand with that of forming *concepts*. This also bears on what is meant by saying that language must be used 'elsewhere' than in purely purposive employ-ments. For when we say that words are used 'elsewhere', this does not mean just that they have a greater quantity of use but that they have a use that is in important respects *independent* of such employments. And one way of expressing this independence is to say that this use expresses not *functions* but *concepts*. This is not to say that the concepts we have are not in the end answerable to the contexts that are their natural home, nor that it is inessential to language that words have practical consequences, which may indeed be illustrated in a very elementary way by Wittgenstein's builders' language-games. Rather, it says that possessing concepts, as opposed to merely employing a system of signals, lies in having the kind of relation to our utterances which we might call the 'articulation of ideas', and which goes beyond the practical application of words in any given sit-uation. Hence, when we do bring words to a situation, they are brought in with an understanding of their *sense*, this having already been established in that other dimension of use. 'Understanding their sense' is of course the same as possessing a concept. We could express the point by saying that we do not just bring words to a situation, we bring *concepts* to it.

CRATES: The central point here is that we must recognize a kind of understanding that belongs with the notions of conversation, sense, nonsense, 'having something to say', and so on, which is different in grammar to—and hence irreducible to—any notion of understanding that can be explained in terms of the grasp of functions alone. This is the qualitative difference that you referred to. Once this is realized and accepted, the main point has been understood. And yet, giving a satis-fying rendition of these complicated differences is—for the reasons we discussed in the previous dialogue—elusive and necessarily circular.

LATO: As is very often the case in philosophy, Crates, it can help to make clearer such distinctions if we consider how we would employ them in describing the development of language in a child.

When the child learns to speak she is not just imitating what the adult is doing; she is learning to *speak back* at the adult. In taking *from* the adult, she is feeding what we might call her own 'will to speak'. Watching a child learning to speak is watching the emergence of a *person*,—which cannot be seen in the development merely of a skilled activity.

CRATES:—Which, again, is not to deny that in vital respects the use of language *is* a skilled activity; indeed the most skilled of all human activities.

LATO: Indeed, we do not deny this. We only deny that conceiving of language as a skilled activity can do justice to the conceptual links between the concept of language and the concept of a person.

From the start the child is trying to speak for herself; and her trying to tell us things and her trying to make sense of the things that are being said to her emerge spontaneously out of her efforts to relate to other speakers.[15] In a discussion of Wittgenstein,[16] Rhees mentioned the connection between language and thinking; and it might make more vivid the general point here if we remind ourselves that the child is learning to *think*—to think about herself, to think about what is going on around her, to think about others and to tell others about these things. All of this belongs to the circumstances in which the child is trying to make sense of the world about her and to engage coherently with the constantly changing environment in which she finds herself. The child's learning to speak and her coming to find her place in the world are the same. The use of language is expressive of and integral to being a thinking, willing subject.

In coming to have things to say, the whole of the child's orientation towards the people about her is under transformation. She is acquiring the attitude towards the adult which is not the attitude towards someone showing her how to get things done but is the attitude towards someone who is *telling* her things. And when the child herself speaks, she expects a response *in kind* from the adult;—she is treating the adult as someone who is listening to what she has to say. More generally, we may say she is acquiring an attitude towards herself, or a sense of herself, as someone to whom others can speak and expect a sensible reply and who can speak to others and expect the same.[17]

The way in which interpersonal attitudes illuminate this notion of 'having something to say' might again be made clearer by considering an objection. The connection between trying to make sense and the notion that the use of language is an expression of the life of a person was characterized again by Gaita in terms of the way that the individual's 'humanity' shows in his relations to language. Gaita's way of expressing this point arose out of his criticisms of another friend and colleague of Wittgenstein, Norman Malcolm. Malcolm attempted to show that, in spite of the impoverished nature of their 'language', Wittgenstein's builders *are* talking sense after all.[18] Malcolm attempted to circumvent the criticisms of Wittgenstein by painting a picture of the builders—but without increasing their vocabulary—which showed them more as people with a life than as the 'marionettes' that Rhees judged them to be.[19] Gaita's response was to agree that an injection of humanity into the situation was needed but that this must manifest itself *in* their having things to say and in their trying to talk sense. Gaita concluded that:

> He [Malcolm] gives some eloquent examples of their humanity, but he fails to connect their humanity to their speech: it remains external to it. Everything that displays their humanity fails to enter their supposed speech and vice versa. The chuckling, the head slapping and so on in Malcolm's example, do not alter the unrelievedly purposive character of the builders' utterances of 'Slab', 'Beam', etc. That is the deep lesson of Malcolm's failure. (Gaita, 1991, p. 108)

Gaita then developed this thought by considering whether a machine might ever speak. He argued that unless a machine has a life like ours in which speech has a comparable place, then whatever else it may do it is not *speaking*. In the course of the discussion he referred to Wittgenstein's remark: 'My attitude towards him is an attitude towards a soul. I am not of the *opinion* that he has a soul.'[20] Wittgenstein introduced this into a discussion of how psychological concepts have a place in our lives; but I think it may be generalized, for one manifestation of the attitude towards a soul is the recognition of others as fellow speakers; and this is shown in the way that we engage with them *in* our speech, and in our trying to understand them *in* what they have to say to us.

CRATES: Lato, you started by explaining how Rhees had followed two closely woven themes. Perhaps you might just remind us of these and of the conclusions we have arrived at?

LATO: If we are using a genuine language and not merely a system of signals, then we *have things to say*. This has to do with that fact that the use of language is not just a tool that we become skilled in the use of, but is integral to our constitution as persons. Having things to say is a primary expression of this. In the second place, it is essential to this that what we say has *sense*,—which is different from it merely having a function. This goes with the fact that in language we form concepts and express thoughts and ideas. There is sense and meaning only when words run through our lives in every direction and in all kinds of circumstances, when they are used in all kinds of connection with one another, and when this is at the service of 'having something to say'. Making sense is not merely a matter of determining what is allowed in the language or with 'the correct way of using various expressions'.[21] Rhees remarked:

> But 'what it makes sense to say' is not 'the sense that expressions have'. It has more to do with what it makes sense to answer or what it makes sense to ask, or what sense one remark may have in connexion with another. (Rhees, 1970c, p. 80)

Recognizing that a child is growing in her having things to say and not just signalling her wishes, desires or intentions goes with the observation that she is getting to be able to handle just such connection-making between sensible remarks.[22] And the context for recognizing this lies in seeing the way that the development of language goes with the development of the life of the child. Gaita sums it up: 'having something to say' is *'[l]iving a life and speaking out of it'*.[23] When we have grasped the difference between this and what we observe in the efforts of the builders on Wittgenstein's building site, we will see first how 'our lives are penetrated by speech' and second how it is not speech unless it *does* penetrate our lives in this way. Only *then* do utterances have sense and are there relations of sense between utterances. Only *then* can we be said to be in the possession of *concepts*.

3   Speaking and knowledge of grammar

CRATES: Armed with this richer understanding of what speaking a language amounts to, perhaps we can now return to the question of how we make clear to ourselves in philosophy the grammars of our concepts.

In the previous dialogue, we argued that the conception of language as a purely functional system of signals lends itself to the incoherent idea that the workings of language may, like any other fact of the world, be completely described from an external, or independent, point of view. On the contrary, whereas the grammars of our expressions and language-games do have aspects that may be described externally, the understanding of the grammars of our concepts that we seek in philosophy is one which takes for granted that the language-games and their concepts are already understood. Therefore, a different kind of relation is involved,—one which is not reducible to the external relation of observer to fact. For this reason, we distinguished between external and internal accounts of the grammars of our concepts and the expressions used to articulate them.

The foregoing discussion of the nature of speaking enables us to see further into the nature of this relation. In particular, it will help us to see that our relation to language is not exhausted in our relations to *rules*; for language is taken up into our lives in other ways that must be accounted for if we are to understand the immediate circumstances of the possession of our concepts. This becomes most strikingly evident when we examine certain of our concepts that are most deeply woven into the fabric of our system of concepts as a whole; for it is these concepts in particular whose employment is most distant from the simple application of a rule.

We will see—and this is pivotal to our whole enterprise in this book— that different concepts stand in quite different relations to us as speakers according to how our grasp of them is constituted in our speech and our lives. It will then follow naturally that if individual concepts enter into our understanding in different ways, then the treatment of them in philosophy should reflect those differences. This, we shall argue, will apply most markedly to those concepts—and their congeners—that are directly to do with the use of language. For we shall argue that the grasp of *their* grammars lies not so much in the grasp of the use of any words in particular (though that will be an element) but in *our whole relation to language*—or, in some cases, to whole areas of discourse. Hence, we will need to acknowledge a different conception of the knowledge of the grammar of a concept than we are used to in philosophy,—one that will amount to much more than an understanding of the rule governing the use of any one or set of expressions.

LATO: A useful way of approaching this will be to take a step back and look at how Wittgenstein's ideas on the genesis of philosophical problems developed. Again we can turn to an account by Rhees in which he traced, from the mid-1930s to the late 1940s, the transitions in Wittgenstein's views of the nature of language and of what philosophical difficulties have to do with language.[24]

Over the course of this period, Wittgenstein's views on these topics certainly underwent considerable development. And yet much of the motivation behind Rhees' attack on the examples of the builders' language-games came from his feeling that they showed that Wittgenstein had still not completely shaken off the earlier attitudes towards language, and hence towards the nature of philosophical problems themselves. Rhees was troubled by what he saw as the continuing resurfacing of this remnant of the earlier view in the later work.

For the sake of making the clearest contrast, we can focus on the most unequivocal expression of this earlier view which is to be found in Wittgenstein's discussions of 1933–34.[25] At that time, Wittgenstein had arrived at the idea of philosophical confusions as confusions of the grammars of particular expressions. These confusions can take different forms. For instance, the idea of the meaning of a word as a mental entity is an example of the confusion of looking for a 'thing' to correspond to a substantive, while the difficulties we feel about *time* may come from confusing the grammar of measuring time with that of measuring length. Words that give rise to special difficulties are often what Wittgenstein called 'odd-job' words, of which 'meaning' is again an example. These cause trouble because we do not recognize the irregular way in which they function but see a law in the way they are used.[26] Roughly speaking, then, the conception of grammatical confusion here is based on the model of entanglement in the rules governing the moves within a game or technique.[27]

These are, of course, illustrations of philosophical difficulties that are confusions to do with language, but Rhees noted that when Wittgenstein asked what led people to treat expressions in these ways his answer was 'the craving for generality'. This attitude manifested itself, for example, in 'the tendency to look for something in common to all the entities subsumed under a general term',[28] or in the way we are tempted to employ the methods of science in responding to philosophical questions.[29] And the point of Rhees' drawing attention to this was to suggest that Wittgenstein had not advanced beyond thinking of the root of philosophical difficulty as lying in an attitude that is not in itself 'specially connected with language', as he put it.[30]

CRATES: No doubt there is a number of reasons why Wittgenstein was not able to make this step. One possibility, perhaps, lay in the influence of the functional view of language and in the technical perspective on the grammars of expressions that is closely related to it. For if language is conceived of as an operating system that we merely observe externally— that is, as essentially an empirical object—then it is perhaps natural to suppose that confusions about such expressions originate in some general habit of thought rather than in something intrinsic to our relations to language, that is, intrinsic to *how* our lives are 'penetrated' by it.

LATO: I am sure that is very likely. We do not have to deny for a moment that many philosophical problems have their origins in the misuse of particular expressions; neither do we have to deny that we can examine the troublesome aspects of these expressions from the point of view of the techniques for using them—as Rhees himself did.[31]

What we find problematic may often be satisfactorily exposed and disposed of in just this way. But one consequence of observing the *difference* between the 'technique centred' and the 'person centred' conceptions of speaking is that we can no longer assume that the grammar of a concept can be reviewed merely by reference to the rules governing the *application* of the expressions corresponding to it. For this will depend on the relation between any such rules and those larger relations to language exhibited in the life of a person who can speak. A clearer view of what it is to speak a language will show us that lying behind such confusions with linguistic expressions is a confusion about language that is not grammatical confusion, in the narrow sense, but is a confusion stemming from a rather more direct kind of misapprehension of what our relation to language is and of how it penetrates our lives.[32] It is here that we *do* find a source for our perplexity that is 'specially connected with language'.

Rhees remarked that 'misunderstandings of the logic of language' express perplexity 'as to whether something can be said or not', and he went on:

> It is a confusion or uncertainty connected with being able to speak, and so perhaps with learning to speak: a confusion in connexion with what it is that one was learning as one learned to speak: with what saying something is and what understanding is. This sort of confusion or uncertainty (which is not just a confusion of the grammars of particular expressions) has led men to the scepticism which runs in one way or another into all the big questions of philosophy. (Rhees, 1970c, p. 74)

Later he spelled it out again:

> If language really were a technique, then the problems of philosophy might seem to be confusions between different parts of the technique. And it is plain that it is not that. If it were, there would be no connexion between philosophy and scepticism. You should not understand what was meant by the notion of the distrust of understanding. And certainly we could not understand why

philosophy should have been thought as important as it has; or why the problems of philosophy should have distressed people in the measure that they have. (Rhees, 1998, p. 112)[33]

The difference between this kind of confusion and the 'confusion of the grammars of particular expressions' is one that may be observed especially in our relations to the concepts that are *to do with language and speaking,*—in the contexts in which we can be said to have these and related concepts, and in how having these differs from having others. So we need to focus our attention now on the nature of our possession of these concepts.

To this end, we can consider again the kind of thing we might say of a child learning to speak. If a child can speak at all, there are all kinds of observations we might make about him. Here we may recall some of the responses characteristic of being able to speak: we see that he recognizes that he is being spoken to; we see that he is trying to *tell* us something; we see that he believes or is doubtful about something he is being told; we see that he knows that he is being told to *do* something; we see him express frustration at being misunderstood or with his inability to express himself clearly; we may see that he is not sure what *we* mean by saying something; or again, we may see his recognition that what some-one says doesn't make sense. In each case, we are thinking of various modes in the child's relations to language, but importantly we are not thinking *expressly* of his grasp of the technique for using any particular expressions.[34]

Now although we are *not* thinking of his competence in the use of any such expressions, there does remain a sense in which, in talking of these relations to language, we are talking of something that is integral to the child's grasp of the concepts we are using to characterize those relations, namely the concepts of speaking, telling, believing, meaning, and so on. In the child's very entry into sensible discourse, and in his ability to handle conversation, he shows that he is beginning to get hold of these concepts. Getting hold of them belongs to 'being able to speak'.

One may feel uneasy with the suggestion that the first steps in understanding these concepts is constituted in the formation of such relations and in being able to handle language in these ways. But the sense in speaking in this way lies in the fact that their formation is not just part of the development of a competency but clearly belongs to the *understanding* of language taken as a whole. It is integral to the 'making sense of the world' that is emerging in the child's coming to have things to say about it.

There are also important continuities between the formation of these relations and a more typical notion of what possessing such concepts amounts to. Indeed we maintain that there is a priority here. Forming these concepts begins in the way that we make these distinctions as part of coming to be able to speak, and only shows itself secondarily as something articulated *in* speech—in their *explicit* application. For one can surely only begin to employ expressions such as 'speaking', 'meaning', and so on, as an extension of those circumstances where the kinds of relations to language that we have referred to are already in evidence. What we shall refer to, therefore, as our *implicit* understanding of these concepts is presupposed.

CRATES: We should perhaps emphasize again here that we do not mean to diminish the part played in having these concepts that the various expressions like 'sense', 'nonsense', 'speaking', 'meaning', and so on, are worked into conversation and that many of the activities of correcting their use, which are shared with any other word or expression, will be present. Our argument is that what we learn when we acquire these concepts cannot be made intelligible from the point of view alone of a mastery of a technique for applying such expressions within a language-game.—In these respects having these concepts differs from having the concepts 'lemon', or 'sitting down', or 'dwelling house'—to use Rhees' examples.[35] There is a different concept of understanding here, and I believe it is this that he had in mind when he said:

> We could say that someone knows the grammar of 'language', or knows what language is, if he has learned to speak. (Rhees, 1970a, p. 47)

This is where the analogy between explaining games and explaining language comes to an end. And it suggests that we may find the root of philosophical perplexity about language—and other phenomena related in one way or another to language—as being to do with this implicit understanding and to which 'confusion of the grammars of particular expressions' may be only secondary.

To develop this argument further, I think we need to say more on the nature of the *implicit* understanding of our concepts that we have spoken of. We can do this by looking more closely at some examples and then relating this to the question of how the expressions corresponding to the concepts ('meaning', 'speaking', and so on) do in fact acquire meaning. The concepts we have chosen to give special attention to here are *belief* and *time*.

4 The grammar of 'Belief'

A child learns to express beliefs as she learns to speak. In learning to talk in elementary ways about things in her life, and in learning to follow the things that are said to her, the child is beginning to express beliefs and to recognize others' expressions of belief. The expression of belief is a *mode* in the use of language that the child acquires spontaneously as she learns to speak.[36] We might say that the use of words to express beliefs is *primitive* to the use of language. Clearly there could be no such thing as the child *beginning* by having belief explained to her. She could only follow an explanation if she were already in some command of this way of using words. Neither could belief—as a phenomenon within human life—have emerged directly out of training. No doubt there are functional relations between utterances and actions that are relevant to understanding what belief is. But, as we have argued, the child is not just learning to perform certain operations; for learning to express beliefs belongs to the emergence of the child's having anything at all to *say* and to seeing others as having things to say. It is in the context of these growing connections that it makes sense to say—and indeed I think we *would* say—that the child who is learning to express beliefs is coming to know or to understand what belief *is*, and is beginning to form a concept of it, in a way that we would *not* say that one of Wittgenstein's builders is coming to know what signalling is.

This will emerge more clearly if we look at the way that these surroundings lie behind the explicit application of the concept. For it is here that the continuity we have just spoken of between this understanding and understanding 'the grammars of particular expressions' becomes important.

LATO: It is certainly true, as we have said, that much of what we might call 'knowing the grammar of "belief" ' might be understood in terms of knowing the techniques for applying the concept. It will lie, for example, in being able to make elementary checks of whether someone really does believe what he is saying, or in knowing the grounds for challenging and questioning beliefs, or in being able to say why a belief is unreasonable, and so on. Much of this might be taught—or certainly developed—by explanation. But learning to apply the concept in these ways depends on and is pervaded by the kinds of relations to language that we have been trying to illustrate.

This dependence is internal. For a start, any application of the concept will depend on the things that are said being *understood*,[37] which must already mean standing in a relation to what is said as to an expression of belief. In certain circumstances we may indeed be unsure whether a proposition is being used to express a belief. These are the circumstances in which we may resort to criteria to make a decision. Moreover, because we may understand the proposition *before* we ask whether *as a matter of fact* it is being used to express a belief, this may suggest that the grammars of the concepts of proposition and belief are not shared but 'fit' one another—to use one of Wittgenstein's metaphors.[38] But it does not follow from the fact that we may often find ourselves in such circumstances, that we can understand propositions in general independently of what it is for them to express beliefs. For the circumstances in which we apply such criteria cannot be the circumstances in which the concepts *proposition* and *belief* are determined. For example, we cannot introduce belief into the life of the child, or convey to her what belief is, by introducing her first to propositions (and explaining their sense) and only later showing her how to use them to express beliefs, if only because unless that is grasped at the same time she will not have been introduced to propositions and in making 'utterances' she will not be saying anything.

What is central to recognizing an utterance as an expression of belief is already at work if we have understood what is said. It is therefore fundamental to our primary recognition of expressions of belief that we do so without making a *judgement* that 'here is a belief' or, in the primary instance of where we do make such a judgement, without the employment of criteria. Without the primacy of such recognition, the application of the concept would in any case be empty,—or at least it would only be the concept of an external property of utterances and therefore of an external or functional relation between utterances and actions. Hence it belongs to my grasp of the meaning of the word 'belief' that I can express beliefs when I speak and that I understand beliefs expressed to me when I am spoken to. This is why I say that the relation between the two is an internal one, and it justifies the claim that the relations to language that come directly with my ability to speak constitute part of my implicit understanding of the concept of belief.

I believe that Wittgenstein was touching on a similar point when he remarked:

> One does not learn to obey a rule by first learning the use of the word 'agreement'.
> Rather, one learns the meaning of 'agreement' by learning to follow a rule.

If you want to understand what it means 'to follow a rule', you
have already to be able to follow a rule. (RFM, p. 405)

Being able to follow a rule here is not merely a condition without
which you would not be able to learn the expression, in the sense of
needing to have an outward acquaintance with the thing to which the
word applies. Nor is it meant in the trivial sense that learning any
expression means being able to follow rules. Rather, 'already to be able
to follow a rule'—having *that* relation to language—is itself partly
constitutive of having the concept of a rule. That is why we learn the
meaning of 'agreement' *by* learning to follow a rule.

CRATES: Similar considerations surely apply to recognizing that one is
being spoken to, or being unsure what something means, or recognizing
that one has either failed or succeeded in understanding something.
Again our implicit understanding of the respective concepts shows in
the overall manner of our linguistic responses rather than in the
employment of the corresponding expressions as such.

In conclusion, Lato, we may contrast this kind of understanding—
which in an important sense still belongs to an understanding of the
grammar of the concept—with what Rhees called 'the grammars of particular expressions', which, roughly speaking, refers to anything that
might be imparted by means of definition, training or demonstration, or
through any account of the grammar of the concept that takes for
granted our implicit understanding of it. Knowing the grammar of
'belief'—and related concepts—has a dimension that is significantly
lacking in the case of 'games', for example, which arguably amounts to
little more than knowing in what circumstances we call things games
and the difference it makes to other things that are said and done that
we call something a game.

5   The grammar of 'Time'

LATO: We have suggested that parallel to what is peculiar in the way we
possess the concepts to do with language are differences in how the
expressions corresponding to them acquire meaning.

The kind of relationship that holds between the ability to speak and
the use of expressions like 'belief' or 'rule' carries with it that their meanings are related in a quite different way to the employments of language
in connection with which we use them than is the meaning of 'game',
for example, to the playing of games (and the language that goes with it).

To illustrate this, Rhees contrasted the grammar of 'reading'—one of Wittgenstein's own examples—with that of 'sitting down'.[39] In the case of 'reading' we cannot point to examples of it and hope thereby to explain its meaning. He remarked:

> And it is true that we cannot point to what is really meant. But not because it is hidden from us. It is hard to give an account of 'reading', for instance, because its *meaning* lies in the language-game in which we use it. As one cannot say this about 'sitting down'. All the puzzling words we study here are words having to do with the grammar of 'language'. (Rhees, 1970a, p. 49)

Here I think we can assume that what Rhees calls 'lying in the language-game' would encompass the relations to the language-game that we have been accounting for in connection with belief and would apply generally to the concepts to do with language we have been discussing. However, the principle also applies, *mutatis mutandis*, to those other kinds of concepts that we have referred to, such as *cause, time* and psychological concepts. So we may examine the example that Rhees himself referred to: *time*.[40]

CRATES: When a child is learning to express an intention, hope or expectation, or to anticipate an event; or if we see that he knows he has to wait for something to happen or for someone to do something; or if he is learning to recall and recount something that happened the day before, or is learning to tell the time; or if he is remembering he has to do something;—in all of these things, and many more, he is learning the various ways of expressing temporal relations and is on the way to forming a concept of time. This does not stop, of course, with these isolated situations; and if all that we describe is his engagement in such language-games conceived of as complete units in themselves, we will not have described his grasp of the concept of time proper. That would only come in the way the child showed himself capable of talking continuous sense expressing appreciation of past, future and present. For example, if the child's ability to make connections between different remarks in different contexts in respect of their temporal content were constantly breaking down, then I think we would say that this represented a fault in the child's grasp of the concept *time*. We might express the general point by saying that possession of the concept of time is manifested in the ability to pass freely between the various language-games in respect of their temporal content. Our grasp of the concept is pervasive of our speech, so pervasive in fact that it enters our speech just about every time we open our mouths.

Turning to the use of the *word* 'time', I show that I know the full import of its meaning in the way that I am able to use it in connection with the fact of my talking continuous sense in contexts where temporal conceptions are embedded. If you can talk sense in such circumstances then you can follow the sense that I talk and see whether I am able to use the word 'time' correctly in these connections. This, I think, is the only kind of context in which we can talk in any comprehensive way of my having grasped what the word 'time' *means*, and so it follows that the word's meaningful use is responsible to the concept as it is thus grasped and expressed. It cannot be done merely by pointing to something or giving a rule or definition for the use of the word; none of these would be of any use unless the concept had already been grasped.

LATO: So we are saying that the expression of the concept *time* in general conversation is prior to the meaningful use of the expression 'time', just as those relations to language that constitute our implicit understanding of the concepts generally to do with language are prior to our employment of the corresponding expressions. It is only through their connections with these manifestations of the concepts in our speech that we can speak of the expressions having meaning; and it is the office of these expressions to bring into the foreground, and to articulate, concepts that are already at work in our speech or in the way we handle language. The accountability of the use of the word 'time' to what is already established in our speech is, I think, reflected in Rhees' remark:

> It may never have struck me before that some form of language—say geometry—does or could belong to the 'meaning' of 'time'. (Which helps to show the sense of 'Don't look for the meaning, look at the use.') This is not like the uncertainty of borderline or doubtful cases— 'Would you still call that a dwelling house?', 'Would you still call that a fruit?'—where the answer may be: 'As you like.' (Rhees, 1970a, p. 49)

The meanings of the words 'fruit' and 'dwelling house' would be learnt by explanation of one sort or another. As far as the meanings of these expressions are concerned, they lie essentially in the way they are employed within language-games in the making of judgements or in our general talk about houses and fruits. Explanations can of course be reviewed and any difficulties we get into with these concepts will not go deep. But in the case of *time* and similarly deeply rooted concepts, we have tried to show that the way *they* form part of our relations to reality is not, in their origins, as concepts that are applied in the making of judgements; for having them is *structural* to discourse. In the case of *time* we have a concept that belongs to the sense of much of what we say. In the cases of *belief* and *meaning*, or the other concepts to do with language, we are looking at something lying in our whole relation to language.

CRATES: And so in the cases of the *words* 'time', 'belief', 'meaning', and so on, we are dealing with expressions whose introduction into the language does not so much *determine* as *reflect* boundaries between concepts—boundaries that are taken for granted in the very course of speaking and which pervade our speech. Failure to adhere to these limits would mean, in the case of the concepts to do with language, a loss of grip on language or, in the case of *time* or *cause*, a profound disturbance of our ability to talk sense and not merely an uncertainty or muddle in their specific application. If it did make sense to speak of moving these conceptual boundaries, then this would represent not merely a shift in the judgements we make but wholesale changes in the way we speak or wholesale changes in our relations to language.—Or rather, it would no longer be clear that we *were* speaking or making sense. It is therefore the very coherence of our lives as concept possessing agents that supports the meaningful use of these expressions, not merely the adherence to definitions or explanations.

6 Philosophical problems and Grammar

LATO: This brings us back to Rhees' original characterization of 'misunderstandings of the logic of language' as:

> ... confusion or uncertainty connected with being able to speak, and so perhaps with learning to speak ...[and]..(..not just a confusion of the grammars of particular expressions) ... (Rhees, 1970c, p. 74)

The deep difficulty in philosophy is not just difficulty in the face of the complexity, the variety or the confusing appearance of the rules governing particular expressions but a confusion or uncertainty that arises out of a failure to acknowledge the understanding that lies in our broader relations to language,—in our *ability* to speak and converse. It is, as it were, perplexity *in the face of* being able to make sense. This is perhaps why Rhees was wary, or at least equivocal, about speaking of this misunderstanding as the misunderstanding of the *grammar* of a concept, as this might suggest something relatively trivial, namely,

'confusions between different parts of the technique'—or the 'entanglement in our rules', as Wittgenstein put it.[41] On such an interpretation of
grammar, we would not be able to understand scepticism if philosophers
were interested only in the *grammars* of concepts. A similar sentiment
was expressed by Rhees when he attacked the idea—sometimes
attributed to Wittgenstein—that philosophical problems are no more
than linguistic confusions:

> Such reflection may help us to understand how it is that language—
> thinking and speaking and the understanding that there is in life
> among men—has led men to wonder what things are. A start from
> ideas of 'linguistic confusions' may issue in philistinism; and
> generally has.
>
> If we look only at usages, we cannot understand how it is that
> language may express ideas.
>
> We cannot understand the central ideas of philosophy—such ideas
> as reality, truth, things, intelligibility, understanding—we cannot
> understand the rôle they play in language unless we try to under-
> stand what language is. We cannot understand how it is that puzzle-
> ment about them and puzzlement about language (about what
> 'saying something' is, for instance) are so run into one another that
> we can hardly distinguish them. So that scepticism regarding them is
> scepticism regarding the reality of discourse. (Rhees, 1969a,
> pp. 134–135)

We are in full agreement with Rhees' underlying thought here. If we
do depart from him—as we have already been arguing—it is because we
believe that it is still valid, and indeed valuable, to characterize the root
of philosophical problems as arising out of difficulties with the
grammars of our concepts, even in those cases that we would characterize as arising directly in connection with 'being able to speak' rather
than with the use of particular expressions. For as Rhees himself was at
pains to argue, having concepts at all belongs with the idea of having
'something to say', which *is* 'living a life and speaking out of it'. We
should therefore *expect* the grasp of the grammars of the concepts that
are most intimately connected with 'being able to speak' to be something very deeply seated in and indeed *structural* to our lives. So it seems
to me that we should not abandon the notion of grammar in these cases
but, if anything, expand it to include them. It does not trivialize
'scepticism regarding the reality of discourse' to express it as puzzlement
over the grammar of 'discourse'.—They are the same. Likewise, the

difficulty we experience in seeing clearly into the grammars of the concepts to do with language may equally be expressed as the feeling of uncertainty or discomfort in our relations to language, to our selves and to the world.

CRATES: Lato, given that the implicit understanding of these concepts is such a pervasive feature of our speech and our lives, there is one puzzling aspect to this that might strike our reader. For one might wonder how it is that we are then so easily distracted in this understanding when we come to reflect on the grammars of these concepts in philosophy. The origin surely cannot be found merely in confusing similarities in the outward manner of language-games, or in 'pictures' lying in surface grammar. Such causes are the province of 'confusion of the grammars of particular expressions'. Neither can it be a failure to be struck by facts on account of their great generality. We have already argued that the recovery of facts will generally only play a secondary rôle in the elucidation of the concepts that are at the bottom of philosophical difficulties.

The answer, I believe, is that our confusion has its roots—or at least one very important root—in the very intimacy of our relations to these concepts,—in the way that the very fabric of our lives as persons who can speak is constituted in these relations. These form part of our grasp of the concepts *without* explicit acknowledgement, since they are prior to the explicit acknowledgement of *anything*. Our understanding of them shows not in the way that we acknowledge these relations but in the very fact that we can speak to one another. There is, therefore, no natural context for their acknowledgement; and so when we do turn our attention to them, we inevitably pass as a matter of course to those dimensions of their grammars that *are* handled explicitly,—dimensions in which we may indeed give definitions, explanations and demonstrations and may employ criteria in their application. In this way our reflections on the concepts fail to attach to the circumstances in which they were determined, thus exposing ourselves to reconstructing them in ways that are almost bound to be distorted.

LATO: I am sure that something of the kind must be at work; in fact there is an example provided by Wittgenstein that illustrates just this possibility:

> ... it looks as if the definition—a proposition is whatever can be true or false—determined what a proposition was, by saying: what fits the concept 'true', or what the concept 'true' fits, is a proposition. So it is

as if we had a concept of true and false, which we could use to determine what is and what is not a proposition. (PI 136)

In the apparent absence of any other way of showing our relations to
the concepts *truth* and *proposition*, it may look as if the question 'Can
this be true or false?', in providing the criterion for judging that 'here is
a proposition', showed how the concept *proposition* might be determined. It would then be original to having the concept *proposition* that
we are able to make such a judgement using this as a criterion: having a
concept of truth would be prior to having the concept of a proposition.
This falsifies the relation between the concepts *truth* and *proposition*.
Now as Wittgenstein remarked:

> ... a child might be taught to distinguish between propositions and
> other expressions by being told 'Ask yourself if you can say "is true"
> after it. If these words fit, it's a proposition.' (PI 137)

In other words, we can perfectly well imagine circumstances in which
we might apply 'is true' as a criterion, and no doubt this does form at
least a part of having a concept of it.—In the surface handling of these
concepts we treat them as pieces that 'fit' one another. This is fine. But
these are not the circumstances in which the concept is determined, for
clearly the child could only follow this instruction if he already distinguished propositions—both in their truth and in their falsity—in his
own speech or in responding to the speech of others. In other words—
in the sense in which we have described—the child will already have the
concepts *truth* and *proposition*.
Wittgenstein rectified this false relation by saying:

> And what a proposition is is in one sense determined by the rules of
> sentence formation ... and in another sense by the use of the sign in
> the language-game. And the use of the words 'true' and 'false' may be
> among the constituent parts of this game; and if so it *belongs* to our
> concept 'proposition' but does not '*fit*' it. (PI 136)

And of course nothing short of a rounded exposition of what speaking
a language is—which must include how language belongs to our engagement with the world and with the people with whom we share it—will
do to illustrate what the use of the propositional sign is and what the
words 'true' and 'false' mean.

Such an exposition will not try to explain what speaking is—or what belief is, or what truth is—from top to bottom; rather, it will bring what *can* be made explicit in the grammars of the concepts—or in the techniques for using them—into contact with the understanding of the concept that lies embedded in our relations to language. An important part of giving presence to this understanding will be to describe the circumstances in which these relations exist—some attempt at which we have made. But they will not be the descriptions of the life with language that we require if they do not at the same time engage with those relations in which that understanding lies,—otherwise they would remain an external account. As Rhees remarked:

> Suppose I describe what the two men are doing while they are building, as Wittgenstein does in the *Investigations* (pp. 3 and 5). If this does illustrate speaking for you, then you must not only understand what they are doing, but you must understand what they say. My description must show that they speak a language which each of them understands, and which you also understand, if the illustration is to help you. (Rhees, 1970c, p. 72)

The description can only show this to the extent that we already recognize them as persons who are speaking—that we already stand in that relation to them—and that means that our understanding of the concepts of a person and of language are already up and running and determining our perception of the illustration. Just as the confusion itself has its origins in 'uncertainty connected with being able to speak',[42] so that must remain the arena within which we strive for clarity.

What Wittgenstein's example shows is how a preoccupation with what *can* be made explicit in how the words 'true' and 'proposition' are employed can conceal from us the deeper connections between these concepts. And it is just this sort of dislocation that is at the root of the problems of truth, language and scepticism.

7   Conclusion

CRATES: Lato, in this dialogue we have tried to move on from the idea of the use of language as an operation with signs according to a rule to a richer conception of *speaking* as a manifestation of the life of *person*,— these concepts being mutually constitutive.

Part of our purpose—apart from the fact that we think these insights of intrinsic interest and importance—has been to make more clear the context in human life in which we may be said to possess concepts. It is important to understand that concepts are only possessed within our capacity for speech in the way we have described. We have not denied that language remains in an important sense a rule-governed activity—thus maintaining the link with action and the operational aspects of language—but, in regard to the concepts of belief and time, we have tried to show that important aspects of how these concepts are embedded in our lives are far removed from this. In the case of *time*, the possession of the concept can only be seen properly where it is pervasive of speech and in our knowing 'what it makes sense to say'. The same may be said of *belief*, although in this case we also have to take fundamental aspects of our whole relation to language as being constitutive of our possession of this concept.

Furthermore, we have tried to illustrate something of how the failure to observe these relations may be at the bottom of the puzzlement we experience when thinking about these and related concepts. However, establishing the importance of this richer understanding of the nature of speech for a proper understanding of concept possession is only one step towards a comprehensive understanding of the latter. It is only one step towards an understanding of what indeed it is that we possess when we possess a concept and of the great variety of conditions under which we possess different concepts. In our first dialogue, we explained that the next step towards examining both the formation of concepts *in general* and some of the ways in which specific concepts are possessed—and especially those of particular importance in philosophy—will be to resist some very pervasive but pernicious theories of concept possession. In particular, we cited mentalistic and rationalistic theories; and we stated that an important entrée into combating these will be to reveal the *instinctive* base of language use. This will return our discussion in the next dialogue to *operational* aspects of language, but we have also stated that this does not conflict with our views on the nature of speaking, which are only that this operational mode does not and cannot *explain* what it is to speak a language. We might also add that understanding the instinctive base of language is also essential to an understanding of concept-formation and to an understanding of the specific circumstances of the possession of particular concepts. So turning our attention to this matter is not merely a prelude to discussing these further issues but an introduction to them.

Dialogue 4   An Instinct for Meaning

1   Introduction

LATO: Wittgenstein was fond of quoting from old Augustine's description of how he learned to speak—or at least how he *imagined* he learned to speak.[1] He was especially interested in this because it contained two assumptions,[2] which together became major objects of criticism in his own discussions—indeed they ramified the whole of his later philosophy.

Augustine described a process in which he observed his elders *naming* objects, this being visible in the way they acted towards these objects. This he took to be the principal process of language acquisition and it illustrated the first assumption: the monolithic view of language as a system of names.

The second assumption lay in the idea that concept-formation and the employment of language are grounded in an articulate *subjective* mode of understanding that is prior to or anticipates the use of language. This is the conception of an 'inner world' of meanings that is known as 'mentalism'. It emerged in Augustine's account where he spoke of seeing and grasping that 'the thing was called by the sound they uttered when they meant to point it out',[3] which he clearly supposed to be pre-linguistic. It also manifested itself in his descriptions of an inward process of making connections of meaning and of training oneself to utter words corresponding to these meanings.

In his response, Wittgenstein strove to show the diversity in the functioning of language and concepts, and that it does not consist exclusively of names. He developed the idea that the use of language (and the expression of concepts) is to be understood *essentially* in connection with human activity, for which mentalist explanations of this kind are neither required nor can be given a coherent presentation.

110

CRATES: As an aside, Lato, when we speak of an 'essential' connection with action, we must again underline that this is a grammatical statement to the effect that the concepts to do with language and action are *logically* related. It should not be taken to exclude the possibility of logical relations between linguistic and psychological concepts in *other* dimensions, such as between concept-formation and sense perception, for example. The objection to mentalism is that it tries to forge a relation between the grasp of meaning and subjective states that would sever or short-circuit the relation between meaning and action. It is not that there is no conceptual connection between language and subjective states. With this *caveat*, we may now explore the essential nature of this relation between the concepts of language and action, which is our current interest—while our special interest in psychological concepts will be addressed later.

LATO: Yes, indeed. This emphasis on the fundamental rôle of action takes us directly to the spontaneous or instinctive nature of language use. By developing our understanding of the logical relation between the concepts of language and of instinctive behaviour, we will both combat the confusions inherent in Augustine's account and reveal important dimensions to the way that our concepts are acquired and possessed.

CRATES: From your conversations with Wittgenstein it is apparent that this notion of the instinctive nature of language is heterogeneous, relating in different contexts to quite different aspects of language use. There are *different* senses in which we may speak of the instinctive nature or language, as we outlined in our first, synoptic dialogue.

In the first place there is the distinction, which you introduced, between the notion of instinct as referring to specific innate behavioural tendencies contrasted with the notion of it as referring to the groundlessness of action or language use. I then distinguished the two different situations in which we apply these notions: the first being the groundless nature of rule-governed linguistic behaviour as such; the second being where specific ungrounded primitive linguistic reactions combine in specific behavioural contexts in the formation of particular concepts. Our main interest is in developing our understanding of these two situations, though we will continue to bear your distinction in mind, so that we do not get confused over which senses we are working with.

Again I think it will be helpful to remind ourselves of the fact that this remains a *grammatical* investigation: we are not invoking a concept of instinct as an *explanation* of language use—which would make it look as if we were fluctuating between different concepts of instinct in our supposed explanations—rather we are trying to elucidate the concept of language by linking it in different respects to the concept of instinct. It is essential to understand this.

The value in treating these different situations *en suite* comes first from the fact that *together* they provide a continuous argument against mentalism and rationalism. But it also serves our larger purpose, inasmuch as the different situations in which we may speak of the instinctive nature of language simply reveal different aspects of the way our concepts are embedded in our lives.

So, Lato, perhaps you would start us off with the first of these, which has to do with the instinctive nature of language *as a rule-governed activity*. We agree that it will be interesting to trace Wittgenstein's discussion of this topic as it unfolds, which will help to make clear how different elements enter into the argument.

2 The instinct for rules

LATO: Wittgenstein's first response to Augustine was to describe a series of very simple linguistic transactions in a shop. He described the different ways in which the 'words' functioned and then the fact that, without further ado or explanation, the shopkeeper *acted* in certain ways. This was followed by descriptions of more complex linguistic functions and their circumstances.[4] His aim was to establish the primacy of the link between the determination of meaning and the function of the words in the active lives of the participants. All of this conformed with his definition of a language-game as 'language and the actions into which it is woven'.[5]

He certainly made *some* references at this stage to the mental processes accompanying the use of language and to how a preoccupation with these may lead to misunderstandings.[6] But it was only later that he turned his attention more explicitly to mentalistic accounts of language,[7] when he attacked one of its most familiar manifestations: the interpretation of the understanding of an ostensive definition (e.g., pointing to or 'meaning' an object, its colour, or its shape) as a mental, spiritual, or 'occult' process:

> And *here* we may indeed fancy naming to be some remarkable act of mind, as it were a baptism of an object. As we can also say the word 'this' *to* the object, as it were *address* the object as 'this'—a queer use of this word, which doubtless only occurs in doing philosophy. (PI 38)

He also attended briefly to the supposed rôle of memory in determining, or grounding, *future* applications of a (colour) word.[8] But he did not treat this topic thoroughly until his discussions of the rule-governed aspects of language were well under way. It was then that the issues of mentalism and rationalism became critical. These discussions began in earnest where he introduced the example of a pupil who has been given a formation rule for writing down a series of signs or numbers.[9]

CRATES: Before you launch into this, Lato, I think again there is a general point to be made here about the great emphasis that Wittgenstein placed on the investigation of rule-governed behaviour as an entry into understanding the nature of language—and especially his preoccupation with examples employing the extension of numerical series. I draw attention to this because of the concerns we raised in the previous dialogue regarding the nature of speaking.

Wittgenstein's emphasis on the nature of rules is not proof *in itself* of a disposition towards a narrow, operational view of language. He had other valid concerns about rules. In the first place, he wished to isolate and examine a particular and very important aspect of language use, namely the nature of the *commitment* to the particular use of a word that we make when we learn to speak. In other words, the discussion was intended to shed light on the nature of *logic* and *necessity*—which were of prime interest. But it also served to bring out—though probably in an oversimplified way, as we shall examine later—important aspects of speaking as *behaviour*, which may otherwise be difficult to see. By establishing the logical links between language and action, he provided clear-cut contexts in which the assumptions of mentalism could be extracted and disposed of.

But now do carry on with your exposition, Lato.

LATO: The puzzle that Wittgenstein set himself here was this. When we teach the pupil the rule for the extension of the numerical series, we are at the mercy of his *reactions*;[10]—he may continue the series in the way we intend, or he may just go off in a different direction. And of course, if he does fail to react in the way we intend—in the 'right' way, that is—his learning will grind to a halt.[11] But what if he *does* go on in the right way and is able to 'get the system'? How will we *now* characterize the nature of this understanding? The *criterion* of his understanding is, of course, his correct application of the rule; and yet his understanding does not *consist* in his having made a correct application;[12] neither does the pupil say that he 'understands' on the basis of observing his own success.[13] Rather, his understanding would seem to consist in that state of mind from which the application flows.[14] This is the conclusion that compels us. This is where we are beguiled by the attraction of a mentalistic explanation.

CRATES: Indeed it seems to fit nicely with common experience; for we are all familiar, directly and subjectively, with the phenomenon of suddenly realizing that we have understood a rule—of a game, or of the use of a word. We exclaim 'Now I can do it!',[15] which may well look like a manifestation of the said state of mind.

LATO: But when Wittgenstein then asked whether that state of mind was the understanding,[16] he suggested that we should examine the circumstances in which we express our understanding;[17] a theme that he then developed with reference to the example of learning to read, which is evidently very closely related to acting in accord with a rule. And the lesson he drew from that discussion was that we cannot give an account of reading in terms of the various experiences that may accompany it; neither is there any one act or process of deriving the words from the page that we might hold up and say '*This* is reading'.

CRATES: So when we express ourselves as being guided by the letters, when we can say 'Now I can read', we are *speaking for ourselves* and not on the basis of some external observations of our behaviour. But neither can this be explained in terms either of a mental state or of reported experiences—these being phenomena that I interpret through the *medium* of the concept of being influenced or guided.[18] No, we are speaking *out of our lives*—which is surely related to Gaita's definition of 'having something to say' as 'living a life and speaking out of it'.[19]

LATO: Yes, I believe it is. Following this discussion, Wittgenstein returned to the phrase 'Now I can go on!' as used to express the moment of grasping a linguistic rule.[20] Clearly this is closely akin to saying 'Now I can read', and in just this same way it is *not* the description of a state of mind or experience. At best we might call it a signal.[21] So, what is it? How shall we describe it? Again, we might express this by saying that it is essential to the grammar of 'human life', and essential to the nature of our *form of life*, that when we speak, we speak *from* it: the utterance of the phrase is an *expression* of our lives. It is a fundamental and characteristic feature of our form of life that we react like this. It is the primary expression of our realization that we can now *speak* with this word, and is constitutive of that realization.

We anticipate our ability to do certain things without either inner or external 'evidence'. If I suddenly remember a tune and am certain that I can sing it, this is not the expression of an experience; neither does it mean that it must have occurred to me in its entirety.[22] It is just a fact of life, without which we would not be the creatures we are.

CRATES: So how can we now apply these thoughts to Wittgenstein's examples of extending arithmetical series?

LATO: If I give the pupil a series of numbers to work out according to the formula +2, I know what I mean or intend him to do at any stage in the series even if I may never have worked it out myself to that point.[23] Now of course there is no guarantee that the pupil will find it natural or obvious to do what I would do at any stage, nor that I might not break-down myself. Again, his ability to follow my course of action may cease;[24] he may not be able to make any sense of or understand at all why I go on as I do. Conversely, he may protest that his own way of continu-ing it is in *accord* with his understanding of the rule. Now how does this bear on *my* certainty with respect to each application of the formula? My subjective certainty appears to be linked to something given in the formula, which, it seems, could only be worked out in one way.[25] And there is apparently nothing given absolutely in the formula that both constrains the individual to work out the series in one way rather than another and which corresponds to *my* subjective certainty (and to pro-pose a further qualification or formula would only push the same problem a step further back).[26] The mentalistic conception of rule-following—which supposes that if I know how to extend the rule, then I must have something present to mind that anticipates all future applications—and the conception of the rule expression as, in some determinate way, containing *a priori* the possibility of all future applications are of a piece.[27]

The answer is that the sense of the rule-expression hangs together with the application in practice:[28] obeying a rule is a practice;[29] the essence of the language-game is a practical method.[30] Wittgenstein remarked:

> The rule can only seem to me to produce all its consequences in advance if I draw them as a *matter of course*. As much as it is a matter of course for me to call this colour 'blue'. (PI 238)

CRATES: So, removing the priority of both the rule expression and the mental accompaniments leads to the conclusion that any *justification* for how we are to obey the rule finds bedrock in the practice itself.

LATO: Just so; which is expressed in another remark:

> Then I am inclined to say: 'This is simply what I do.' (PI 217)

CRATES: And this, I believe, explains the further remark:

> When I obey a rule, I do not choose.
>   I obey the rule *blindly*. (PI 219)

For unless I am already following a rule there is no *choosing*; unless I am already following a rule there is no 'seeing'. Again it is important to emphasize that we are talking about *bedrock*. There certainly remains a sense in which, *in ordinary circumstances*, we do not follow rules 'blindly'. I have in mind the fact that rules are not learned in isolation. As we discussed in the second dialogue,[31] the learning of many linguistic rules is surrounded by descriptions of the circumstances in which the rule is to be applied, the actions to be carried out, and so on. And if we are asked to justify *why* we go on in a particular way, we will refer to other rule expressions, and so on, which are *not* a matter of dispute. We will try to show, for example, that anomalous results will ensue if we carry on in this way rather than that. To this extent we *do* go into the learning of the rule with our eyes open. But of course this will not do as a *general* account of what it is to learn to follow a rule, as it already takes for granted that we are following rules in the explanations we are employing. At this level, resort to mentalistic conceptions of an intelligibility given prior to the practice of language, and which determines its application, are of no help.[32] The subjective certainty with which we realize that 'Now I can go on' is, therefore, not a certainty derived from the direct introspection or intuition of a necessity determined *a priori*. Rather it is itself a primary manifestation of our selves, *qua* willing subjects, as rule-following creatures. It is the subjective correlate of an otherwise outward manifestation of our lives; and of course we should *expect* there to be such a correlate, for we are *persons*, not automata.

LATO: We have arrived at the point where Wittgenstein had established the primacy of *practice* in our discussions. To speak of 'primacy' here is to speak of the *essential* 'blindness' of linguistic practice;—and this is to speak of its essentially *instinctive* nature. The notion that the use of language is driven ultimately by blind, instinctive, ungrounded ways of acting was given expression by Wittgenstein in a variety of ways. It might be helpful to have some of the most striking of these before us:

> What *counts* as its test? [i.e. an empirical proposition]—'But is this an adequate test? And, if so, must it not be recognizable as such in logic?'—As if giving grounds did not come to an end sometime. But the end is not an ungrounded presupposition: it is an ungrounded way of acting. (OC 110)

> Giving grounds, however, justifying the evidence, comes to an end;— but the end is not certain propositions' striking us immediately as true, i.e. it is not a kind of *seeing* on our part; it is our *acting*, which lies at the bottom of the language-game. (OC 204)

> You must bear in mind that the language-game is so to say something unpredictable. I mean: it is not based on grounds. It is not reasonable (or unreasonable).

It is there—like our life. (OC 559)

I want to regard man here as an animal; as a primitive being to which one grants instinct but not ratiocination. As a creature in a primitive state. Any logic good enough for a primitive means of communication needs no apology from us. Language did not emerge from some kind of ratiocination. (OC 475)

Now I would like to regard this certainty, not as something akin to hastiness or superficiality, but as a form of life. (That is very badly expressed and probably badly thought as well.) (OC 358)

But that means I want to conceive it as something that lies beyond being justified or unjustified; as it were, as something animal. (OC 359)

Not only rules, but also examples are needed for establishing a practice. Our rules leave loop-holes open, and the practice has to speak for itself. (OC 139)

The essence of the language-game is a practical method (a way of acting)—not speculation, not chatter. (CE, p. 399)

To begin by teaching someone 'That looks red' makes no sense. For he must say that spontaneously once he has learnt what 'red' means, i.e. has learnt the technique of using the word. (Z 418)

CRATES: So to summarize the position so far, Lato, we have arrived at the notion of the instinctive nature of language *in general*. By this we mean that the following of rules *as such*—and linguistic rules in particular—is continuous with human *action* and, moreover, that it is ultimately ungrounded. And the point of insisting on this grammatical point is to combat those views which assume some process of reasoning that lies prior both to action and speech, for such a conception of reasoning makes no sense.

In reaching this conclusion, we are not committing ourselves in any way to the idea that action is therefore prior to intelligence, nor that rules and language are prior to reason. For intelligence is constituted *in* our forms of behaviour—instinctive behaviour too may be intelligent though not 'rational'—and speech, we might say, is the highest form of intelligent behaviour. So the notion of the instinctive nature of language that we are currently developing works, on the one hand, as a part of the defence against the attraction of mentalism and rationalism as general explanations of the use of language; it also represents one aspect of how language—*qua* rule-governed activity—is embedded in our lives.

But this is not the end of the matter, for—as we have already indicated—there are further contexts where a notion of instinct may perform a similar service, namely where we are concerned with the formation and possession of *specific* concepts. Wittgenstein was preoccupied with these too. So let's now turn our attention to them.

3 Forms of life, primitive reactions and concept-formation

LATO: I think we can best introduce this by exploring first of all Wittgenstein's notion of the human *form of life*, which plays an important though largely implicit rôle in his investigations. It is important because it facilitates the identification of the characteristic circumstances into which a language-game is woven and its concepts embedded.

The responses that form the groundwork of our language-games belong to the larger picture of human life that Wittgenstein referred to as the 'hurly-burly':

> How could human behaviour be described? Surely only by showing the actions of a variety of humans, as they are all mixed up together. Not what *one* man is doing *now*, but the whole hurly-burly, is the background against which we see an action, and it determines our judgement, our concepts, and our reactions. (RPP2 629; see also Z 567)

The particular and characteristic weaving together of these fundamental linguistic and behavioural reactions that make up the human 'hurly-burly' is what Wittgenstein referred to as our 'form of life', and so clearly it was central to his thinking. Unfortunately, because of the infrequency of his use of the phrase, it is a notion that has been subject to much interpretation. His explicit uses of it—he sometimes substituted the phrases 'facts of living' or 'ways of living'—were, as I recall, as follows:

> What has to be accepted, the given, is—so one could say—*forms of life*. (PI, p. 192)

> Instead of the unanalysable, specific, indefinable: the fact that we act in such-and-such ways, e.g. *punish* certain actions, *establish* the state of affair [sic] thus and so, *give orders*, render accounts, describe colours, take an interest in others' feelings. What has to be accepted, the given—it might be said—are facts of living.[33] (RPP1 630)

> It is easy to imagine a language consisting only of orders and reports in battle.—Or a language consisting only of questions and expressions for answering yes and no. And innumerable others.—And to imagine a language means to imagine a form of life. (PI 19)

Here the term 'language-*game*' is meant to bring into prominence the fact that the *speaking* of language is part of an activity, or of a form of life. (PI 23)

'So you are saying that human agreement decides what is true and what is false?'—It is what human beings say that is true and false; and they agree in the language they use. That is not agreement in opinions but in form of life. (PI 241)

Can only those hope who can talk? Only those who have mastered the use of language. That is to say, the phenomena of hope are modes of this complicated form of life.[34] (PI, p. 148)

I want to say: it is a feature of our language that it springs up // it grows // out of the foundations of forms of life, regular actions // that it springs up from the soil of firm forms of life, regular forms of actions. (Wittgenstein Nachlass, 1937, Vol. XV, 148)[35]

I want to say: it is characteristic of our language that the foundation on which it grows consists in steady ways of living, regular ways of acting.[36] (CE, p. 397)

And in a similar vein, he said:

Language, I should like to say, relates to a *way* of living. (RFM, p. 335)

And that was all.

CRATES:—Which is not a lot to go on.

LATO: Quite. Which is why I feel that the sensible approach to its interpretation should not rest too heavily on a minute examination of the remarks themselves—which can only lead to endless and fruitless debate—but should resort to an interpretation that operates best within his philosophy as a whole. It is in the light of this that *we* take it as referring to the mode of life of the individual taken as a whole and in its most general and fundamental aspects. It refers to what is not optional in the pattern that she shares with others of her kind and which makes up what we recognize as characteristic of human life. It might also be said to belong with the *instinctive*, in the sense that these patterns are not the *product* of reason or thought.

We shall not discuss all the various interpretations in detail, however one variant that we might mention briefly is the interpretation—put forward by Peter Hacker—that a form of life should be understood to be a *cultural* rather than a *biological* entity.[37] I think that this distinction is spurious because—as we shall discuss later—Wittgenstein thought it was important to see language as *extending* our pre-conceptual lives. To be sure, what makes the human form of life different from animal forms is *linguistic culture*; but that does not mean that what is animal in our constitution is not also constitutive of our form of life.

Other commentators have argued that we have to make a choice between the notion of our form of life as the mode of our life *taken as a whole* and the notion of it as some *particular aspect* of our lives—such as *hope*—so that our form of life might be also be thought of as a composite of such lesser forms.[38] But, again, the need for such a choice seems spurious. It is not an explanatory concept but a guide to exploring the grammars of our concepts of life and language. There is no especial reason why we should avoid using it to refer either to the mode of life taken as a whole or to an aspect of it—be it hope, intention or whatever; but for most purposes, we may take 'form of life' to mean that larger framework of life. It is the 'given' *within which* what is grounded or reasoned is generated.

CRATES: And the justification for this, as you suggest, comes from the way that we see such a conception at work *throughout* his discussions, which were frequently devoted to describing the structure of our lives— how we relate to ourselves, to others and to the world about us—and how language fits into this structure. This is nothing other than an unfolding account of our form of life. Moreover, it is a form that is inherent in our lives; it is what emerges spontaneously or instinctively as our lives develop, either in response to innate tendencies or in response to the promptings of our teachers. And if it did *not*, we would cease to recognize what is most characteristic in human life: our language and the life that goes with it. It is the base from which we then go on to learn new forms of behaviour, which, by becoming second nature, then *extend* the form of our life.

LATO: Fine. So let's now look at some examples of the discussions that illustrate the unfolding of this conception. Wittgenstein frequently described how primitive linguistic reactions are woven together with characteristic modes of behaviour to form the cornerstones of language-games. These remarks were often combined with references to the fact that the emergence of these reactions belongs to concept-formation. Perhaps the fullest treatment of this was in his lengthy discussion of the formation of the concept *cause*, where he stated the general point quite explicitly:

> The origin and the primitive form of the language-game is a reaction; only from this can more complicated forms develop.
> Language—I want to say—is a refinement. 'In the beginning was the deed.'[39] (CE, p. 395)

Elsewhere, Wittgenstein used the notion of 'spontaneity' to express the ungrounded, instinctive nature of the newly formed language-game, that is, that the newly generated element is not anticipated in thought:

Something new (spontaneous, 'specific') is always a language-game. (PI, p. 191)

'We decide on a new language-game.'

'We decide *spontaneously*' (I should like to say) 'on a new language-game.' (RFM, p. 236)

What is essential for us is, after all, spontaneous agreement, spontaneous sympathy. (RPP2 699)

Perhaps his most striking descriptions of primitive reactions that go to form the foundations of language-games are these:

It is a help here to remember that it is a primitive reaction to tend, to treat, the part that hurts when someone else is in pain; and not merely when oneself is—and so to pay attention to other people's pain-behaviour, as one does *not* pay attention to one's own pain behaviour. (Z 540)

But what is the word "primitive" meant to say here? Presumably that this sort of behaviour is *pre-linguistic*: that a language-game is based *on it*, that it is the prototype of a way of thinking and not the result of thought. (Z 541)

– Being sure that someone is in pain, doubting whether he is, and so on, are so many natural, instinctive, kinds of behaviour towards other human beings, and our language is merely an auxiliary to, and further extension of, this relation. Our language-game is an extension of primitive behaviour. (For our *language-game* is behaviour) (Instinct) (Z 545)

The contribution of sympathetic responses of this kind to the determination of the language-games of pain and sympathy in the third person is complemented in the first person by the replacement of expressions of pain by linguistic responses:

'So are you saying that the word "pain" really means crying?'—On the contrary: the verbal expression replaces crying and does not describe it. (PI 244)

And again:

Primitive pain-behaviour is a sensation-behaviour; it gets replaced by a linguistic expression. 'The word "pain" is the name of a sensation' is equivalent to ' "I've got a pain" is an expression of sensation'. (RPP1 313)

Similarly:

> What is the primitive reaction with which the language-game begins, which can then be translated into words such as 'When this word occurred I thought of ...'? How do people get to use these words? (LW1 133)

> 'You said the word as if something different had suddenly occurred to you as you were saying it.' One doesn't learn this reaction.
>   The primitive reaction could also be a verbal one. (LW1 134)

> 'The word is on the tip of my tongue.' What is going on in my consciousness? That is not the point at all. Whatever did go on was not what I meant by those words. It is of more interest what went on in my *behaviour*. What I said, which pictures I used, my facial expression.—'The word is on the tip of my tongue' is a verbal expression of what is also expressed, in a quite different way, by a particular kind of behaviour. Again, ask for the primitive reaction that is the basis of the expression. (LW1 828)

What is primitive to the language-game determines what kind of language-game it is. A reaction that is primitive to a language-game is always instinctive: a new language-game is not *any* newly contrived way of speaking—such as might have been invented by giving a definition—as what is primitive to *that* will reside not in what is defined but in the terms of the definition. A genuinely new language-game will be irreducible, that is, 'specific'.

CRATES: Can I just underline the point here, Lato, that, in referring to specific reactions as determining the nature of a language-game, we have moved on in our conception of instinct as an element in the use of language. We have passed from the notion of instinct as a way of expressing just the groundlessness of linguistic practice *in general* (the groundless nature of rule-following) to the notion that the *specific characteristics* of a language-game are determined fundamentally by specific kinds of response which, in that rôle, are essentially instinctive or ungrounded and are not the product of thought. The mode of these spontaneous responses is *constitutive* of the grammar of the concept. We have now moved quite clearly into another and distinct situation in which the concept of linguistic instinct, or spontaneity, may again be used to defend against mentalistic and rationalistic prejudices.

LATO: As I have said, Wittgenstein's most continuous treatment of the relation between instinctive behaviour and concept-formation occurred in his discussions of the concept *cause*. He described a variety of primitive reactions that he identified as being of the kind that belong both to the origin of the language-game of cause and effect and to language-games closely related to it. His remarks were directed principally against the notion—which he found in his former teacher and colleague Bertrand Russell—that the origin of this language-game might be found in an *intuition*. This notion of intuition we might construe as belonging to mentalism. Wittgenstein held that this origin is rather to be found in the reactions themselves. I think I might repeat these at length, as they illustrate a number of the issues at stake:

1   *We react to the cause.*
Calling something 'the cause' is like pointing and saying: '*He's* to blame!'

We instinctively get rid of the cause if we don't want the effect. We instinctively look from what has been hit to what has hit it. (I am assuming we do this.) (CE, p. 373)

2   [On cause and effect, intuitive awareness]:
A sound seems to come from over there, even before I have investigated its (physical) source. In the cinema the sound of speech seems to come from the mouth of the figures on the screen.

What does this experience consist in? Perhaps in the fact that we involuntarily look towards a particular spot—the apparent source of the sound—when we hear a sound. And in the cinema no one looks towards where the microphone is.

The basic form of our game must be one in which there is no such thing as doubt.—What makes us sure of this? It can't surely be a matter of historical certainty.

'The basic form of our game can't include doubt.' What we are doing here above all is to *imagine* a basic form: a possibility, indeed a *very important* possibility. (We very often confuse what is an important possibility with historical reality.) (CE, p. 377)

3   There is a reaction which can be called 'reacting to the cause'.—We also speak of 'tracing' the cause; a simple case would be, say, following a string to see who is pulling at it. If I then find him—how do I

know that he, his pulling, is the cause of the string's moving? Do I establish this by a series of experiments? (CE, p. 387)

4   The primitive form of the language-game is certainty, not uncertainty. For uncertainty could never lead to action.

....

The simple form (and that is the prototype) of the cause–effect game is determining the cause, not doubting.

....

The basic form of the game must be one in which we act. (CE, p. 397)

5   The game doesn't begin with doubting whether someone has toothache, because that doesn't—as it were—fit the game's biological function in our life. In its most primitive form it is a reaction to somebody's cries and gestures, a reaction of sympathy or something of the sort.

....

'The game can't begin with doubting' means: we shouldn't call it 'doubting', if the game began with it. (CE, pp. 381–383)

And here is another example of a primitive reaction that may anticipate a language-game:

You can 'see the d<uck> and r<abbit> aspects' only if you are thoroughly familiar with the shapes of those animals; the principal aspects of the double cross could express themselves in primitive reactions of a child who couldn't yet talk. (LW1 700)

In these remarks it is evident that Wittgenstein was saying that these characteristic reactions—in some cases linguistic and in others apparently non-linguistic—are integral to the formation of various language-games and essential to the possession of its concepts. Closely related to this was his assertion that language-games may be viewed as *extensions* of primitive behaviour:

Believing that someone else is in pain, doubting whether he is, are so many natural kinds of behaviour towards other human beings; and our language is but an auxiliary to and extension of this behaviour. I mean: our language is an extension of the more primitive behaviour. (For our *language-game* is a piece of behaviour.) (RPP1 151; cf. Z 545 and also Z 540 and 541 above)

I can easily imagine that a particular primitive behaviour might later develop into a doubt. There is, e.g. a kind of *primitive* investigation. (An ape who tears apart a cigarette, for example. We don't see an intelligent dog do such things.) The mere act of turning the object around and looking it over is a primitive root of doubt. But there is doubt only when the typical antecedents and consequences of doubt are present. (RPP2 345)

In this way I should like to say the words 'Oh, *let* him come!' are charged with my desire. And the words can be wrung from us,—like a cry. Words can be *hard* to say: such, for example, as are used to effect renunciation, or to confess a weakness. (Words are also deeds.) (PI 546; see also CV, p. 53e)

In these passages and elsewhere, we take the view that Wittgenstein did not intend a *concept* to be thought of as an extension of behaviour; rather, the behaviour—the character of which is partly determined in the way that language and its concepts are integrated into it—may be seen as an extension of the more primitive, non-conceptual behaviour that precedes it. Thus the primitive behaviour of the ape is the non-conceptual counterpart of that human behaviour in which doubt is expressed in both actions *and* words.—'I doubt' is a *deed* of doubting.

CRATES: So there are two main themes to be explored here and which offer the opportunity of taking us directly into some very fundamental aspects of concept-formation and the nature of our possession of concepts. The first is the rôle of both primitive *linguistic* and primitive *non-linguistic* reactions in concept-formation. The second is the idea that we might fruitfully think of the possession of our concepts (or a significant suite of them) as in some sense constituting an extension of our behaviour—or indeed as an extension of our form of life.

But this, Lato, is where you say you began to run into trouble with a number of Wittgenstein's associates and followers, who did not share your favoured interpretation of these remarks. In particular, it seems that Wittgenstein was accused of holding a *foundationalist* theory of concept-formation.

LATO: It is true that Wittgenstein's remarks on instinctive behaviour and its relation to concept-formation received much critical comment in the years following his death. We should pay attention to these critical voices, which I believe express significant but widespread misunderstandings of Wittgenstein's standpoint—misunderstandings that are still common within the philosophical fraternity. This is especially important because these are voices that otherwise had been supportive of his philosophy—and of course one must pay special attention to the criticisms of friends!

Elizabeth Wolgast's views are representative of this critical perspective and she touched upon most of the difficulties generally experienced with Wittgenstein's remarks on this topic.[40] Much of what we have to say will be in agreement with positions put to me by Rush Rhees.[41] But he too expressed misgivings, which will also need to be addressed.

Wittgenstein's remarks gave rise to speculation not just because of their paucity—which allowed varied interpretation—but specifically because they invited interpretation as advancing a *theory* of the genesis of our concepts from instinctive forms of behaviour. And of course, this is problematic for Wittgenstein's avowed philosophical method just because 'we may not advance any kind of theory'.[42] We have been at pains to emphasize that, for Wittgenstein, to speak of the *instinctive* nature of language is essentially a *grammatical insight*. For whereas speaking may be pre-meditated on any particular occasion, we cannot conceive of speaking *as such* as something pre-meditated. It is this that establishes the link between the concepts of speaking and of instinctive behaviour. But the problem with his remarks on instinctive behaviour and concept-formation is that their grammatical nature is not always as obvious as one might wish. It is this that allowed Wolgast, among others, a platform from which to claim that Wittgenstein was making assertions about concept-formation that were both speculative and not entirely intelligible.

4   Wolgast's interpretation of Wittgenstein

The remarks that troubled Wolgast were those where it seemed to her that Wittgenstein spoke of 'primitive reactions' as if they gave rise *directly* to our language-games and the concepts embedded in them. Moreover, she observed that Wittgenstein did not talk in this way when speaking to a wider audience (except in a limited way, which I shall refer to later) but only on isolated occasions that were apparently not intended for the public ear.[43] This fuelled her feeling that this idea was really spurious to his central insights and should be dispensed with.[44] Her analysis of Wittgenstein's position, as it emerged in these remarks, was roughly as follows:

Wittgenstein's suggestion was that our concepts are *generated* from pre-linguistic forms of behaviour. His most developed example of this process was his treatment, already referred to, of the concept *cause*.[45] Here he spoke at length of how the concept might have emerged out of instinctive behaviour, and proposed that the language-game was generated from our spontaneous reactions to events impinging upon us. He illustrated this by reference to reactions such as the response to receiving a blow,[46] or feeling the pull on a string.[47] Language 'draws on' such reactions for its concept of cause;[48] they are the foundations on which the concept is grounded.[49] This was not merely a conjecture as to how our concepts might have arisen out of certain forms of behaviour, but was apparently thought of as something upon which the very *possibility* of forming such concepts depended. On the basis of this interpretation, she concluded:

> ....[w]e could not have the concept of cause if we did not react as we do, and the same applies to other concepts. (Wolgast, 1994, p. 591)

CRATES: Wolgast clearly took Wittgenstein, against the better judgement to be found in the main body of his discussions,[50] to be espousing a *foundationalist* account of language—not, perhaps, in the traditional sense of wanting to provide a rational justification for our concepts, but in the sense of demonstrating at least some kind of inevitable pathway of derivation from primitive behavioural reactions to the language in which the concepts become embedded.

LATO: Yes, and the thrust of her argument against this 'theory' was that what he presented as a philosophical account of concept-formation was at best only speculation about historical facts of which we know nothing.[51]—At worst it was incoherent.

The heart of her anxiety lay in her concern over the apparently *ambiguous* nature of the primitive reactions in question. In her discussion of the example of *cause*, she remarked:

> In the situation described, let us agree that I'm angry and look for the one who hit me. But is this a reaction to the blow, to cause of the blow, to the pain, or the anger? How can one determine which? Once such questions are raised, it becomes clear that the reaction itself is ambiguous. If, for instance, someone inarticulate or an animal were to react in similar circumstances, we would have trouble distinguishing one from another. (Wolgast, 1994, p. 592)

Her conclusion was:

> The crucial difficulty with the account is ….the ambiguity that surrounds the question *what* language game they ground. Does

pulling back from a hot object give rise to the concept of cause, of fear, of caution? What would show us *which* of them originates with it? (Wolgast, 1994, p. 597)

We may obtain a more precise understanding of the significance of this ambiguity by examining the instance in which Wolgast *was* prepared to accede to Wittgenstein. She accepted his claim that without its characteristic expressions the language-game with 'pain' would lose its point.[52] I also assume that, as far as the concept-founding mechanism is concerned, she would have approved Wittgenstein's suggestion that the teaching of the concept is effected through the *replacement* of pain-behaviour by the use of the word.[53] By attaching the word 'pain' to natural expressions of pain, the child learns both new pain-behaviour *and* the concept; for the word also belongs to the language it is learning. All this is possible because of the clearly unambiguous nature of expressions of pain, so that the use of the word can, in an important sense, be identical with the reaction. To cry out and to use the word 'pain' are *the same* to the extent that they are both driven in the same measure by one's being in pain; the difference being that 'pain' also belongs to a language, so that its use may also be a move in the game. On the principle that the *ontogeny* of the child's formation of the concept repeats the *phylogeny* of the concept, we may imagine that the origin of the concept pain lay in some process by which 'pain' came to replace pain-behaviour.—By such a process of replacement we *cannot but* have formed the concept.

By contrast, if the reaction is ambiguous it cannot be identical with any one of its possible interpretations. For if a form of words were to enter the language just by replacing such a reaction, the resultant language-game would be obliged to embody all of the possible interpretations together, as it were.[54] The alternative concepts that seem to be anticipated in the reaction could then only be separated out from one another by their being further determined in some *other* way. But of course this would destroy the whole point of invoking primitive reactions in the first place. Hence, an ambiguous reaction cannot of itself be the foundation for or explain the genesis of any one of the possible language-games. If the language-game is imagined to emerge ineluctably out of a primitive reaction, the ambiguous nature of the reaction then shows that it cannot.

Wolgast concluded that the case of pain is exceptional; ambiguity among primitive reactions is the rule. Therefore any attempt to model a general account of concept-formation upon them will be incoherent.[55] This is a conclusion with which we can agree. What we refute is that

Wittgenstein held, or that his remarks imply, any such theory of concept-formation,—or indeed any theory *at all*.

5   The ambiguity of primitive reactions

CRATES: To clear a path out of Wolgast's difficulties, Lato, perhaps we might begin by restating her account of the ambiguity of primitive reactions in a more perspicuous form as follows.

One circumstance in which we might say that a piece of behaviour is ambiguous is where we recognize that for its proper interpretation the behaviour requires to be placed in a larger context. For example, we could easily imagine a situation where we are unclear whether a crouching cat is resting or hunting, and could equally easily imagine what would settle it. The ambiguity arises here because in an important sense we just do not see enough of the action; it is solved by observing the larger course of action to which the episode we observe belongs.

It is important to note here that it is not merely a contingent fact that our interpretation requires that we view the behaviour in the larger context. Resting and hunting are concepts of a *course of action*. To this extent the concepts determine what is to *count* as seeing enough of the action for the purpose of making such a judgement. So the problem of interpretation arises because the perspective demands *conceptually* that we see more of the behaviour than in fact we do see. In such cases, we might say that the ambiguity is not an *intrinsic* property of the phenomenon we are observing; rather, it is a feature arising out of a conflict between the context we are offered and the larger context demanded by the concepts we wish to apply.[56]

But—if I understand this correctly—the ambiguity that Wolgast had in mind was of a different kind. In her argument, the reactions appear to be *intrinsically* ambiguous. This is because we appear to be able to ask whether the child's reaction is to the *pain*, the *blow*, or the *cause*, even though the larger context that would settle the issue—language-games within which the separate concepts might be expressed—does not exist. If I may repeat the remark you quoted:

> But is this a reaction to the blow, to cause of the blow, to the pain, or the anger? How can one determine which? Once such questions are raised, it becomes clear that the reaction itself is ambiguous. If, for instance, someone inarticulate or an animal were to react in similar circumstances, **we would have trouble distinguishing one from the other.** (Wolgast, 1994, p. 592) (my emphasis)

But this surely is to understate the difficulty—unless Wolgast is simply being ironic—for the lack of the larger context renders the attempt to make the distinction *meaningless*, not just troublesome. What we are dealing with here is the kind of difficulty that arises when we try to force primitive behaviour into categories for which—in the lives of such creatures—the context does not yet exist; where to describe the creature in those terms at all is already to *presuppose* an appropriate linguistic capacity. Unlike the case of the cat, it is not that we are not in a position to know whether the reaction is to the blow or to the cause of the blow; the distinction makes no sense.

The underlying logic of Wolgast's criticism, therefore, is not merely that, in an ordinary sense, the primitive reactions are ambiguous and so admit of a variety of interpretations; it is rather that there is no question of an 'interpretation' until we provide precisely the linguistic context that they are supposed to explain; we *then* find that the same reaction might just as easily be at the root of a variety of such contexts. This logical circle shows us that primitive reactions cannot ground concepts: the genesis of such concepts cannot be explained merely in terms of the dressing up of primitive reactions in 'words'.

LATO: On this principle, we can agree with Wolgast.

6 Primitive linguistic reactions

But there is also another matter to clear up, which involves—we believe—a substantial misunderstanding by Wolgast of Wittgenstein's intentions in his discussions of the concept *cause*. Wolgast took it for granted that whenever Wittgenstein spoke of primitive reactions—and the like—he was always speaking of *pre-linguistic* behaviour. Leaving aside, for the moment, what Wittgenstein had in mind when he *did* speak of pre-linguistic reactions—which is a matter that we shall deal with in due course—it is highly questionable whether he intended his examples to be understood in this way. Even a cursory examination should show that he was imagining reactions that *already* belong to language-games—that is, 'language and the actions into which it is woven'.

Wittgenstein wanted to distinguish the cases where we recognize 'a cause immediately' from the ones where we recognize a cause as a result of 'repeated experiments'.[57] Regarding the first of these, he described various situations in which we 'react to a cause'—for example, when we react to a blow, or to a voice in the cinema, or to someone pulling at the other end of a string. Now to be sure, he spoke of these reactions as *instinctive*, but there is nothing to suggest he was thinking of them as anything other than belonging to an 'up and running' language-game in which we call something 'the cause'.

CRATES: What he was trying to do, clearly enough I would have thought, was to clarify one particular form of the language-game in which the concept *cause* enters and to dispel certain myths surrounding it.

LATO: Yes. Specifically, he was attacking Russell's attempt to interpret this instinctive use as a kind of *intuition*. Wittgenstein was saying that in such instances what we have is not some kind of direct insight into a causal relation (the intuition), but just an instinctive reaction: in certain circumstances we unhesitatingly speak in causal language. This is a direct reaction to events which does not demand explanation in terms of an intuition, that is, in terms of some subjective state or act accompanying the use of the expression.

So the examples he gave were clearly intended to be elementary forms of the language-game,[58] *not* 'pre-linguistic' reactions that must lead ineluctably to a language-game of a particular logical structure. Elsewhere, as I have said, Wittgenstein did indeed speak of the 'pre-linguistic' prototype of 'a way of thinking',[59] but in the current discussion he spoke quite explicitly of the prototype of a language-game as the most elementary form in which the game is played:

> The simple form (and that is the prototype) of the cause-effect game is determining the cause, not doubting. (CE, p. 397)

There is every reason for supposing, therefore, that this is how we should understand the examples he discussed on this occasion. Indeed in another very important remark, as you will recall, he stated:

> 'The basic form of the game can't include doubt.' What we are doing here above all is to *imagine* a basic form: a possibility, indeed a *very important* possibility. (We very often confuse what is an important possibility with historical reality.) (CE, p. 377)

This tells us that Wittgenstein conceived of what he was doing as an investigation into the *logical* structure of our language-games, *not* natural history, that is, not an explanation of the origin of the language-game.

Let us see how this interpretation fits the following statements, and then consider Wolgast's reaction to it:

> Certainly there is in such cases a genuine experience which can be called 'experience of the cause'. But not because it infallibly shows us

the cause; rather because *one* root of the cause-effect language-game is to be found here, in our looking out for a cause.

We react to the cause.

Calling something 'the cause' is like pointing and saying: '*He's* to blame!'

We instinctively get rid of the cause if we don't want the effect. We instinctively look from what has been hit to what has hit it. (I am assuming that we do this.)

Now suppose I were to say that when we speak of cause and effect we always have in mind a comparison with impact; that this is the prototype of cause and effect? Would this mean that we had *recognized* impact as a cause? Imagine a language in which people always said 'impact' instead of 'cause'. (CE, p. 373)

CRATES: Wittgenstein was evidently thinking of simple situations in which we react instinctively to being hit, and so on, by using expressions such as 'He's to blame'. In other words, he was describing an elementary language-game,—the kind of *prototype* language-game (in the sense described above) out of which the more complicated forms might develop. Even where he spoke of a reaction being at the 'root' of the language-game, we may interpret the reaction as a linguistic one. Using an expression like '*He's* to blame!' is a direct reaction that *itself* expresses the concept *cause*. We do not have to suppose that the possibility of using such a phrase with this meaning depends upon a *prior* conception of causality,—one derived from intuition or repeated experiment. Similarly, in the case of 'impact', we do not have to posit a further step: an act of recognizing the impact as a 'cause'—by an act of intuition. The concept of a cause is already manifest *in* such elementary, instinctive uses of language. They are primary expressions of it. Having the concept of cause is comprised, partly at least, in being able to employ such expressions in these ways—and in other ways too, of course, such as when we do indeed make repeated experiments.

LATO: Exactly. Wittgenstein's discussion belonged to his attack upon the idea that having concepts depends on having some kind of internal representation accessed by intuition; he was not theorizing about the origin of the language-game. This interpretation of his remarks seems fairly obvious, which makes Wolgast's reaction to Wittgenstein's first remark at best puzzling:

Wittgenstein says, 'Calling something the cause is like pointing and saying: "He's to blame!" ' And one wants to say, yes, but that doesn't say *what* the reaction concerns, the blow, its cause, the pain or some-thing else. The point isn't trivial for Wittgenstein. If the cause of the blow isn't distinct from the blow or the pain, the reaction one has isn't clearly ground for the concept of 'cause,' but might be the ground for 'wondering what happened', or even 'pain'. Or nothing. (Wolgast, 1994, p. 592)

CRATES: It certainly is puzzling, because Wittgenstein did not refer to a *non-vocal* reaction that *grounds* the concept; he described simple lin-guistic reactions combined with various actions as being elementary to the language-game and as giving it its character.

LATO: Things also go wrong where she seemed to suggest that Wittgenstein had lapsed momentarily into an empiricist theory of concept-formation when he stated:[60]

Certainly there is in such cases a genuine experience which can be called 'experience of the cause'. But not because it infallibly shows us the cause; rather because *one* root of the cause-effect language-game is to be found here, in our looking out for a cause. (CE, p. 373)

She pointed out, correctly, that an empiricist account of concept-formation is at odds with the whole tenor of the main body of his philosophy.[61] But again, in the present context there was no reason for thinking that Wittgenstein had lapsed. Later, Wittgenstein discussed 'continuous aspect' perception:[62] we perceive the world under the aspect of the concepts we have.[63] The point about such experiences is that they *go together* with the playing of language-games;—they do not precede them. Hence, it belongs to the playing of the language-games deploying causal concepts that we perceive 'causes';—we 'see' things as causing one another, and especially so where our most direct linguistic reactions to reality are concerned, that is, where they are most closely linked to overt behaviour. If we treat Wittgenstein as speaking about basic forms of language-games rather than pre-linguistic reactions, then it is entirely consistent that he should also have spoken of the experiences that accompany them without our needing to suppose that he was making an empiricist assumption.

CRATES: To summarize, then, Lato, the principal message of Wittgenstein's discussions of cause and effect is that *one* point of articu-lation of the language-game of causality—and hence of the *concept* of causality—is a spontaneous or independent linguistic reaction occurring in the context of our daily routines, which does not have to be explained at a more fundamental level by a further rational process of intuition. Such behaviour neither gives rise *to* nor is made intelligible *by* the concept but belongs to the circumstances in which the language-game has the sense that it does have. Its primitiveness therefore speaks of the *structure* of the language-game, not of the paths by which it came into being.

LATO: Agreed. One of the achievements of Wittgenstein's later philosophy lies in its breaking down the picture of the relation of language and thought to reality as 'a view from the boundary'. Rather, language has sense, and thought is *of* the world, in the multifarious ways that words move *in concert* with human activity and social intercourse. Language is of 'the midst'. Talk of primitive reactions, by drawing attention to the integrity of certain linguistic reactions and forms of activity within the language-games, belongs to saying just this.

Wolgast's use of this discussion to try to show Wittgenstein as struggling to give an account of the direct derivation of concepts from *pre*-linguistic behaviour was misguided. Wittgenstein certainly did speak elsewhere of *pre*-linguistic prototypes of language-games—as we have noted previously—so if we are to comment on what he might have had in mind in those other contexts, we must divorce any such treatment from the way he spoke in his discussion of cause and effect.[64]

7   Language as extending pre-linguistic behaviour

CRATES: So, let's now look at those occasions when Wittgenstein *did* speak of language-games as 'extensions' of *pre*- or *non*-linguistic primitive behaviour. I have been especially struck by two you have already quoted, which seem to me to be most emphatic:

> But what is the word 'primitive' meant to say here? Presumably that this sort of behaviour is *pre-linguistic*: that a language-game is based *on it*, that it is the prototype of a way of thinking and not the result of thought. (Z 541)

> Being sure that someone is in pain, doubting whether he is, and so on, are so many natural, instinctive kinds of behaviour towards other human beings, and our language is merely an auxiliary to, and further extension of, this relation. Our language-game is an extension of primitive behaviour. (For our *language-game* is behaviour.) (Instinct) (Z 545)

I can see that these and other similar remarks may superficially be construed in ways that are consistent with Wolgast's interpretation.

Certainly the remarks appear to say something different from what he said in the discussions of cause and effect. At the very least, he *appears* to allow primitive behaviour a rôle in concept-formation that did not show in those other discussions.[65] But we believe it possible to give plausible, intelligible and illuminating treatments of the notion of pre-linguistic behaviour—and of the idea of language-games as *extensions* of primitive behaviour, in certain cases at least—which need not draw us into unwarranted *a priori* speculation about the origins of our concepts or into foundationalism. Indeed, I think I am right in recalling another remark and which would appear to have been overlooked in this debate—where Wittgenstein expressed the idea of language-games as extensions of non-linguistic behaviour while explicitly rejecting a foundationalist interpretation of this relation:

> For think of the sensations produced by physically shuddering: the words 'it makes me shiver' are themselves such a shuddering reaction; and if I hear and feel them as I utter them, this belongs among the rest of those sensations. Now why should the wordless shudder be the ground of the verbal one? (PI, p. 148)

It will be important to commanding a clear view of certain language-games that we clarify the sense in which they can be described as extensions of primitive pre-linguistic behaviour. We will certainly need to be careful to express the point in a way that avoids foundationalism; but it remains an important aspect of language use and concept possession and so needs to be preserved.

LATO: Central to this issue, Crates, is the achievement of a proper conception of the relation between our use of words and the rest of our lives. Happily, this takes us straight to the heart of Wittgenstein's philosophy. Wittgenstein, as we know, defined a language-game as 'language and the actions into which it is woven'.[66] Part of what he was trying to do with this notion of a language-game was to wean us off the idea of language as an autonomous activity whose essentials lie apart from the way it is woven into our everyday lives and actions. Such apartness is visible, for example, in mentalistic accounts of concepts such as *meaning*. On the contrary, it is in the way in which language goes together with our active lives (and taking into account the points made in the previous dialogue on the nature of speaking) that our intelligent engagement with our environment is constituted. It is this that identifies us as thinking, speaking, conceiving things. It is this engagement *taken as a whole* that shows what it is to speak and to have concepts.—This is our starting point.

There is a variety of contexts in philosophy in which we speak of the dependence of language on behaviour. For example, we may have in mind the way that the use of language depends upon constancy and agreement among our verbal and perceptual responses and reactions. These form what have been called the 'framework conditions' that make language use possible. Or, we may be thinking of the way in which certain activities form the *context* for a language-game, and so belong to the provision of its sense. However, the kind of relation that we presently have in mind is where the use of language is bound up rather more intimately with the natures of the activities themselves. This obtains most obviously where the language-games, in the way in which they become part of our lives, are *constitutive* of our selves as persons—I am thinking, for example, of hoping, intending, believing, knowing, and so on. In fact, we have already referred to this in a different context in the fifth section of our second dialogue, where we discussed having the concept *of* a language-game. In particular, we examined the case where we conceive of certain phenomena in human life in terms of specific uses of language occurring in connection with more general features of our form of life. For example, the concepts of hoping, intending, and so on, are concepts of *aspects* of our form of life into which language use is woven in a characteristic way. Hence, true accounts of these aspects— and so also of the concepts—will be accounts of both language use *and* non-linguistic features (actions) and of the relations between the two. Thus we refer to hoping, intending, and so on, as *phenomena*, to emphasize that they are *gross* features of human life and not aspects of our lives whose reality resides only within the verbal arena.

CRATES: One might consider, as an illustration, the example of *greeting*. Verbal expressions of greeting are embedded in the patterns of interaction between people. These patterns of behaviour are not merely the staging for what is otherwise a purely *linguistic* exchange. To say that two people are greeting one another adds up to more than can be explained simply in terms of the use of a form of words in a given context and their further *linguistic* consequences. For if, when people encountered one another, the verbal exchanges were not a part of patterns of behaviour expressing acknowledgement of one sort or another, I do not think we would be inclined to call this greeting in the sense in which we normally mean it. So the concept is of a form of life (or aspect of our form of life) comprising linguistic expressions *and*—independently, as it were—other patterns of behaviour. This is the *phenomenon* of greeting. Hence, that what I say is a *greeting* is partly a function of how it hangs together with larger features of the ways in which we are disposed towards one another.—Language use *and* a certain way of life are *internal* to our concept of greeting.

LATO: This sense in which the use of language forms a part of such phenomena is very important. It is certainly true that, on the one hand, language is the *medium* within which concepts are articulated. But our concern in the present dialogue is to draw special attention to the rôle that the use of language has as a *component* of these phenomena of human life. This distinction is crucial to what we want to say. Put rather more formally we may distinguish between:

1   The use of language to express or articulate the *concepts* of hoping, greeting, intending, and so on. Here the criterion for possessing the concept would lie, for example, in the ability to apply the concepts in judgements, or to talk about the phenomena during conversation.
2   The use of language as a component in the *expression* of hope, greeting, intending, and so on. Here the use of language belongs to the way in which the phenomena are manifested. And our particular interest here will be to show how we may regard this use of language as an *extension* of these phenomena.

To emphasize this contrast, we may note further that where language *does* enter into the manifestation of the phenomenon, it may not actually involve the direct articulation of the concept of the phenomenon at all. For example, we could easily imagine utterances expressing hope in which the *concept* of hope is not articulated: someone is sitting impatiently waiting for a train to leave, he looks at his watch, he says to himself 'Come on! Come on!'. The man certainly hopes that the train will leave very soon. This shows in what he says.

CRATES: Similar considerations apply, we believe, to the other phenomena, or aspects of our form of life, listed above—and many more. In fact we may now examine once more and from this somewhat different perspective our earlier example of a language-game in which this distinction applies: *intention*. Our present reason for this choice is that the phenomenon of intention has a significant, indeed an *essentially* pre-linguistic dimension.

LATO: It is also an interesting example because it is 'ambiguous' in Wolgast's sense; for, while being pervasive of human activity, intention is not uniquely expressed by any one reaction. It is therefore a genuine instance of a primitive feature of human life of the kind that one *might* suppose could generate a concept in the way that Wolgast found objectionable. And for just this reason it is also well suited to elucidating Wittgenstein's notion of language-games as extensions of primitive behaviour while observing this to be neither theory laden nor attracting the problem of ambiguity.

CRATES: Intentionality is a phenomenon within human life. It belongs among our concepts of a *course of action*. It is part of our concept of an *agent*. For these reasons, it is rooted in an elementary way in our concept of action, and so it relates to our lives in a rather more fundamental way than do concepts relating specifically to ourselves as speakers. At the same time, it is linked to speaking because of the way that speaking is related to action through the formulation and expression of intentions. So we might say that, for a speaker, intentionality is comprised both through there *being* courses of action *and* in the way that such courses of action may be expressed in language.

It is important to keep these two aspects apart and not to subordinate the notion of a course of action to the relation between expressions of intention and actions in accordance with those expressions. One mode of intentionality is where a course of action is initiated by premeditation. Here one is certainly tempted to say that the action's being intentional lies in its being in accord with the expressed intention; that its being an intended act consists in its standing in an internal relation to the linguistic expression. But premeditation cannot be sufficient to an account of intentionality in general, as it already *takes for granted* the notion of a course of action. Moreover, the fact that the notion of a course of action has a dimension that is intelligible *independently* of the relation between actions and verbal expressions of intention is manifest in the observation that the concept of intentionality clearly applies more widely than to premeditated actions.

LATO: We may even speak of *natural* expressions of intention in dumb animals. As Wittgenstein remarked:

> What is the natural expression of an intention?—Look at a cat when it stalks a bird; or a beast when it wants to escape. (PI 647)

CRATES: So the notion of *being on a course of action*, and therefore of intentionality, cannot be reduced to the relations between actions and verbal expressions of intention. Moreover, if there is an order of priority, then it is surely the other way about: natural, or 'primitive', intentionality is in an important sense a *pre-requisite* for the language-game of expressing intentions. This belongs with what I meant just now by saying that premeditation takes for granted the notion of a course of action. Perhaps, Lato, you would explain this in more detail.

LATO: This notion of a *course of action* is quite fundamental to our concept of a person—more fundamental, it may be argued, than that of speaking and therefore of the verbal expression of intention. The reason for this ought to be obvious: speaking *presupposes* acting, while acting does not presuppose speaking (although undoubtedly certain kinds of action do). In the first place, speaking itself is behaviour and the use of words is intentional, so that anything done *in* language presupposes acting. Second, language is a form of behaviour whose nature lies in the way it is woven into other such forms. What makes anything language is at least partly a function of its relations to other forms of coherent behaviour, or courses of action. The possibility of speaking depends upon a coherent life. Intentionality belongs to this coherence, and the life of a child that is learning to speak is pervaded by intentional acts. The child learns to speak and he learns to formulate intentions, but it would be nonsense to say that acting intentionally *as such* is learned;[67] for if the child can be said to be learning anything at all, then he is *already* engaged in intentional acts, in the primitive sense.

CRATES: So, intention *qua* being on a course of action is more elementary to the concept of intention—that is, to the phenomenon of intentionality—than is the expression of intention in words.—An individual can only express intentions if he can *already act*. The concept of expressing intention in words presupposes and contains the concept of intention in the primitive sense. We might also express this by saying that, in its primitive form, intention is pre-linguistic: it is a *pre-requisite* for being able to participate in language generally and in the language-game of expressing intentions in particular.

LATO: Yes. In this respect intention differs from greeting. Here too we may conceive of a primitive or animal form of greeting without speech—there are plenty of examples in the animal world that we might wish to call greeting. However—and this is the important point—there would be no conceptual difficulty in imagining the absence of characteristic primitive behaviour expressing greeting *prior* to the formation of the language-game. By contrast, what is interesting about intention—just because it is so fundamental to human life—is that the verbal expression of intention is inconceivable except in so far as it is embedded in a life pervaded by intentionality in the more primitive sense. It is in these contexts that it is philosophically illuminating to speak of the use of language as an *extension* of primitive behaviour.—It is a grammatical remark on our conception of the human form of life.

Let's consider how the language-game of expressing intentions might be 'grafted' onto the life of an infant. Imagine a child getting up to leave the room and being asked what he is doing. He answers, 'I am going outside'. Perhaps the adult will encourage him to say this by *asking* him if he is going outside. Or we might imagine a child being taught to express intentions retrospectively. He might be asked whether or not he *meant* to act in the way he did; or he may be encouraged to *say* what he intended to do. Alternatively we might imagine situations where a child is being taught to formulate intentions: the adult asks the child 'What are you doing today?', and so on. Obviously these are gross caricatures of the process of learning; but the important point is that we *can imagine* the child engaging in various forms of behaviour and the adult encouraging him to respond with appropriate verbal expressions of intention. The child is either being encouraged to say things expressing the intent of past or present courses of action, or he is being prodded into using language to initiate a course of action.

Now, it is important to note that in imagining this grafting of language onto the life of the child, we do not have to imagine that a *reaction*—a primitive expression of intention—is being *replaced* by a verbal expression. Rather, in the right context the expressions are woven into the fabric of the life of the child, either by encouragement or on the child's own initiative. Neither does the *criterion* of the child's having learned to use the expressions correctly lie in him being seen to have successfully 'replaced' anything. It lies in his being able to go on to use the expression appropriately in future contexts, both in connection with his own actions and in the way that the expressions are used in connection with other things that he says.

CRATES: Similar considerations apply to the fact that when the child is learning to use the expression, there may be no guarantee that he will take it in the way the adult intended. This may be partly explained by the vagaries of the process of learning generally, though the 'ambiguity' in the life of the pre-linguistic child—in the sense explained previously— may also be a factor. In these same circumstances the child might be learning to express wants or hopes or any number of other uses of language. But this does not mean that it is wrong to speak of the expressions as being 'grafted' onto the natural behaviour. Again, we do not have to interpret this in a literal-minded way as substituting a verbal expression for a specific reaction. If the child takes the expression 'wrongly', then the adult carries on until the child starts to use it correctly. Certainly the child is learning *new* reactions that cannot be reduced to pre-linguistic ones; but the important point is that these new reactions derive much of their character—their rôle—from their relations to pre-existing ones. This is what it *means* to say that the language-game is 'grafted' onto the reactions of the infant. They bring the child into new relations to his own actions; they bring the child into new relations to himself as an agent. The adult is there to *guide* this new dimension of expression into a life that already exists; and the new expressions take their place among the pre-linguistic modes of behaviour.

LATO: All this adds up to *one* sense in which we may say that the language-game of expressing intention is an *extension* to the life of the pre-linguistic child, or that the pre-linguistic behaviour of the child forms the 'base' for or is 'at the bottom of' the language-game—to use Wittgenstein's phrases. It adds a further dimension of intentionality to the life of the child; it introduces new modes of intending. This conception of language as extending primitive behaviour conforms to what seems to me to be the most natural interpretation of Wittgenstein's own remark that '[o]ur language-game is an extension of primitive behaviour'.[68]

We are drawing attention to the way that Wittgenstein spoke of the language-game as an extension of our relations to other people, emphasizing that the language-game is *itself* behaviour. This shows that he was not thinking of a mechanism of concept-formation, but of how the rôle that the language-game has in our lives derives from the way it is seated among 'natural' forms of behaviour—forms which, at the very least, we are not obliged to conceive of as being 'the result of thought',[69] or which, in cases like intention, *cannot* be so conceived.

8 Rhees on behaviour as the 'Prototype of a Way of Thinking'

We have mentioned Rhees' misgivings about some of Wittgenstein's remarks on these topics. We shall now examine these in more detail. His doubts were expressed to Norman Malcolm, who was an enthusiast for interpreting Wittgenstein as wishing to explain the genesis of concepts directly from primitive behaviour.[70]

Rhees was as keen as we have been to deny that Wittgenstein was promulgating such a theory. Indeed he expounded his own version of Wolgast's argument against the theory on the grounds of the *ambiguity* of primitive reactions,[71] though this time the argument is identified as originating from within Wittgenstein's *own* writings.

CRATES: One more reason for thinking that Wittgenstein did *not* adopt the theory himself.

LATO: Quite so. Most of Rhees' remarks were devoted to examining the rôle of primitive reactions—linguistic or otherwise—*within* language-games. He argued persuasively that when Wittgenstein spoke of primitive reactions, he generally had in mind the kind of primitive linguistic reactions described in his discussions of cause and effect,—this being in accord with our own interpretation of these remarks. However, Rhees was less keen on the notion of language-games as *extensions* of primitive behaviour, or on talk of 'pre-linguistic' behaviour;—so much so, in fact, that he did not mention at all Wittgenstein's use of the latter phrase in his discussion of his remarks on this subject.[72] This is surprising given that this is the phrase that is most strongly suggestive of a theory of concept-formation from roots outside language, and so really *ought* to call for special comment. My feeling is that Rhees was intent on steering away from these ways of speaking because he could only see in them the tendency towards theorizing. Let's trace the course of his argument.

Rhees began our discussion by warning against speaking of behaviour as 'the prototype of a way of thinking' ('a way of thinking' is not equivalent here to a *concept*—as we shall see). He argued that a form of behaviour is only the prototype of a way of thinking when seen as *already* having a place within the language-game; hence it would not be the prototype in an animal as there is no further issue.[73] I think he had in mind here that in the animal the equivalent behaviour is not 'a way of thinking' of a prototypical kind, whereas in a person it *belongs with* our ways of thinking. Thus, what would be regarded as 'mere behaviour' in an animal is treated as a *component* of the articulate expression of thought in a person. Rhees expressed this by speaking of such behaviour as 'something akin to a gesture',[74] to emphasize its belonging to the field of *meaning*.[75]

CRATES: It would appear here that Rhees was trying to treat the primitive gestural behaviour—for which we may find analogues in the instinctive responses of animals—as having similar status to the prototype *language-games*, that is, as instinctive reactions giving character to the language-games. But surely the comparison can only be taken so far. We can agree that such behaviour is not the same thing in the life of a person as its equivalent is in the life of an animal, just because it *does* stand in a relation to the use of language in the person in a way that it does not in the animal. That makes it more like language,—more 'akin to a gesture'. But there remains an important difference between prototype language-games and such behaviour even *within* the language-game, just because the prototype language-games *can* stand on their own (or can be conceived of as standing on their own) as primitive forms of language.—That is why it makes sense to call them *prototypes*. But this will not work with primitive behaviour of no intrinsic linguistic content. *Outside* the context of language, the behaviour is not articulate and is not a 'gesture'; *inside* language its being a 'gesture' *depends* on its relations to ways of speaking and so cannot be conceived of as the prototype for them. The behaviour may be primitive to the language-game—but that is different. From this perspective, then, it is not obvious why we should want to call primitive behaviour of this type the prototype of a way of thinking at all.

LATO: No, it isn't. So let us try another tack. Rhees' interpretation of 'the prototype of a way of thinking' conflicts with other phrases of Wittgenstein's and with his own treatment of them.[76] First, *that* Wittgenstein had in mind something coming *before* language shows in the fact that his phrase 'the prototype of a way of thinking' was clearly intended to be understood in the light of the remark 'that this sort of behaviour is *pre-linguistic*'. Matters get more confused in Rhees' conclusion. Criticizing Wittgenstein's use of another phrase,[77] he said:

> ... and we should not say 'daß ein Sprachspiel *auf* ihr beruht' ('that a language-game is based *on* it'): you wouldn't know what was meant by that. (Rhees, 1997, p. 2)

Here he *did* seem bothered that the phrase was suggestive of a theory of concept-formation; and yet it was surely intended by Wittgenstein to be understood in the same way as 'the prototype of a way of thinking'. My feeling is that Rhees was over anxious to make Wittgenstein's talk of 'prototypes' in this remark consistent with the way he used it elsewhere to refer to primitive *linguistic* reactions (primitive *to* language-games). This goes with the fact that he insisted that Wittgenstein's use of the phrase, '[o]ur language-game is an extension of primitive behaviour' must have referred to an extension of an existing language-game, in spite of the fact that Wittgenstein had just spoken of this behaviour as *pre-linguistic*.[78] But he could not cover up the loose ends. I think we can make more consistent sense of Wittgenstein's remark along the lines we developed earlier in this dialogue. Let us begin with a fresh example.

I think one can safely assert that *running* is, as a matter of fact, a natural, primitive behaviour for humans. We might then suppose a wide variety of sports or games to be *based* on this behaviour. I am not treat-ing the primitive reaction here as itself a game, but it is an activity *around which* games may be formed, so we may say that they are based on it in this sense. This would not be to presume that the game of foot-ball, for example, was generated out of the primitive reaction; it does not mean that instinctive behaviour *must* lead to a certain game—any number of different games might grow up around it in a spontaneous and unpredictable way. Furthermore, we might even say—and again without suggesting any kind of inevitability—that the primitive reac-tion partly *determines* the character of the game, in the sense in which it does *not* determine anything in the game of chess, for example. In other words, running *lends itself* to the formation of some games and not others but does not of itself take any responsibility for generating any of them.—No game could be predicted just from the primitive behaviour. This seems to me to be a perfectly natural sense in which we might speak of a game being 'based' on primitive behaviour. I think we can agree?

CRATES: We can,—though I think we must add one *caveat* here. In this particular example we would probably not wish to speak of the primi-tive reaction as the prototype for the *game*, as running about is not in itself a game. If one thing is the prototype for another, then at least it ought to be something of the same or similar *kind*—of which games and merely running about clearly are not. If, on the other hand, the primi-tive behaviour did show elements of being 'game-like', then we might be more inclined to speak of it as the prototype. For example, if it were a natural instinct for young children to kick things about between them-selves (comparable with a dog's instinct to retrieve, or the game-like behaviour that young animals often show), then we would be more inclined to call this behaviour the prototype of the game of football—here we might also say that the game is based on the reaction in a rather more substantial sense. What we are looking for in a prototype, then, is primitive behaviour that merits description, to *some* degree at least, in terms characteristic of games proper.

LATO: That is an important point, Crates, since turning our thoughts again to language, we might say that this is precisely the point in the argument that creates the most difficulty. For the gulf in *kind* between primitive behaviour and language is surely just too great—one might say. But I believe this depends very much on the *dimension* in which we are looking for the connection. We certainly cannot bridge it by looking for an analogue in primitive behaviour to the articulation of *concepts*.—So much is agreed. But as we argued earlier in this dialogue, language and primitive behaviour show connections in kind in quite another dimension, namely in the *rôle* that they have in our lives. And I would suggest that it was this that Wittgenstein had in mind when he spoke of 'the prototype of a *way* of thinking'.—He did not speak of primitive behaviour as the prototype articulation of a *concept*.

This interpretation was suggested, though not developed, by Peter Winch in his own comments on Malcolm's remarks:

> If we look at the crying, etc. of a small child as the prototype of the adult's use of pain language, we are seeing it—the crying—from the vantage point of our mastery of pain language. (Winch, 1997a, p. 61)

Elsewhere, he made the same point while adverting more explicitly to Wittgenstein's remark—again in response to Malcolm:[79]

> Words are said to be substituted for the original, natural expression of *sensation*. The reaction is a reaction to *being hurt*. What the child is taught is new *pain behaviour*; i.e. this replaces an earlier form of *pain behaviour*. (Winch, 1993, p. 123)

And then with reference to Wittgenstein's remarks on cause and effect, he said:

> And here too the primitive reactions with which Wittgenstein compares our language-game are themselves described in terms taken from that language-game; they are seen from the point of view of that language-game. They are 'reactions *towards a cause*'. (Winch, 1993, p. 123)

Rhees himself made a remark that is suggestive of this. Commenting on Wittgenstein's use of the phrase 'a way of thinking', he cited as a possible example someone saying, 'I can't help thinking about the man we saw on the street. I wonder if they were able to help him'.[80] The example illustrates that 'a way of thinking' is not just 'concepts put together in a certain order', as it were, but has to do with the way in which what we say is a *response* to the events around us. In what he said, the man showed how he was preoccupied about an event, and it is the *preoccupation* that characterizes the way of thinking. Now this, and here we may depart from Rhees, bears comparison with an adult animal's preoccupation, for example, with its injured offspring. To say that the behaviour of the animal is 'the prototype of a way of thinking' (in us, of course, not in the animal) would have sense not because the behaviour is the prototype for *saying these words*—it is not a prototype for language—but because of the way that both are expressions of a certain kind of preoccupation. The way in which the animal responds on a purely behavioural level is (or could be) the prototype for the *kind* of response that *we* express in language. And of course the two expressions of preoccupation are not merely analogous: what makes what the man says an expression of preoccupation is determined in large part by the way that the use of words belongs with the kind of behaviour shared with the animal.—It is an *extension* of primitive preoccupation. We might express the point grammatically by saying that it belongs to the grammar of 'preoccupation' that it may be expressed either in natural forms of behaviour or in language.

CRATES: We may apply these thoughts again to our principal example: *intention*. For we may say that the use of language to express intention is comparable to 'a way of thinking'. Primitive intentionality and primitive expressions of intention have lent themselves to the formation of the language-game of expressing intentions: it is based on them, it has grown up around them. We might also say that primitive intentionality partly *determines* the character of the language-game, just because if the language-game were not woven into primitive intentionality, it would just not be the language-game of expressing *intentions*.— The concept of intention constrains what would *count* as a language-game of expressing intentions. And so we may speak of 'natural' expressions of intention as the prototypes for verbal expressions, not because they are verbal expressions 'in the making', but because they are part of the phenomenon around which the language-game of expressing intentions has grown up and within which the language-game has its rôle. The natural and verbal expressions are both expressions of intention,— and in that sense are things of the same kind. It belongs to the grammar of 'intention' that it may have both natural and linguistic expressions, of which the former are more elementary.

9   Returning to Wolgast

LATO: I want to return to Wolgast for a last time. Rhees was worried about certain ways of speaking about language because he saw in them, and often rightly so, a tendency towards theorizing on how language and concepts generated themselves out of pre-linguistic behaviour. That he saw no other possibilities in these ways of speaking may have stemmed from an inclination to speak only from a perspective *within* the language-games. This allowed him to illustrate how such behaviour has a fundamental, but non-generative, rôle to play in the game, but without him having to acknowledge—as we have laboured the point—that the language-games may also be regarded as forming a part of the larger phenomena of human life. As a result, these larger connections between linguistic and primitive dimensions of our forms of life went unrecognized. Wolgast's failure to acknowledge these same connections is rooted in a similarly too narrow focus on what language achieves for us.

The immediate cause of this shortcoming—which I have already hinted at—lay, I suspect, in her confusion of the two different conceptions of the 'use' of language, referred to earlier: (1) to articulate concepts and (2) to be constitutive of the *phenomena* of hoping, intending, and so on. In her failure to recognize this second conception, she took it for granted that whatever is at stake when we inquire into the relation of *language-games* to pre-linguistic behaviour always amounts to this same issue of how our *concepts* are rooted in pre-linguistic behaviour, namely, concept-formation. As a result, she allowed herself no room for manoeuvre to entertain the kind of alternative we have been expounding. We hear this commonly in discussions of this topic.

The ease with which she made the transition from language-game to concept and then to concept-formation is clearly visible—and, I believe, is rather instructive. For example, commenting on Wittgenstein's remark on pre-linguistic behaviour as 'the prototype of a way of thinking and not the result of thought',[81] she said:

> 'Language is a refinement' and not the original form of expression, which is action (CE p. 395). **Thus the concepts of language begin in** *'behaviour that is pre-linguistic'* (*Zettel* 541) and in situations where doubt and verification are not applicable. (Wolgast, 1994, p. 600) (my emphasis)

Similarly:

> Acting with certainty is **the original of the concept of certainty, the language game of certainty** (Wolgast, 1994, p. 599). ... The crucial difficulty with the account is. ... the ambiguity that surrounds the question *what* language game they ground. Does pulling back from a hot object **give rise to the concept of cause, of fear, of caution? What would** *show us which of them originates with it?* (Wolgast, 1994, p. 597) (my emphases)

And:

> ... I want to explore the way he proposed that primitive reactions could account for concepts. ... (Wolgast, 1994, p. 588)

CRATES: She certainly seemed to start from the idea that it is the *concepts*—or their possession—that are imagined to be extensions of primitive behaviour. This led naturally to the picture of primitive behaviour as if it were, in some sense, already the *expression* of an idea,—where the 'original of the concept' is already embedded or represented in some way in the primitive behaviour. The invitation to a theory of concept-formation is now irresistible, for if we then imagine attaching words to these primitive expressions—or indeed *replacing* the primitive expression with words—this *cannot but* lead to the *concept* being represented in words, as we discussed earlier in the case of pain.

LATO: Wolgast argued correctly that this model cannot work, if only because the behaviour or reaction cannot be uniquely related to any one concept and so cannot take responsibility for generating it. But what she destroyed was a myth of the genesis of language that was of her own creation, not Wittgenstein's. And as far as the actual origin of language is concerned (either of linguistic *behaviour* or the concepts embedded in it), there is nothing in our account that is alien to Wittgenstein's own remark on these origins—a remark quoted approvingly by Wolgast but from which she wrongly thought him departing:

> You must bear in mind that the language-game is so to say something unpredictable. I mean: it is not based on grounds. It is not reasonable (or unreasonable).
> It is there—like our life. (OC 559)

The source of Wolgast's assumption—that what is at issue is the relation between *concepts* and behaviour—may be traced to her own view of language. Our criticism of Wolgast has been founded principally upon grammatical observations of the relations between language and action, both in respect of Wittgenstein's definition of a language-game as 'language and the actions into which it is woven' and in respect of the notion that certain phenomena of human life, such as *intention*, comprise both language *and* non-linguistic behavioural components. Language is a *component* of these phenomena. It is significant that these considerations played virtually no part in Wolgast's discussion. The reason for this appears to be that, although she *did* acknowledge at one point 'the change that language makes in their lives',[82] she seemed inclined to view language rather as an *independent* addition to our repertoire of behaviours: its character does not come especially from the way that it is woven into the rest of our lives, for we have non-vocal behaviour, and then parallel to that we have vocal behaviour.

This conception is evident in her account of language as something developing out of spontaneous vocalizations:

> The reactions I mean are the spontaneous vocalizings of humans— the babbling sounds infants make long before learning to utter words. Such vocal noise-making truly *is* one source of language, and together with the ability to mimic sounds, it is a crucial requirement of mastering a language. (Wolgast, 1994, p. 597–8)

> The instinct to vocalize shows language itself as a kind of doing, a noise-making that later connects with making stylized designs on paper. Seen in this way, we have no purchase on the thought that language is separate from activity: it *is* activity, even a whole family of activities—greeting, expressing feelings, reporting, telling stories, joking, many more. (Wolgast, 1994, p. 601)

> Speech belongs to humans in the way that mimicking sounds belongs to parrots, it grows spontaneously out of the creatures we are; and that is all one need say of language's basis and explanation. One does not need to ground particular concepts in particular kinds of reactions. (Wolgast, 1994, p. 601)

CRATES: So on her account, using language is an *activity*—one among a variety of activities. It is the activity of producing vocalizations. It is vocal *as distinct from* non-vocal behaviour. Vocal behaviour has a character of its own—as do the babbling of the child, or making 'stylized designs on paper', or the mimicry of parrots. It is *within* this activity that we have all that we need to 'explain' language. In other words what we seem to have here is a new version of the view of language that Wittgenstein was trying to get away from, namely the view of language as a kind of autonomous activity whose nature can be grasped without bothering to look at how the *sense* of what we say has to do with the way that language is woven into our actions,—that what we *say* is a *constituent* of our actions. Remember Gaita's 'having something to say' is 'living a life and speaking out of it'.[83]

LATO: We have noted that Wolgast does indeed speak of 'the change that language makes in their lives',—which does suggest a connection with other activities. But the lack of emphasis that this is given leads one to suppose that such connections are to be conceived of only as a *consequence* of using language (the changes that *follow from* our grasp of concepts), not something to which reference must be made if we are to understand what it is to use language at all. Against this we would argue, as we believe Wittgenstein would have argued, that 'vocalizing' is only *language* in the way it *is* woven into other activities—you rightly recall Gaita's words. Thus it is legitimate to inquire about these connections; and it is as part of *this* inquiry that the notion of language as an extension of primitive, non-linguistic modes of behaviour has its place.

Weighed down with her conception of language, it is not difficult to see how it led Wolgast to the interpretation of Wittgenstein as holding that *concepts* are extensions of primitive behaviour. For Wolgast, a sufficient account of language is an account of how concepts are embedded in it, of how we articulate concepts in it—*language* only as the servant of the intellect, one might say. This makes it difficult to see how language is a part of the *phenomena* of intending, hoping, believing, knowing, greeting, and so on. Hence, any account of the use of language in terms of its relations to, or dependence on, pre-linguistic behaviour will almost inevitably be construed as an attempt to explain the origin of its concepts in primitive behaviour.[84]

Wolgast cited the following as an example of Wittgenstein's leaning towards 'foundationalist' theorizing: 'I want to say: it is characteristic of our language that the foundation on which it grows consists in steady ways of living, regular ways of acting'.[85] But in the case of remarks such as these, we should surely begin not by assuming that Wittgenstein was engaged in a transcendental speculation—that is, from some supposed vantage point outside normal discourse—but by assuming that this is a grammatical remark, and then asking oneself *how* it is a grammatical remark. In this case, the remark is saying that the concept of language is the concept of something in the life of a creature whose life is made up of regular ways of acting that do not themselves depend on linguistic activity.—It is a remark connecting the grammar of 'language' with the grammar of 'acting'. We should not be stopped in this interpretation just because his statement has the outward form of a factual speculation. For, as we argued in our second dialogue, it is a commonplace for grammatical remarks to take on the clothing of empirical propositions. Indeed, Wittgenstein himself took pains to remind me of just this point. After a series of remarks that outwardly are factual descriptions of how a child might learn to doubt, he asked:

Am I doing child psychology?—I am making a connexion between the concept of teaching and the concept of meaning. (Z 412)

CRATES: Lato, we began this discussion by referring to the conflict Wolgast felt between Wittgenstein's most public remarks and the remarks on primitive reactions spoken on miscellaneous other occasions.[86] We have argued that the schism is not real but is the product of a limited conception of the framework within which the philosopher studies language,—one that fails to recognize that the rôle of language in our lives is *itself* something of which we have a conception, and hence is a legitimate object for grammatical investigation in its own right.

10 Conclusion

We have been discussing the relations between the concepts of language and instinctive behaviour. The first situation in which language may be said to be based in instinct, and which we have described as 'the groundlessness of language in general', has been explained principally by reference to and in terms of the 'blindness' of rule-following. This has certainly been an important first step in this part of our discussion of the nature of the possession of concepts, and it provides an essential bulwark against mentalistic and rationalistic accounts of language use. It represents an important element in our understanding of that dimension of our form of life that underpins our use of language. On the other hand, it does not take us very far along the road we wish to travel, confined as it is by the extent to which language may be regarded simply as a rule-governed *activity*. It does not as yet touch the sense in which instinctive reactions perform a specific rôle in determining *content*, that is, in forming specific concepts. This is the main situation in regard to instinctive behaviour that has to be examined if we are to understand concept possession and speaking. Here our interest has again centred around the groundless nature of the specific instinctive reactions that contribute to concept-formation. However, we have also looked at the sense in which language and its concepts *extend* our form of life and the constitution of our selves through building upon its more primitive dimensions and modes of behaviour.

Again we emphasize that we have been occupied with this notion of instinct not because it provides the key to *explaining* how language and its concepts came about, but because it represents that dimension of language and its relation to the rest of our lives that allows us to see more clearly the irreducible nature of language-games in general and of the possession of individual concepts in particular.

In the next dialogue we shall extend this discussion. In particular we shall develop some of the themes that we have already introduced—in connection with the possession of the concept of intention and its expression—through a more wide ranging discussion of the possession of psychological concepts and subjectivity generally. In the course of this, we shall also take the opportunity to advance our account of the nature of philosophical reflection and of the particular difficulties we experience in this regard arising out of the manner in which these concepts are possessed.

Dialogue 5   Concepts of the Subject

1   Introduction

CRATES: If we want to judge whether a child has the concept of colour *beyond* the ability merely to make correct judgements as to the colour of an object, we will probably look first at the way that the concept is woven into the child's use of language as a whole: in her ability to talk sense with the concept and to distinguish sense and nonsense in the way the concept is used in conversation generally. We would also look at the way that the child shows appreciation of the *subjective* qualities of coloured objects: the way she makes comparisons among colours, expresses likes and dislikes, makes judgements as to the harmony or disharmony between colours, and so on. And we would look at the way that she reacts to *other people's* judgements about and reactions to colours. These all belong to the child's possession of the concept *colour*, and they show whether she has got hold of the grammar of 'colour'. But what they also show is that her *having* a concept of colour involves not just linguistic competence in a narrow sense, but engages with her subjective relations and responses to coloured objects. Similar consider-ations will apply, *mutatis mutandis*, to any concepts in which subjective reactions such as these play a part, including, for example, our reactions to the pain and suffering of others. It is the rôle of the individual's subjectivity in the possession of psychological concepts that we shall be discussing in this dialogue. We shall occasionally speak of 'subjective concepts', which may be regarded as a subclass of psychological con-cepts, relating mostly to perception and sensation, where we wish to emphasize the subjective component.

We may begin by defending Wittgenstein against the accusation that he leaned towards a behaviouristic conception of language.

LATO: It became a commonplace among critics of Wittgenstein to complain that he ignored what has often been called 'the subjective character of experience'—a response no doubt to his apparent preoccupation with the operational use of language.[1] Moreover, it was said that in the arguments he deployed against various notions of linguistic 'privacy',[2] he attempted, by a reduction of mental states to external behaviour, to *eliminate* the relevance of subjective experience to the formation of concepts. He was aware of this criticism himself:

> Back to 'neglecting'! It seems that I neglect life. But not life physiologically understood but life as consciousness. And consciousness not physiologically understood, or understood from the outside, but consciousness as the very essence of experience, the appearance of the world, the world. (NFL p. 255)

Wittgenstein was thought to deny the reality of subjective experience because an essential component of one of his best-known arguments— or *suite* of arguments, usually collectively referred to as the 'private language argument'—was precisely that meaning *cannot* be (it makes no sense to speak of it as being) determined by reference to our own subjective states. It was then concluded that the supposed subjective quality of experience must fall outside the linguistic equation, so that any reference to it that cannot be analysed into outward behaviour (or, in other philosophies, into 'physical states' such as brain states) may therefore be dismissed as 'metaphysical'.

CRATES: And of course it is not difficult to see why such a conclusion was felt distasteful within the philosophical community because, historically, one powerful reason for the demand for a philosophy of mind was precisely to *accommodate* the evident reality of the subjective qualities of experience. It was the nature of just these qualities and their place in reality that they most wished to understand. And so the struggle in philosophy over the centuries has been to overcome the difficulty of finding a place for them, not to agree to their elimination. So how can we avoid this conclusion? Does it follow necessarily from Wittgenstein's private language argument?

LATO: Our first response, Crates, must be to state that the private language argument is, in any case, being misused if it is used to sanction such a reduction; for it is concerned only to refute certain conceptions of *how* words refer to subjective states,[3] not to deny *that* they refer to them— still less to deny them absolutely or to deny their qualities. The argument certainly has a *bearing* on our understanding of the dimensions within which subjective qualities exist (their grammar).—But that is all. And once the confused conceptions have been dealt with, the remainder of the grammar of subjective concepts stands intact and awaits elucidation. It is here that we will find the accommodation we seek.

CRATES: So let's return to the 'neglect' that Wittgenstein spoke of. How does this become an issue *at all*? From what point of view or in what circumstances does it *matter* that the subjective reality of our subjective states is being ignored?

LATO: The answer surely is that our preoccupation with subjective states is not something that arises for us only as an 'abstract' philosophical problem, but is prompted by *introspection*. In other words, it is something arising as a *reaction* to our own subjective states. The bafflement that people in general—and not just philosophers—commonly feel about the nature of their own mind or soul arises directly out of their introspective reflections. This explains, I believe, why even the very suggestion of scepticism regarding the reality of these states is greeted almost as a personal affront.—It is as if our own reality were being denied to our faces. This, no doubt, is one explanation for the passion that is aroused by puzzlement over the nature of mental life.

LATO: So we are reacting to our own subjective states. This is the kernel of the problem. Equally important is that this reaction is *not* mediated by reference to our own body; it occurs wholly within the domain of the mental. Given this, it is perhaps not surprising, indeed it is *understandable*, that the subject's reaction to his own subjectivity should appear to him as if it were a reaction to a 'something', the essential nature of which is *independent* of its outward expression and only accidentally connected with it.

This, in fact, is the subjective analogue to the situation in grammar. For if the concepts of subjectivity really are not reducible to concepts of external behaviour—and notwithstanding that they are internally related—then it *follows* that the experience we have of ourselves *under the aspect of those concepts* will be an experience of the mind which is to that extent independent of its outward conditions. A consciousness or seeing of the self as a detached entity is perfectly intelligible as a reaction when considered in this light; and it is an experience vividly captured in a remark by Wittgenstein:

> It seems that I can *trace* my identity, quite independent of the identity of my body. And the idea is suggested that I trace the identity of something dwelling in a body, the identity of my mind. (NFL p. 270)

CRATES: Just to clarify that last point, Lato—to remove any possible doubt—it is not the *idea* of the mind as a detached entity that we are saying is intelligible (in the sense of being logically possible) but the *reaction*.—The fact that our reaction to our own subjective states is not mediated by a reaction to our body makes intelligible—or at least makes *explicable*—the subjective impression of the mind as a detached entity. This impression is almost certainly responsible for the genesis of the illusory and unintelligible *conception* of a detached self—but that is a separate matter.

This familiar experience is especially important to our discussion, because it brings home the fact that it is our relations to our own subjectivity that is the field of our perplexity.—It is the reality that we attribute *as subjects* to our subjective experience that we find puzzling and which we wish to do justice to in philosophy. This is why we believe that the root of our puzzlement about the nature of mental life is to be found in our misunderstanding of the *general nature of subjectivity*, of which the more direct question of how words referring to subjective qualities get their meaning is only a facet.

LATO: Agreed. But this approach to the philosophy of mind through the general concept of subjectivity is not novel. It was injected into the philosophical debate in the 1970s in a most striking way by Thomas Nagel in a controversial discussion of subjectivity in animals—which at the time provoked much comment and consternation.[4] It was argued by Patricia Hanna,[5] for example, that Nagel's conception of subjectivity remained vulnerable to Wittgenstein's private language argument. This was disputed by H.O. Mounce,[6] who argued that Nagel was rightly defensive of the irreducibility of subjectivity to objective concepts.

For ourselves, we are not convinced of Nagel's innocence of the confusions Hanna attributed to him. Yet our sympathies are with the understanding of subjectivity as developed by Mounce; and we are in agreement with his criticisms of the kind of account of psychological concepts typified by Hanna—and others such as Hacker—especially on the issue of how psychological concepts are applied, and on the rôle of criteria in these applications.[7] Both these issues will be pursued.

In developing an understanding of subjectivity, we will examine some aspects of the private language argument as they apply here. We will look at some of the difficulties inherent in Nagel's account of the notion that 'there is something that it is like to be a bat', which we believe arises out of a failure to acknowledge the distinction between the practical and the factual modes in the establishment of psychological concepts. And we will examine some of the confusions surrounding the rôle of criteria in the deployment of concepts in general and psychological concepts in particular. More generally, we will develop a critique of some of the ways in which *objectivity* has been invoked as a *condition* for the use of language. This will lead to the core of our discussion in this dialogue, which will be on aspects of the possession of psychological concepts. We shall concentrate on the relation between subjectivity and primitive linguistic and non-linguistic behaviour, one aspect of which, following on from earlier discussions, will be the conception of the language-games of subjectivity as *extensions* of our lives as subjects. Finally, we shall examine how this bears on our relations to these concepts *within* philosophical investigation, which will be treated in ways we have already employed in regard to the concepts *belief* and *time*.

CRATES: Can we also add a *caveat*, Lato, regarding the use of the term 'subjectivity' and other related terms? Unless otherwise stated, 'subjectivity' should not be taken in our discussions to refer to subjective impressions or subjective judgements as to how things appear to us; rather it refers to the properties of the subject *qua* subject, that is, to what is characteristic of mental life in general. In this sense we may say, for example, that 'I am in pain' is a *manifestation* of the subject; it is *not* a judgement as to how things seem to the subject. Only when we speak specifically of subjective impressions or judgements, should the term be taken to refer to how things appear to us.

2   The 'Objectification' of subjective experience

LATO: The change in philosophical perspective—of which we spoke earlier—from the conception of language as a view of the world 'from the boundary' to a view of the world 'from the midst' is the same transition that we require to judge properly the place in our lives of the concepts of subjective phenomena: sensation, mind, feeling, and so on.

The view from the boundary is expressed in the idea that concepts are, as it were, *intelligible in themselves*; that is, as carrying a sense that is determined transcendentally to the circumstances of the language-game *in which they are in fact* determined and employed. And at the heart of this conception is the tendency for the subject to 'objectify' his own subjective relations to his experiences and perceptions. We might call this the objectification of the subject *qua* subject. The most characteristic expression of this tendency is to be seen in the idea of private ostensive definition. This is the idea that there is a legitimate mode of judgement whose terms are defined wholly subjectively—that is, through how things *appear* to the subject—but which nevertheless yields judgements that are, for all that, objective. Hence, one may seem to oneself to be able to define a rule for 'naming' a sensation subjectively and then to go on to make sensible uses of the word which are objectively guaranteed *even though that guarantee is wholly dependent on a subjective judgement that one is using it **in the same way** as in the original ostensive definition.* Even within the confines of purely subjective judgment, then, the subject is presented as standing in a kind of 'Archimedean vantage point' to his own experiences. This is a pervasive notion. Indeed the whole of the centuries-old egocentric empiricist epistemology is based on it. It is one version of the idea of the 'privacy' of meaning and language; while the private language argument is designed to show that this is not an intelligible conception. Let's outline the argument.

First of all, 'the' private language argument is not one but a complex of arguments.[8] For present purposes, however, we may consider it as having two principal struts. The first revolves around this question: if we seem to ourselves to be able to give a definition of a word 'privately'— that is, *subjectively*—what does this really establish? Have we established a rule for the use of the word? We will not have established anything unless we are knowingly—that is, *objectively*—able to use the word in the same way on future occasions. But as the connection we are supposed to be establishing between the word and the sensation (or perception, or whatever it is) is wholly dependent on a *subjective* judgement, then all we can ever obtain by this procedure is the impression that we are following a rule; and so, for all that, we are *not* following a rule. It can make no sense to speak of a language founded on subjective judgement, for the only connection between the private ostensive definition and subsequent uses of the word would be further subjective judgements that it is being used in the same way.—In other words, the subjective judgement that the word is being used in the same way would be *internal* to the subsequent use—which will therefore remain a subjective use in this sense. So no objectivity will have been established for the use of the word.

The second strut is that any act of naming must take for granted a technique (convention) within which there is such a thing as *naming*.— There must be both a *rule* and a linguistic *rôle*. Both of these were important to Wittgenstein and are, in any case, strongly connected. For in an obvious sense we cannot go so far as to make judgements *at all* (subjective or otherwise) if there is no linguistic framework for them, and it cannot make sense to speak of such a framework being established within the confines of purely subjective circumstances.

So the development of the private language argument will require us to demonstrate (1) that there is something incoherent in the idea of following a rule 'subjectively' and (2) that there is no room, in the circumstances as described, for the essential accompanying linguistic apparatus.

CRATES: So we may say, then, that the overarching principle, as far as establishing a language is concerned, must be a demand for *objective* circumstances. Only then can the judgement that a person has learnt a rule, or grasped a concept, make any sense. The conclusion of the private language argument is that the necessary investment of objectivity into the language-games expressing subjective states must be by means of their outward manifestations, not in their purely introspective modes. Expressed grammatically, the concept of a language-game is the concept of something rooted in objective circumstances and that this holds also for the concepts embedded in it.

LATO: At this point, Crates, it may be helpful to remind ourselves of a distinction we made in our second dialogue. Among our concepts are those of the language-games in which other concepts are expressed. Our main example was *intention*: we have both the concept of intention *per se and* the concept of the linguistic *expression* of intention. Hence, we may distinguish between the elucidation of a given concept and the elucidation of the concept of the language-game of which that concept is a component. In the latter case, the concept of the language-game is the concept of the circumstances in which a person may be said to *have* the concept. And belonging to these circumstances will be features relevant to the judgement that the person is following a linguistic rule. One root of the demand for objectivity, therefore, arises out of the grammar of the concept *language-game*. And it is in supplying the facts that surround the language-game, and which are *essential* to it, that this demand is satisfied.

Now, as we discussed at length in that dialogue, there will be cases where, when describing the circumstances of the language-game, our description will contain facts that function as criteria for the application of the concepts embedded in it. For example, if we are to give an account of the language-game of investigating symptoms and diagnosing diseases, we may include a description of the symptoms of measles and, hence, the criteria for employing the concept *measles*. In this kind of case, the description of the circumstances that justify the application of the concept of the disease does *not* take for granted the concept itself. In other words, we can understand the description of the symptoms without assuming that we already have an understanding of the concept *measles*. In this instance, then, we easily satisfy the need for the circumstances of the language-game to be seen to be objective.—The objectivity of the account lies straightforwardly in the ability to give an account of a set of factual circumstances. But in other situations, which we also discussed previously, the objectivity of the language-game may not be so easily located.

I am thinking particularly of the situation where the concepts embedded within the language-game are also needed for the description of its circumstances. For example, a description of the circumstances in which sensation concepts are employed will need to use and to take for granted an understanding of those very sensation concepts. This is the circularity we spoke of in the second dialogue. In this situation there will be no such thing as an *independent* description of the criteria for applying the concepts, as there are no criteria for the application of sensation concepts. So although the concepts enter into the description of the circumstances of the language-game, no further facts are adduced in support of *them*, just because they have no criteria; hence the description is to this extent circular and so thus far it will not have established the objectivity of the language-game. But this does not mean that, to this extent, there is no demonstrable objectivity in the *circumstances* of the language-game. For in this kind of case, the objectivity lies just in the agreement in linguistic reactions among participants, not in any agreement over the facts that the language-game is based on. Hence, the demonstration of *its* objectivity will rest on a recognition of this agreement. We may also note—again as we discussed previously—that the determination of concepts through practice, in this case a shared practice, is more fundamental than by reference to facts. Hence, the agreement in reactions is in any case at the bottom of the objectivity of *all* language-games, including those where facts do enter into the determination of concepts.

CRATES: Perhaps we should just add here that, as in the case of measles, there is also objectivity in these circumstances to the extent that they *can* be described without circularity. Our point, then, is that the recognition of agreement in reactions is placed within the recognition of those circumstances. Together these determine our concept of objectivity for this kind of language-game.

So the important point here, for our present purposes at least, is that the objectivity lies in the *agreement* rather than in the *kind* of reaction. There is therefore nothing to exclude subjective reactions from being among those that may go to determine concepts—as long as they are *shared*, or at least *able* to be shared. This is why there is no essential conflict between the demand for objectivity and the possibility, as we shall argue, that the grasp of the concepts embedded within the language-game may, in an important sense, be an expression or outgrowth of our lives as *subjects*,—the limiting factor here being that the subjective component may not function as a ground or justification for the concept. The *kind* of subjective reaction may be a determining factor for the grammar of the concept of which it is a component. Moreover, the individual's reactions *qua* subject may be conceived of as a part of her capacity to form the concept,—of her *understanding* of the concept.

The main thrust of the private language argument, then, is to make a case against a particular and pervasive conception of how words refer to subjective states. The positive account of how such words refer *begins* with the argument that what is required is an established technique forming the substratum of the practice of speaking, this being an *outward* manifestation of our form of life. A full account of the establishment of psychological concepts, on the other hand, will need to demonstrate the rôle adopted by the subjective dimension of our form of life as a determinant of these referential relations.

I know, Lato, that we intend to return to this later in the dialogue, but first we need to re-establish confidence in this very notion of subjectivity, which the confused responses to the private language argument we referred to earlier have tended to undermine.

3   Nagel's impasse

LATO: The destructive effect of the private language argument on private ostensive definition—and hence on empiricism and egocentric subjective epistemologies generally—was taken in many quarters to be a denial that the formation of the concepts of subjective experience can itself incorporate the subjective dimensions of our lives. Indeed, it was commonly felt that Wittgenstein must have been *some* sort of behaviourist since this seemed to follow directly from the argument that the rules for the use of psychological concepts must be laid down in the objective circumstances of outward human behaviour and transparent to any independent objective observer. And, as I have just intimated, it was hardly a step at all—or so it seemed—from *this* condition to the belief that whatever mental words *mean* must be exhausted in the objective behavioural phenomena constituting those circumstances. The bland defences either that the distinction between pain-behaviour *with* and *without* pain just is written into the language-game or that 'pain' simply does not *mean* 'behaviour'—but without at the same time giving a full account of *how* these differences are supposed to be constituted—seemed just to avoid the issue and were not on their own very reassuring. It was Thomas Nagel who attempted to break out of this impasse, while at the same time claiming to acknowledge the force of the private language argument.[9] His discussion—and our response to it—is complex, so I hope you will bear with me, Crates, if I introduce it at some length.

By observing that wherever we recognize an animal as being *conscious* then 'there is something that it is like to *be* that organism—something that it is like *for* the organism',[10] Nagel returned the notion of the subjective character of experience to centre stage. And he did so in a way that could not easily be denied, as it seemed to represent a genuine grammatical insight apparently making no direct appeal to private ostensive definition. For in the case of an animal, reference to its life as a subject of experience can be made, and the reality of its subjectivity affirmed, without any question of private ostensive definition being raised at all. Unfortunately, Nagel's use of this formulation to defend the irreducibility of subjectivity ended in failure, in our view, not so much because of the formulation is necessarily faulty but for other reasons, which are of interest. The formulation also points towards a notion of the subjective quality of experience that we do wish to preserve, so this is reason again for pursuing the matter.

Nagel objected to those 'physicalist reductionist' philosophers who would wish to make an *essential* translation of the subjective mode into an objective mode of discourse about physical states; that is, a translation that effectively eliminates, or analyses away, subjective concepts as a distinct class. His own aim, however, was not so much to deny the possibility of a physicalist theory, but just to demand that such a theory must do justice to *subjectivity* by recognizing it as retaining some distinctive characteristic of its own. However, to make subjectivity compatible with physicalism, an account of subjectivity would be required that involved at least some kind of objective re-presentation of the subjective—otherwise it would not be possible to marry it to the objectivity of a physicalist theory. Nagel believed that we are not yet in a position to do this, nor is it clear how it might be achieved.—Hence we are not ready to embrace a physicalist account.[11] In his concluding remarks, however, he did come up with one possibility: he speculated upon the idea of an 'objective phenomenology'; that is, a system of universally intelligible concepts for describing 'what it is like' to have any given subjective experience, even to those to whom the experience is profoundly alien. He conceded that this language might not be able to convey *everything*—though he did not say what remaining kinds of things might continue to be objectively inexpressible, or how we should treat that fact.[12]

Regardless of what other merit we might find in his attempt to defend the reality of the subjective, the fact that he entertained the possibility of such a phenomenology at all showed, we believe, that he was not in the end prepared to let go of the idea that the individual's relations to the qualities of his own subjective states can still be modelled on a grasp of 'facts about what it is like *for* the experiencing organism' that go beyond that which is manifested in the individual's outward being.[13] This must be the correct interpretation of his view otherwise the intelligibility of the phenomenology would be wholly relative to the mode of life in question, in which case it could not transcend the differences between modes of life. And so in spite of his protestations to the contrary, it is difficult to see how the view can avoid being just another objectivist reconstruction of subjectivity and a re-emergence of the inner 'Archimedean vantage point' against which the private language argument is directed. So it will be interesting to examine why he couldn't seem to resist being pulled back in this direction.

CRATES: This objectivist reconstruction of subjective concepts—that is, that knowledge of what the perception, sensation, and so on, 'is like' can be modelled on knowledge of *fact*—is, as we have noted, a pervasive and insidious influence.—We still see it everywhere. So I agree it will be helpful to look at another manifestation of it by tracing the way it winds itself through Nagel's analysis. This will help further to identify the critical points that we will need to make to defend the integrity of the concepts of subjectivity. Nagel got himself onto the horns of a dilemma, which, we believe, can be explained in terms of one of the familiar confusions over concept-formation that we have already discussed. Once this is sorted out, we can then make the case for holding on to the subjective mode and to this notion of subjective quality expressed in the idea of 'what it is like' to have a certain experience.

LATO: I agree. But let us take a step back. It is striking that Nagel founded his account on a factual *belief* that animals, as well as humans, 'have' experiences; it is as if we were 'of the opinion' that they have experiences.[14] In an aside, while discussing the attribution of experiences to robots, he remarked:

> Perhaps anything complex enough to behave like a person would have experiences. But that, if true, is a fact which cannot be discovered merely by analyzing the concept of experience. (Nagel, 1974, footnote p. 436)

And then:

> I assume we all believe that bats have experience. After all, they are mammals, and there is no more doubt that they have experience than that mice or pigeons or whales have experience. (Nagel, 1974, p. 438)

It is important that Nagel's account, *qua* philosophical account, *begins* with the attribution of subjectivity to other creatures as a factual matter which he assumed did not raise conceptual issues.—As a consequence, he was already implying that the exercise of psychological concepts is of the kind that begins by considering whether something is the case or not.[15] In other words, his conception of the language-games in which subjective concepts are articulated was that they belong with those that, in the relevant respects, are founded on fact and not on *practice*. We, of course, maintain that the former are secondary to the latter. This predetermined the form of his account by presenting as the central issue how we accommodate facts about subjective experience, and it emerged in the way he treated the central example in his discussion: the understanding of the subjective lives of creatures of a form of life fundamentally different from our own: bats.

Having stated that bats have experiences, Nagel argued that, given the well-known peculiarities in the way that they perceive their environment, the experience that bats have of the world must be radically alien to ours. His conclusion on the nature of a bat's experience was expressed by saying that 'there is no reason to suppose that it is subjectively like anything we can experience or imagine'.[16] And as this was in the nature of a supposition, it led to the idea that since the bat certainly does have experiences 'this implies a belief in the existence of facts beyond the reach of human concepts',[17] and to the conclusion that a knowledge of 'what it is like to be a bat' is unavailable to us.[18] Now this idea—that we cannot have knowledge of what their experience is like—is notoriously difficult to fix. Nagel denied that this should be taken in a simple epistemological sense—that is, that we are unable to *find out* what their experience is like—but in the sense of it following from our incapacity to share the 'bat's point of view' and so to form a conception of what their experience is like.[19] But this is where we believe the confusion sets in.

If we say—turning to the linguistic analogue to this situation—that through the formation of different concepts we can express different facts, so that the content of those facts is unavailable to us if we don't have or are unable to form those concepts, then that's fine. Here we are dealing with the simple observation that if we do not share the mode of experience and the language that goes with it, then we are not in any position to follow any perceptual reports that emerge out of it,—we just do not share their form of life. But if, on the other hand, we are thinking of these alien concepts as being in some way *informed* by facts of subjective experience, then, to those who do not share the form of life, these are facts that clearly will remain unavailable in another way. What we cannot help feeling is that there is some such conception still at work in Nagel's account, bringing with it the idea of a realm of *facts* relating to the quality of a bat's experience that is beyond human concepts. This would also explain the origin of Nagel's 'objective phenomenology', as it would suggest that if those concepts could be imparted to us in some *other* way, then we might yet understand the quality of the otherwise alien experience. These two situations are being run together, we believe, because there is an underlying assumption—perhaps originating from a form of pragmatism—that concepts are ultimately all founded on facts and that this goes as much for perceptual concepts as for any other.

Let's try to impress this point a bit further by broadening the context.

The idea that the experiences or perceptions of alien creatures may be beyond our comprehension evidently has a parallel in the more frequently discussed question of how we may fail to understand the beliefs and concepts of a radically alien society.[20] Certainly the two conceptions share an essential property inasmuch as the way to mutual understanding is barred in both cases as a result of the incommensurability of our respective lives. The present case, however, introduces a new and distinct element insofar as it relates the incommensurability specifically to the bats' mode of natural perception rather than to their social structures and systems of belief.[21]

Now I think it would be true to say that when faced with a radically alien society it would *not* be the most natural way of expressing what we fail to comprehend in them to say that there are *facts* available to them to which *we* have no access. I think that would be regarded as secondary to the more fundamental difference, which would be a difference in the *way* that they construct the world as evidenced in their behaviour and concepts. It would be more natural to say that they stand in a different kind of relation to the world and to themselves, and that this kind of relation is alien to us. So it is only the facts expressed *by means of* the concepts that are unavailable to us, which is already covered by saying that we just do not share their concepts.

Where we *might* speak more naturally of the facts being unavailable to us is where the concept is *founded* on fact—rather than on practice—so that if, for example, I don't know what facts the concept of measles is based upon, I won't know what the state of a person is if I am told he has measles. But of course, those underlying facts would themselves only be genuinely unavailable to us—in the sense in which we have been speaking of it—if we failed to share the concepts in which *they* were articulated. So we still haven't gone beyond the situation where it is only facts expressed *in* what is said that remain truly unavailable to us.

CRATES: So, just to clarify this point, we do not deny that we may not understand what is expressed in the behaviour of a bat, or in what is said by someone with a different perceptual system from our own, just because the form of their life is different—thus making any fact so expressed unavailable to us. Moreover, even in those legitimate instances in which concepts are founded on fact, we have still not advanced beyond the principle that facts are expressed *in* what is said.

What we are concerned with now is how this might get muddled up with the idea that the unintelligibility of the behaviour or of the analogous concepts is because certain facts of subjective experience are unavailable to us because we do not share their perceptual point of view.

LATO: Yes. As it happens, in important respects we do understand bats' relations to the world: they perceive the world using a perceptual system employing echo-location. Hence, the facts of what they perceive will also be intelligible to *us*,—for example, that they can detect or 'observe' the position of a flying insect in complete darkness.[22] But of course these are not what Nagel had in mind—or so it seems to us—when he spoke of facts about the subjective qualities of a bat's experience that are beyond our ken,—which are facts that would distinguish between sensible qualities within a subjective realm. These are not facts expressed *in terms of* the concepts, or through the behaviour, but facts that are supposed to underlie their sense.

CRATES: So to break out of the dilemma we have to move away, once more, from the assumption that concepts—except in the kinds of situation we have previously described—are based on facts.

LATO: Nagel passed as a matter of course from the notion that 'there is something that it is like to be a bat' to a concept of *knowledge* of what it is like, in this factual sense. But these are not coextensive. The original purpose, in the context of the philosophical debate, of the statement that 'there is something that it is like to be a bat' was, as we have indicated, to emphasize that '[t]he subject too is real'—where 'real' means that the concept of the *subject* is irreducible.[23] Moreover, in addition to reminding us of the reality of the subject, it also reminds us that it is essential to consciousness that it has a *form* that is expressed outwardly in different ways. But the fundamental *form* of our experience is yielded up by means of the use of *concepts* (or modes of behaviour) that are not themselves comprised of any subjective knowledge of fact. In other words, the essential 'there is something that it is like to be a bat' is that which is expressed in the way we differentiate experiences by means of concepts, not by individuating facts; and in the analogous case of animals, it is expressed in the *form* of their behaviour. Moreover, in both cases this is *primitive*. And so, if we do still wish to speak of 'knowledge' in this context, then this has to be interpreted in terms of the understanding of the form of our experience that lies in our ability to *use* the concepts that we have acquired. Here we might recall a point from the second dialogue, that it is not just in the grasp of facts that we grasp what the world is like but in the formation of our concepts.

The distinction between differences in concept and differences in fact may be a confusing one to apply when reflecting on the nature of perception or subjective experience. It is no doubt very natural, when introspecting or reacting to differences in the subjective qualities of colours, sounds, and so on, to feel that here are differences that *ought* to be describable. When we feel compelled in this way, we are trying to interpret the concept rooted in *practice* as if it were one rooted in *fact*, which I am then puzzled to find I cannot put into words. But if the difference is one of concept rather than fact, then it *is* put into words just in the way the difference shows in how the different concepts are deployed.—It shows in judgement pure and simple, not in articulated differences between facts. The same principle applies in the case of simple judgements of sameness or difference in a subjective quality: the judgement is primitive. It is a confusion to hold that below the threshold of what is captured through our concepts is a realm of fact that is not expressible *in* what we say, but upon which the sense of the concepts depends.

4   The subjective and the objective modes and 'What it is like to be a ... .'

CRATES: Lato, having disposed of some false conceptions of subjectivity, we are now in a position to adopt a clearer view of the *modus operandi* of subjective concepts and how they are seated in our lives. To this end we will be wise not to abandon altogether this notion of 'knowledge of what an experience is like'—even to the extent of accommodating this feeling of what 'ought to be describable'—but will try to develop it in ways that avoid the pitfalls.

LATO: It is certainly true that there has been pressure from certain quarters in philosophy to abandon this notion. Nagel's use of 'there is something that it is like to be a bat' was seized upon and criticized by Norman Malcolm,[24] who took it to be just another proposition resting on a belief in private ostensive definition. We have argued that he was probably right to find Nagel guilty of this fallacy; but we believe that there is a narrowness in Malcolm's view that caused him to overlook other important contexts in which we *may* intelligibly speak of 'knowing what it is like' to have a particular experience, and that these are important to an understanding of the nature of the possession of these subjective concepts.

The essence of Malcolm's argument is that if we do wish to speak in this way, then it can only legitimately mean (1) that we can in an ordinary way describe what the experience is like—he cited the case of the experience of being a lorry driver,[25] where we may refer to the various individual experiences that go to make up the composite experience of being a lorry driver, and hence what this experience is like—or (2), in the more fundamental situation of knowing 'what it is like to *see*',[26] that we have 'the ability that a sighted adult has of making visual discriminations, reports and judgements'.[27] Generally, we may say that on this view the meaning of 'knowing what it is like to have an experience' is coextensive with the ability to describe what we see or with the ability to make perceptual judgements. This approach became popular among those who believed that they were defending a Wittgensteinian position. Thus we found Hacker concluding as follows:

> We are no doubt tempted to say that such a person does not know what pain is *like*. But what is it to know what pain is like? Does the yelping dog whose paw has been trodden on know what pain is like? No, for whatever 'knowing what pain is like' means, it does not mean the same as 'being in pain'. Is it to have 'knowledge of certain kinds of experience'? But what does that mean? If I have toothache, do I *have* *knowledge* of a toothache? Am I *acquainted* with toothache? Do I *know* nausea or cramp? These are slightly curious, quasi-poetic expressions. They are either philosophical nonsense, or they signify no more than having had the sensation. One can indeed say 'I have known fear' or 'I am acquainted with grief', but this simply means that I have been afraid and have grieved. So too for knowing toothache or being acquainted with headache. What then do I know when I know what

pain is like? Either I can say or display what it is like, or it is ineffable. But if it is ineffable, then knowing what pain is like amounts to no more than to *have* or to *have had* a pain. But then the thesis that one can possess the concept of pain only if one knows what pain is like merely reiterates that someone who has mastered the use of 'pain' but has never had a pain does not know what the word 'pain' means, which is absurd. The criteria for possession of a concept, for mastery of the use of a word, consists in one's correctly using and explaining an expression, not in one's medical history. (Hacker, 1987, pp. 146–147)

My difficulty with this approach is that it stops with the criticisms that we have already made of Nagel and does not allow for how we *react to* and *reflect on* our experiences, or for how these responses ramify our lives. These are also constitutive of our concepts of experience and perception; they are components in the determination of the concepts of subjective quality and knowledge of their qualities,—and they are not reducible to the formulae offered by Malcolm and Hacker.

At the most elementary level, the concept of subjective *quality*, in contrast to the concept of perceptual judgement, is determined in the distinction we make—as outlined in the introduction to this dialogue— between the judgement that an object is such and such a colour and the judgement as to *how* the colour strikes us. This is a grammatical distinction. These two modes of judgement betoken different conceptual relations to objects. And so there really oughtn't to be an objection to characterizing the latter as a relation to a subjective quality. The only condition that we must insist on is that this kind of response *determines* the concept, such that it would make no sense to say that the response depended on some *prior* appreciation of subjective quality; that is, on a judgement originating under some other regime, namely private ostensive definition. The responses are *primitive* to the determination of the concept of subjective quality.

CRATES: This notion of subjective quality is perhaps most evident when we are making aesthetic judgements, for example when we are savouring or generally appreciating the qualities of colours: the way they combine, whether they clash or are in harmony with one another and so on. Similar considerations would apply to sounds or to any other context where subjective responses of this kind are made.

LATO: When we look at the way these sorts of judgements and comparisons are made, the language we use very frequently—but not always—imports terms from other contexts, or other language-games.

These are often referred to as 'secondary' uses of words. For example, if we say 'The sound of the lute is *brighter* than the guitar', 'brighter' has been borrowed from its literal context, where it is used to make judgements of light intensity. These secondary uses are *figurative*, but in an important sense they are not metaphorical. Wittgenstein often referred to the secondary use of colour words to describe sounds:

> The secondary sense is not a 'metaphorical' sense. If I say 'For me the vowel *e* is yellow' I do not mean: 'yellow' in a metaphorical sense,— for I could not express what I want to say in any other way than by means of the idea 'yellow'. (PI, p. 184)

These uses of words are the product of a need to find a means of expressing a subjective quality,—a need that can only be satisfied by taking, without *justification*, a word from an alien context. Moreover, as there is no justification for their entry into discourse, their use is also *primitive*. And again, just because these linguistic reactions are indeed primitive, they *determine* a concept of description and thereby a concept of subjective quality also.

Furthermore, whereas these secondary uses depend on a primary use, in an important sense they are themselves *subjective*.—They are not governed by any rules allowing them to be projected into the new context. Hence, they can only be understood as *qualitative* responses to our subjective states. And they acquire currency within the language-game just because they are primitive and can be shared among language users.

This drive to find words to express subjective qualities may well correspond to the feeling of what 'ought to be describable' that we referred to earlier; but this has to be understood as a response arising out of our own subjectivity, not as the discovery of facts below the threshold of what can be put into words.

CRATES: It might be interesting to reflect on some of the many other contexts in which subjective quality may manifest itself.

Imagine a person who has seen others receiving and reacting to electric shocks but who has never experienced a shock himself. We might imagine his surprise on receiving a shock for the first time: 'I didn't know it would be like that!'—perhaps he had expected it to be more like touching something hot, or like a muscular spasm, or hitting the 'funny bone' in his elbow (perhaps it is a bit like that!). The point is that 'knowledge of what it is like' may be an expression of *expectation* and may lead to the conclusion that we had never experienced the like before. Again it should be emphasized that this notion of what the experience is like is not intended as an *explanation* of the expectation—which would bring us up against the private language argument once again. Rather, *that* we have expectations of such sorts is part of what determines a concept of subjective quality.

We might also think of more complex cases. It is a commonplace for people who have experienced profound depression to insist that unless others have experienced it themselves they cannot really know 'what it is like' because it is not really comparable with anything else in ordinary life. They will have been struck by the fact that it was not like anything *they* had previously known, nor could it have been anticipated from their own previous experience. Perhaps they will have tried to convey it to others, but realized the futility of it. 'Knowing what it is like' in this sort of case goes beyond the mere sense of the uniqueness of a sensation.— It goes together with a multitude of other changes in the thoughts, feelings and beliefs of the sufferer and is pervasive of his life. It is in these sorts of circumstances that the sufferer becomes aware that another does not 'know' what it is like to experience depression. And of course the point of speaking in this way is to draw attention to the fact not just that the other has not had the experience but that, in his behaviour and in what he says, he shows that he does not *understand* the experience. The sufferer finds himself at a distance from the comprehension of others.

This is an interesting case because it differs, I believe, from both the cases we cited earlier—that is, of not being able to understand a foreign culture and of not 'knowing what it is like to be a bat'. On the one hand, it is not like failing to understand the alien culture, if that *just* means not being able to follow the ideas and beliefs of the culture (it might mean more than that). And it is not like the case of the bat; for it does not arise just out of the lack of a shared system of perception. Rather, it arises out of an inability to understand a *pervasive* quality of their state of mind,— an inability having to do with the failure to make connections of thought and feeling, or with not being able to understand how the sufferer might be driven to certain thoughts and actions. Two people who share the experience will understand one another in the things they have to *say*, in being able to follow each other in the connections of thought and feeling that they make, in the way that their beliefs undergo changes, and in their responses to the problems of life. 'He knows what it is like' says that he has an understanding that has evidently grown naturally out of his own personal experience.

In all these sorts of situations, it is surely natural to want to character-ize the responses in terms of the appreciation of, or indeed the *knowledge of*, the subjective qualities of the experiences. It could only be *a priori* prejudice to want to deny such a conception or to reject it as an insignificant part of people's lives—the Philistinism of positivism. And of course it is not to be understood just in terms of the one person having had the experience and the other not.

LATO: By contrast it would at least be *possible*, I suppose, to imagine a people who made all the perceptual judgements of the kind that Malcolm and Hacker referred to, but who did not compare their experiences in the myriad ways that we do and who lacked the widely ramified types of responses of the kind we have been describing. Here I think we *would* have the right to say that there is no room in the lives of such people for any notion of the subjective quality of experience, because they lack subjective responses to their own experiences. But these are not the kind of people we are dealing with and would hardly be recognizable as human beings.

Crates, the kind of understanding that we have been describing just now may be described as *intersubjective* understanding. It is realized in the way that people are able to compare experiences and share their understanding, and it provides a genuine and substantial context for speaking of a *knowledge* of what the subjective state is like. Moreover, it is of the very nature of intersubjective understanding that it arises out of the way that people engage with one another but not from purely external observations of each other. We will also find that this plays a very important rôle in the possession of psychological concepts generally. Clearly an understanding of the nature of this engagement will be central to an understanding of how these concepts are embedded in our lives. But if we are right to contrast this with the idea that these concepts might be determined by external *observation*, then it will be important to examine this contrast. This brings us to the difficult question of the rôle of criteria in the application of psychological concepts.

5   Concepts and the application of criteria

An understanding of the rôle of criteria in the possession and application of a concept is central to a philosophical understanding of its grammar. It is a matter that is also directly related to this question to which we keep returning, namely the extent to which a concept is determined by reference to facts rather than in the establishment of a practice. So it will be illuminating to approach the question of criteria with this distinction in mind.

In the decades immediately following Wittgenstein's death, it became common for philosophers to allot criteria a central rôle in his account of the employment of concepts. We may follow the words of Hacker, who exemplified this trend. He stated the position quite unequivocally:

> Criteria, then, can be seen as those conditions which non-inductively justify the assertion of a sentence and in terms of which the sense of the sentence is to be accounted for. (Hacker, 1972, p. 283)

And then:

> In the *Investigations* he [Wittgenstein] suggests that the criteria for '*p*' are the circumstances which would justify one in saying that *p* (e.g., *PI*, §182). His numerous investigations into specific psychological and dispositional terms employ the concept of a criterion extensively in precisely this sense. (Hacker, 1972, p. 288)

We find a similar sentiment expressed by Hanna:

> Concepts require criteria of application; and if a concept is to be applied to others, one must be able to say from an objective standpoint whether these criteria are satisfied. If this cannot be done, there is no justification for such an application. To persist in doing so puts one in the position of claiming to give a 'subjective' justification, which as Wittgenstein notes (PI, I: 265), is no justification at all. (Hanna, 1990, p. 352)

In the first place, we may note—according to Hacker's first remark, at any rate—that the criteria for applying a concept are apparently the *determinants* of the meaning of the concept, inasmuch as they determine the sense of the sentences containing it. However, this did not mean that Hacker imagined a simple equation between the presence of the criterion and the fact of the thing for which it is a criterion; for, as he also stated, in any given circumstance the relation between the criteria present (or absent) and the fact asserted (or denied) is not one of *entailment*.[28] For example, a person may show pain-behaviour but not *be* in pain.—He may be pretending. This position has the virtuous consequence, within the criterial account of psychological concepts, of enabling behaviourism to be avoided—at least on the formal level—for it will be a part of the grammar of psychological concepts that *in particular circumstances* the absence of the state of mind will not follow from the absence of criteria (and *vice versa*). This shows that the mental state cannot be identical with its outward expression.

Second, we should note that criteria are identified, on this view, as the circumstances *justifying* the application of a concept. Identifying these circumstances will be an operational part of the application;—they are not just facts that may be referred to retrospectively, or by a third party, in explanation of the application of the concept:

> Learning language involves learning to recognize (but not necessarily to describe) the circumstances justifying the use of an expression. Thereby one acquires tacit intuitive knowledge of the criterial rules justifying the employment of the expression. Thus one test for whether '*p*' is a criterion for '*q*' is whether one could come to understand '*q*' without grasping that the truth of '*p*' justifies one in asserting '*q*'. (Hacker, 1972, p. 292)

CRATES: So on this view, the application of a concept is based on the observation of facts—either as stated explicitly or recognized as such—that justify its application. Now I am sure we can agree that there will be very many situations in which the application of a concept will operate in more or less the way that Hacker described—we have already argued that facts are often integrated into concepts—but such an account, as we have also stated previously, will not do as a *general* account of the use of concepts. For regardless of whether the criteria are applied implicitly or explicitly, in either case it was supposed by Hacker that the criterion must be *conceptualized*, as this is the only sense in which the criteria can be *recognized*. But this can surely only mean that the application of the criterion is itself a conceptual act that must *itself* be based on criteria, and so on *ad infinitum*.[29] Clearly there is something wrong here, Lato.

LATO: Well, in the first instance we should not be fooled by his notion of the 'tacit' application of criteria,—which is ambiguous. When we apply a criterion explicitly, the recognition of the criterial circumstances will obviously not involve the application of the concept for which those circumstances are the criterion—which would obviously be circular. For example, if the criterion for a disease is a rash of a certain sort, then the description of the rash cannot depend on employing the concept of the disease for which it is a criterion. Now in the case where the criterion is applied *explicitly*, any such circularity will—or ought to be—obvious enough. But in the situation where the criterial concepts are only applied *tacitly*, it may not be so easy to distinguish the genuine case from the circular one.

A genuine case of tacit application, for example, would be where an experienced ornithologist is able to identify a bird by its 'jizz', that is, without noting any specific features; while the *justification* for the identification would demand a specific description of the identifying plumage characteristics. Contrast this with 'I am in pain', which to the philosophically unwary may also be taken to be a judgement based on a tacit criterion—though not Hacker in this case, who explicitly denied that such first person 'avowals' are based on criteria.[30] A typical formulation of this—which is at the bottom of much empiricist philosophy— is that we perceive the 'essence' of the sensation, which is then used as the criterion that *this* is a pain, or whatever it may be. Or perhaps it is believed that the judgement is, as it were, the criterion for itself.[31] The underlying factor here is the temptation to assume that wherever it is not evident that a criterion has been *explicitly* applied, then sure enough there must have been an *implicit* application—which we then go in search of. But this is surely an empty conception. We may certainly agree that whenever a criterion *is* applied, the criterial circumstances are conceptualized (logically) prior to the application and, moreover, that this remains the case whether the criterion is applied explicitly or implicitly, in other words it will always be possible to *produce* criteria. But to prevent the infinite regress, we will need to acknowledge that in the bedrock of language, criteria are *not* applied at all and that in these circumstances conceptualization *begins* with the judgement itself. Moreover, we have no grounds as yet for assuming that the criterionless application of concepts only occurs in first person subjective judgements—which would then have to form the base for *all* other judgements.

CRATES: So the alternative to Hacker's and Hanna's accounts of criteria may certainly begin by acknowledging that many concepts are, to a greater or lesser degree, founded on facts, and that to this extent their application does involve identifying these facts (implicitly or explicitly) and employing them as criteria. But it will also have to acknowledge that a general account of the application of concepts must recognize that ultimately it is not founded on the recognition of facts but on the exercise of linguistic practices—at whatever level they may enter into human life—which are not based on criteria.[32]

This will apply both to the *application* of concepts and also to their *determination*. In other words, to the extent that the exercise of a concept is rooted in a practice and not founded on facts, the sense of the concept cannot be accounted for by reference to any fact. This is essentially the same point we argued for in the second dialogue, that the establishment of a *practice* is, in the end, more fundamental to the constitution of concepts than the absorption of facts. Hence, where the exercise of a concept is not by the application of a criterion, its exercise will be rooted in a primitive *reaction*. We have already discussed *first* person reactions expressing mental states as one criterionless and non-factually based mode in which psychological concepts are determined and articulated. In the following discussion, we will try to show how a similar principle applies to *third* person attributions of mental states. But before you launch into that discussion, Lato, perhaps as a preliminary I could make some points about facts, practices and concept-formation.

There is no doubt that facts do often play an important rôle in determining psychological concepts and that the interplay between the factual and practical components in this process is complex. Moreover, the extent to which and the *mode* in which individual concepts may embody facts is itself highly variable, thus increasing the complexity. This is especially the case where third person uses are at issue. An elucidation of the employment of psychological concepts in these circumstances will therefore demand an examination of this complex balance between and interweaving of the factual and the practical components. Hence our examination of the nature of the *practice* of employing psychological concepts will have to maintain contact with this wider discussion.

There is also another dimension to this that we must always include. As we have been emphasizing throughout, understanding a concept is not merely a matter of being able to operate a sign correctly to achieve a particular end. It is not just a matter of producing the right reactions. Rather, the concept that is expressed through a given practice is a function of the way that the practice is related to or is a component of our form of life—which itself does not merely comprise a series of such reactions. For otherwise we are not *saying* anything with the concept. For this reason, the whole character of that form of life will also have to be taken into account.

One of the ways in which we can keep this other dimension constantly in view is by reminding ourselves of that sense in which the possession of the concept may be regarded as an *extension* of our form of life,—which is an extension of our lives as *persons*.

6 Psychological concepts: criteria or primitive reactions?

LATO: In our very last discussion of psychological concepts, Wittgenstein said that we cannot account for such concepts merely by describing the external circumstances which are the direct context for judging that a person is in a given mental state. He said:

> I am trying to describe the laws or rules of evidence for empirical sentences: does one really characterize what is meant by the mental in this way?
>
> The characteristic sign of the mental seems to be that one has to guess at it in someone else using external cues and is only *acquainted* with it from one's own case.
>
> But when closer reflection causes this view to go up in smoke, then what turns out is not that the inner is something outer, but that 'outer' and 'inner' now no longer count as properties of evidence. 'Inner evidence' means nothing, and therefore neither does 'outer evidence'.
>
> But indeed there is 'evidence for the inner' and 'evidence for the outer'.
>
> 'But all I ever perceive is the *outer*.' If that makes sense, it must determine a concept. But why should I not say I perceive his doubts? (*He* cannot perceive them.)
>
> Indeed, often I can describe his inner, as I perceive it, but not his outer.
>
> ....
>
> *No* evidence teaches us the psychological utterance. (LW2, pp. 61–63)

He was suggesting here—in the first and last remarks, at least—that psychological concepts are not rooted in the facts that might count as evidence for a mental state in a particular instance. Moreover, treating observed external cues as evidence for the inner is not in any case central to our encounter with the mental lives of others.

CRATES: These views seem to be an advance upon the view he expressed on earlier occasions and which is summarized in his 'An "inner process" stands in need of outward criteria',[33] which appears to be a slogan for the 'evidential' account. This latter remark has been taken as evidence of Wittgenstein's commitment to a theory of the meaning of psychological concepts based on criteria. But is it so certain that the remark *should* be treated in this way?

LATO: I certainly take his use of the phrase 'inner process' to be ironic, meaning that if we *are* to think in terms of an inner process then we are indeed committed to a notion of outward criteria. It is not that he approved of construing the relation between the 'inner' and the 'outer' in this way—this is why he placed the phrase in scare quotes. Be that as it may, let's develop our discussion in the light of what came out more clearly in his later remarks and consider the following picture of the language-game of *pain*.

Let us suppose, for the moment, that psychological concepts *are* among those which, in their third person applications at least, are dependent on facts, the observation of which would therefore count as criteria for their application. In the practical situation, then, our judgement that a person is in pain would be based on our observations of his pain-behaviour, the typical manifestations of which we could of course describe. These third person attributions would evidently differ in grammar from first person avowals, which it is agreed are not based on criteria. It would therefore be the latter and not the former which constituted the instinctive root of the language-game, and they would do so in this way: 'the verbal expression of pain replaces crying ....'.[34] Hence, 'I am in pain' would be a primitive reaction within the language-game; indeed its utterance would itself be one of the facts that, in the third person context, would be taken as a criterion for the judgement 'He is in pain'. 'I am in pain' would also supply the subjective component of the language-game; for it would both be a cornerstone of the language-game *and* be recognized as a direct expression of the individual's subjective state. And insofar as the meaning of 'pain' is determined in the third person situation, this would be quite secondary to its determination in the first person situation. Indeed it would depend on the latter.

This is consistent with Hacker's observation that the relation between the fact of the criterion and the fact of the pain is not one of entailment,[35] for this certainly would be the case if the concept were determined exclusively *by means of* the criteria for its third person application. It may well be a *part* of our concept of pain that it is manifested in certain ways in outward behaviour; but this does not go to the root of the concept, which is determined by its first person utterances.

CRATES: That is certainly how the Wittgensteinian position was often presented—in outline at least—and no doubt there is much that is correct about it, especially in regard to the rôle of first person utterances in determining the concept. But such a simple dichotomy between the inward and the outward components of the determinants of the concept of pain is false. We will shortly try to correct this picture by examining Hertzberg's account of the interrelations between the primitive reactions that characterize the language-game.[36] But I suggest we begin by drawing attention to a closely related situation where the establishment of facts *does* play an important rôle in forming judgements. It is important not to confuse this with the main issue at hand.

If I want to see whether a child is learning to use 'pain' properly and am observing his behaviour—both in expressing his own pain and also when applied to other people—I am not concerned with exercising the concept *pain* but, once again, the concept of the *language-games* of expressing pain and of recognizing pain in others. The latter concept is partly constituted in the ability to recognize an array of facts, such as that the child only uses the word where the person of whom he speaks has given expression to pain in appropriate circumstances, or where the child himself is expressing his pain in appropriate circumstances. These facts belong to the criteria for saying that the child is using the word correctly. If the child is not able to react appropriately, we will be justified in saying that he has not got the concept *pain*. This judgement will have been one based on the facts of the matter. But whereas there are criteria that a concept has been correctly applied, it does not follow that there are criteria for *its* application—either as applied in his own case or when applied to others—just because the concept *of* a language-game is a different concept from the concepts *within* the language-game. There are criteria for deciding that a child has correctly applied 'pain', that is, that he only says of people actually in pain that they are in pain. But it does not follow that the child employs a criterion in making his judgement. So the point I want to establish before we continue is that we should not be fooled into thinking that third person attributions of 'pain' are based on external criteria just because judgements as to the correctness of the child's use of the concept make use of external criteria.

In fact, we will see that even the latter types of judgement cannot depend wholly on external criteria. For when we observe that the child has made the correct use of 'pain', the determination of the facts that show this is dependent on *our* judgement that the third person actually is in pain. In other words, we have to have made the same judgement that we are attributing to the child. So although, as I say, the observation that the child is using the term correctly is not *in itself* an exercise by myself of the concept *pain*; nevertheless my observation does depend on the (logically) prior exercise of that judgement, otherwise I would not be in a position to make the observation about the child. So the determination of those facts is itself subordinate to our *own* judgement.

Our present purpose, then, is to examine third person judgements more closely. And we shall argue that they are *also* criterionless. It is in order to show that the determination of the sense of these judgements is not fundamentally by means of agreement on *criteria* that we need to examine the rôle of primitive reactions in determining the character of the language-games in question.

And so to Hertzberg.

LATO: Hertzberg began with the observation—which we introduced in the fourth dialogue—that within a language-game certain responses are *independent*; that is, they are not dependent on any other judgement and are therefore primitive to the language-game. But his account has the additional virtue that its perception of the foundations of the language-game does not identify only first person expressions of pain as primitive but extends this to include reactions to third persons; indeed he went even further in identifying as primitive the recognition of responses of sympathy (or repulsion, or indifference) *between* third parties. This immediately releases us from the picture of the language-game as a simple dichotomy between, on the one hand, first person modes of judgement that are criterionless and, on the other, third person attributions that are based on facts, that is, where what is observed as fact is taken as the criterion for the attribution. This is just because third person reactions, being primitive, must also be criterionless.

The logical basis of this extension is that if the recognition of expressions of pain *as such* were not essentially primitive, then it would have to take the form of a hypothesis that the behaviour we observe is *caused* by the mental event.[37] This causal model would require that the concept of pain be established independently of the concept of what constitutes its expression; and for this, it would be necessary to turn to the well-known argument by analogy from one's own case. But this is an argument without credibility,[38] since it is in any case dependent on the discredited notion of private ostensive definition. Now we may justify a judgement on some particular occasion, for example that here we have an expression of pain, by comparing it with acts recognized independently as belonging with the behavioural expression of pain. But if this is not to lead to an infinite regress (which would also undermine the determination of the concept), expressions of pain must at some point be recognizable without recourse to such further justification.[39] Hertzberg is arguing, then, that not only are first person expressions of pain primitive, the recognition of behaviour as an expression of pain is also primitive. This primitiveness is manifested not just in the recognition of others' expressions of pain, but in the whole circle of mutual understanding. For example, it would be a primitive reaction for a person to see someone's response to a third person as a reaction to their distress. He concluded:

In such cases, then, it is not as if I brought the pieces together and concluded that the situation is one revolving around someone's pain.

Rather, I see the situation under the aspect of pain, and this way of seeing it, as it were, brings the pieces together in this particular way. (Hertzberg, 1992, p. 33)

CRATES: So this seeing of the situation 'under the aspect of pain' indicates that our recognition of the nature of the particular responses is founded on something that we bring *to* the situation and within which we view it, namely an overall conception of the person as a conscious, sensitive agent. It is a way of looking at our fellow humans, and not just a readiness to make certain judgements from which to draw certain conclusions. And this, of course, tells us something of how the concept *pain* is embedded in our lives. This relationship between humans is what has been called the 'attitude towards a soul',[40] the nature of which we must now explore.

7 Intersubjectivity: the 'Attitude towards a Soul'

LATO: Hertzberg was careful to avoid the conclusion that the demonstration of the independence of the primitive reactions within the language-game is *all* that is required to give an account of what is primitive to the possession of the concept *pain*, or psychological concepts in general.[41] For no judgement that is defined in observational terms, even if it is primitive to a language-game, amounts to an application of the concept *pain* unless it is at the same time a manifestation of the 'attitude towards a soul', which is also primitive to the language-game.

As you have just reminded us, Wittgenstein stated that we are not of the *opinion* but are of the *attitude* towards others as having souls. This observation is part of the elucidation of the concept of the intersubjective responses between human beings, and it says that this relation is essentially an attitudinal one *within which* judgements are made. Opinions lie too shallowly in our lives to characterize the essential nature of the recognition between souls, which is a pervasive feature of the relations between persons. The attitude provides a framework for and gives sense to opinions; it is not itself *founded* on opinion. Only a soul can be in pain; and unless I already see him as a soul, I am not judging that he is in pain. There is no doubt that behaviour is usually the immediate context for the *judgement* or *belief* that the other is suffering; but the possibility of such a belief depends on it being at the same time an expression of this attitude,—which is not an attitude towards the behaviour as such.

We must examine this distinction between attitude and opinion as it applies here; but for the moment we may consider a variation of your own.

CRATES: The attitude towards a soul embraces not just the possibility of a *suffering* soul but conscious life in general. For example, imagine that I am helping someone in a building task. In the course of the work we will employ visual signs and signals of all kinds, such as holding up a tool inquiringly or pointing. I will be watching out to see if he is watching *me*—to see that we are working in co-ordination, perhaps, or to check that we are working safely, and so on—and, of course, we will be talking freely about the things that are open to the view of us both. So it is written into everything I do that the other *can see*; and the same goes for him. My whole orientation towards him—and his orientation towards me—is appropriate to two persons living in a shared visual space. This orientation is not founded on the general *belief* that people can see. The mutual interaction within the shared visual space is the 'given' *within which* the language-games of seeing are established and their sense determined. Hence I may wonder whether he has seen *this* or not, or I may notice that he doesn't see so well. But these judgements depend on my living a form of life in which my recognition of sighted-ness is an implicit and pervasive feature of my behavioural and linguistic relations with people, such that the *judgement* of the recognition of sighted-ness is secondary. The 'given' is the intersubjective mode of life;[42] intersubjectivity is the *attitude*.

If the attitude were not given, then the application of the concept of seeing to third persons would have to be rooted in learned judgements based on observation; but in that case they would not be intersubjective. The intersubjective mode is irreducible; it cannot be derived from observation without running into the confusion of treating the determination of psychological concepts as *essentially* founded on external criteria. If I say 'He's seen me, I must leave', I make this judgement on the basis, for example, of my seeing him look up and register my presence and start towards me. But when I say he has seen me, I do not mean this string of observations about his movements, nor that I now have certain expectations of his next moves. The sense of what I say depends on my having a concept *seeing*, which provides the framework through which I observe his behaviour; and my having the concept *seeing* has, in its foundations, my attitude towards persons insofar as it shows in my daily uncalculated interactions with them.

LATO: Turning again to 'pain', I *recognize* expressions of pain and expressions of sympathy. And so in what I say and do I show that

I believe that he is in pain, or that he cares about others in pain. But my understanding of the nature of the state he is in—and hence my grasp of the sense of what I am saying in making that judgement—is dependent on it being a part of my attitude towards him. For we judge that the person has the concept in the way that its entry into his judgements and his conversation goes together with his attitude. This is characteristic of our form of life. One mode in which the attitude towards a soul shows itself, for example, is in the expression of sympathy: 'it is a primitive reaction to tend to treat the part that hurts when someone else is in pain'.[43] Indeed sympathy is woven in innumerable ways into the patterns of interaction between people. Again, the sympathetic attitude is not directed towards the *behaviour*; it is an attitude towards the suffering *person*. We may certainly say that the belief that the person is in pain occasions the sympathy.—It is part of our concept of pain that it is a proper object for sympathy. But that is not because we have determined the nature of pain first and have then formed a concept of sympathy to 'fit' it. For the recognition of pain as warranting sympathy (or shock or revulsion or cruel indifference, for that matter) is part of our understanding of its nature. The concepts *pain* and *sympathy* are internally related: the grasp of the concept *sympathy* belongs to the grasp of the concept *pain*. And as sympathy is itself a manifestation of the attitude towards a soul, our grasp of the concept *pain* is partly a function of that attitude. Wittgenstein remarked:

> How am I filled with pity *for this man*? How does it come out what the object of my pity is? (Pity, one may say, is a form of conviction that someone else is in pain.) (PI 287)

Sympathy is not, of course, the only manifestation of this attitude that provides a context for the determination of the concept *pain*. As in the case of *seeing*, the grammar of 'pain' is an element in that larger structure: the grammar of 'consciousness'. Pain is a *mode* of consciousness. Only if my relation to the sufferer is part of a comprehensive relation to others as conscious beings, am I in a position to recognize his behaviour as an expression of pain.[44] It would be senseless to attribute pain to a creature that exhibited no other manifestations of consciousness other than the immediate behavioural reactions that we normally recognize as expressing pain. The general recognition of consciousness must be a pervasive feature of my engagement with him.

Hence *all* the different kinds of responses—in virtue of all the different modes in which conscious life is expressed—form the substrate of our recognition of a person as being in pain. It lies, for example, in the way I point to the cause of the pain, or in the way I shout a warning, or in the way I rub or protect the painful place, or in the way I inquire about his pain: what it is like, whether it is becoming intolerable, and so on. Our understanding of 'pain' is rooted in the attitude towards a soul, which is a primitive feature of our form of life.

8 Intersubjective concepts and the extension of primitive intersubjectivity

CRATES: The attitude towards a soul is a pervasive feature of our form of life, having both conceptual and non-conceptual components; that is, it manifests itself both in what we have to say and in natural behaviour. We may *also* recognize the intersubjective attitude in *purely* non-linguistic modes in that more primitive arena: the behaviour of animals—though we may not wish to call this the attitude towards a *soul*, because that usually also connotes features which, just because of their conceptual nature, are lacking in animals. Thus, when an animal calls out to another, or strikes out, or makes a gesture, or when it engages in play with another, the behaviour is the behaviour towards another hearing, feeling, seeing, *conscious*, creature.

I emphasize again that this is not to suggest that animals have even a primitive conception of the mental life of other animals. Rather, it is to suggest that it is an aspect of animal interactions that we can conceive of them as relations between subjects and not only as relations of a subject to an object. It is a feature of their form of life that their relations among themselves are different in kind from their relations to inanimate objects—even mobile ones. Hence there is no obvious reason why we should not characterize the former as *intersubjective* relations. So the conclusion is just this, that intersubjectivity is not exclusively a relation between persons possessing concepts, it may also occur on the purely non-linguistic behavioural level,[45] as in the case of animals—and of course in pre-linguistic children too.

The question now arises as to whether intersubjectivity at this behavioural level may be demonstrated to be *logically* more primitive than intersubjectivity at the conceptual level. Referring once again to the human form of life, the concept of intersubjectivity is the concept of an aspect of that form of life that may manifest itself either linguistically or behaviourally. We may argue, then, that it is another of those concepts—like *intention*—where we may perhaps view the linguistic form as an *extension* of the natural form. The interesting question is whether there is an *essential* priority in the transition from the natural to the conceptual components; for if there is, then this adds greater philosophical significance to the proposition that the conceptual mode is an extension of the natural.

LATO: Indeed. We might start by conceding that there *are* instances in the life of the human subject when it *does* seem clear, even in the most direct expressions of subjective states, that there is a conceptual mode at work having no behavioural analogue. Thus, the 'secondary' uses of language to describe subjective qualities—which we have already touched on briefly—have no obvious non-linguistic counterpart. But I think these cases must be exceptional. For it is surely impossible to conceive of a child learning the language-games of seeing and hearing, for example, except in circumstances where the child and the adult share a visual and aural space, this sharing being manifested through pervasive features of their natural modes of interpersonal behaviour. And we may argue along similar lines with the concept *pain* among a myriad of others: we may not conceive of the child as learning the concept except where she is fully engaged inter-subjectively with the adult right across the shared aspects of their lives—crying for help, being soothed, and so on. As we argued in the previous section, the intersubjective attitude is the *context* for the formation of concepts.

And we might consider another, related case. In a great number of contexts, the employment of a concept may *itself* be viewed as the exercise of an attitude in its own right, rather than the exercise of a *judgement*, as in the above case. And no doubt in many instances this attitude will *not* have been anticipated in any pre-conceptual behaviour. This surely applies in the case of the moral attitude—by which I mean the treatment of others and oneself as moral agents—where, to avoid falling into naturalism, we must surely say that what is characteristic in the moral attitude must arise *spontaneously* and *simultaneously* with the grasp of the concepts.[46]—The moral attitude, being primitive to the language-game, has no analogue in non-conceptual primitive behaviour (which, incidentally, is not contradicted by the observation of 'social order' in the lives of non-conceptual animals). With this kind of example in mind, there may be a temptation to speculate that the intersubjective attitude *in general* might have come into being simultaneously with the formation of psychological concepts. However, where we are concerned with the most basic features of our form of life, I do not think that the genesis of intersubjective conceptual attitudes is conceivable except as a function of a child's dispositions as a whole: we judge the child to have mastered the intersubjective use of language against the background of her broadly established modes of interpersonal engagement with her fellows. It is the latter that determine our concept of intersubjectivity at the most fundamental level.

CRATES: We should perhaps remind ourselves again here of the context for this kind of questioning. We are elucidating here not so much the concepts of mental life as the concepts of the interrelations between subjects, of which the language-games with psychological concepts form a part. In our discussion of intention in the fourth dialogue, our aim was to show that the language-game of expressing intentions is, in a quite fundamental sense, an extension of natural intentionality. This means that the concept of the language-game of expressing intentions takes for granted the concept of the natural expression of intention. Now of course the recognition of intention in others—which is the same as the recognition of other persons as *agents*—is also a form of intersubjective understanding, a mode of the attitude towards a soul, otherwise, it would be reducible to the mere anticipation of physical movements. The recognition of agency is written into the whole way that the child relates to the adult. For example, it would make little sense to speak of the child as being in the process of learning to *speak* unless we have already conceived of the child as capable of recognizing the intentional nature of the adult's behaviour towards him.

In conclusion, the recognition of expressions of subjective states in others is primitive to our language-games. Moreover, when we make the judgement that this person is in pain, we are already seeing him through the perspective of the attitude towards a soul. This form of judgement adds up to more than the exercise of a verbal technique based on the recognition of a particular phenomenal circumstance. Rather, we are bringing to bear a concept whose sense derives from circumstances part of which are constituted by the intersubjective attitude that is fundamental to our form of life and which is extended in the development of the language-game. When we *say* that the language-game is intersubjective, this is an expression of our conception of the relations between persons *as* persons, certain essential features of this language-game being autonomous of the language-games of describing outward manifestations of behaviour.

LATO: And of course this notion of intersubjectivity is also constitutive of our concept of *speaking*.

9   Philosophical investigation in the subjective mode

In these final sections of this dialogue, we shall examine from various points of view how the ways that these concepts are seated in our lives affect our relations to them *within* philosophy. In the present section, and following on from the previous sections, we shall concentrate on the problem of how philosophy deals with what we have been referring to as the *subjective* dimension of their possession.

Because the possession of psychological concepts is not simply a matter of the exercise of a technique but has to do with the way that they become a part of the fabric of our lives as persons, our relations to the concepts are complex—as we have illustrated previously in the cases of *intention* and *belief*. In the case of *belief*, we saw that the possession of the concept is a part of our whole relation to language and the world; while in the case of *intention*, we saw that it is partly a function of the rôle of language-games as expressions of intention. We have also seen how the possession of psychological concepts belongs with the 'attitude towards a soul'. These aspects of their possession complicate the processes of reflecting upon them in philosophy and—especially where a subjective element is involved—create a situation that may appear puzzling at first sight.

We have said that a distinctive feature of psychological concepts is that our understanding of them engages with the subjective states of which—in certain modes of their use, at least—they are an expression. To conceive of someone as being in possession of them is to conceive of certain uses of language as integrated into the subjective mode of his life. However, if the subjective mode belongs to the *understanding* of the concept, then it looks as though the improved understanding of the concept that we seek in philosophy will itself partake of this subjective mode. *Prima facie* this is an uncomfortable position for the philosopher, as it seems to clash with the need for objectivity. How can we address this?

CRATES: There is one apparently obvious solution to this, which we might illustrate by referring again to the 'secondary' uses of language to express the quality of a subjective experience. As Wittgenstein pointed out, secondary uses of language have their source just in what we are *inclined* to say. It just seems right that *these* words fit *this* experience and no further justification can be given,—or at least, to the extent that further justification can be given, the use is not secondary. Understanding what is said by someone who uses linguistic expressions in this way depends on our *sharing* the reaction; there is no other guide. Now it is essential to such uses of language that they have a *primary* use and that the shared understanding of this primary use is integral to the phenomenon of secondary uses. In other words, it would make no sense to speak of understanding the secondary use if the understanding of the primary use were not also shared.[47] Moreover, primary uses of words are governed by *rules* inasmuch as there are right and wrong ways of using them.

Nevertheless we cannot say that the secondary uses of language *as such* are governed in the same way by rules, except insofar as they have to be recognizable as secondary uses of language. Hence, an account of the grammar of a secondary expression will tell us what *kind* of expression it is, but it will not in itself lead to any further insight into what it means to say, for example, that 'Wednesday was fat'.[48] From the point of view of elucidating the grammars of these sorts of expressions, then, it surely does not matter that the subjective aspect of the understanding does not enter into the elucidation, since what we are concerned with is just the *kind* of proposition that they are. We are not concerned to improve our insight into the *particular* sense that the uses express but only into the *kind* of sense that they have. Applying this to the philosophical understanding of psychological concepts, we might feel inclined to employ the same principle: we can eliminate what is grasped on the subjective level, for we only wish to see more clearly the *kinds* of concepts that they are, and this can be determined by looking at how their uses bear on the uses of other expressions in given concrete circumstances.

LATO: Yes, this would appear at first sight to dismiss the problem. But I think a closer examination will show that the analogy does not really work.

We argued in the second dialogue that in philosophy we may find accounts of concepts that amount to no more than delineations of what propositions are allowed, what connections are allowed between the concepts, which concepts are most closely related to one another, and so on. This corresponds to a purely 'formal' conception of philosophy. We also argued that this is not an adequate conception given the nature of philosophical problems, as these arise in response to a puzzlement emerging from *within* our understanding of a concept. Hence the elucidation we require in responding to this puzzlement will be one that draws on our understanding of the concept and which should deepen our reflective understanding of it. The disturbing consequence of the foregoing discussions is that it now looks as though the philosophical understanding of psychological concepts depends on what is subjective in our understanding of them, which therefore seems to undermine the objectivity demanded by philosophy.

CRATES: In fact we did go over this point—or a very closely related point—in the fourth section of the second dialogue; but I think it worth reiterating in the light of our recent discussions.

LATO: Agreed.

That this appears to present a difficulty is, I suspect, because of an inclination to interpret this as harking back to the idea of an understanding depending on subjective *judgement*. But, as we argued in the first section of this dialogue, this is not the notion of subjectivity that is relevant in this situation; for to say that the language-games with 'pain' depend on their being bound up with both my expressions of pain and my intersubjective responses to other persons is just to say that *together* they belong to the 'given'. Ultimately, all use of language is without ground, without *justification*. The subjective mode just is a given dimension of our form of life; it is one of the channels through which we follow a rule 'blindly'. And its being a part of the way in which language has a rôle in our lives does not imply that language may be founded on subjective judgements.

That the demand for objectivity is not compromised by the fact that our understanding of certain concepts lies in the subjective mode may perhaps be illustrated by considering the circumstances under which we judge that a child has a grasp of such concepts. If we are to give a complete account of the circumstances in which we determine the correctness of a child's employment of a psychological concept, we too must understand the concept in all the senses that we wish to test in the child's understanding. This is reflected in the concrete situation; for observing that a child has got hold of a concept will involve understanding what the child is *saying*—which of course emerges out of our *conversation* with the child. Hence, if establishing that the child has a given concept is a factual matter, and if the grasp of the relevant concept is bound up with the subjective mode of our lives, then we just have to accept that our recognition of the fact that the child understands the concept is partly a function of our own lives as subjects. If having the concepts *at all* involves our subjective relations to things—in this same sense of our relations to things *as subjects*—then our recognition of the facts that show that the child has the concept must engage with this understanding also. The same will apply at the philosophical level, where reminding ourselves of these same facts will be integral to the elucidation of the language-games in which psychological concepts are embedded.

CRATES: There is nothing especially paradoxical, then, in claiming that the understanding that is required when elucidating the grammars of psychological concepts is one that engages with the subjective mode. For if it did not, then the philosophical investigation could not deepen our understanding of the concepts. This is in the nature of philosophical reflection. Above all, we should remind ourselves that a philosophical elucidation is not a *justification* of a concept; and the objectivity of philosophy is the same as the objectivity of discourse—it is not a *transcendental* objectivity.

LATO: Quite.

10   Concepts of the subject and natural uncertainty

We have referred to the discomfort that we might feel in philosophy in having to engage with the subjective mode in the possession of a concept—uncomfortable at least to the extent, as you say, that we still think of philosophy as viewing the concepts of everyday discourse from a distance. But there is another situation where philosophy's frustration with these concepts is more rooted in reality. I am thinking here of the situation where uncertainty is *written into* a concept. In this kind of case, the perplexity we experience with it is not a culpable confusion but the reflection of a native equivocation at the very origin of its formation.

Consider these statements by Wittgenstein:

> Think of the uncertainty about whether animals, particularly lower animals, such as flies, feel pain.
>
> The uncertainty whether a fly feels pain is philosophical; but couldn't it also be instinctive? And how would that come out?
>
> Indeed, aren't we really uncertain in our behaviour towards animals? One doesn't know: Is he being cruel or not? (RPP2 659)
>
> For there *is* uncertainty of behaviour which doesn't stem from uncertainty in thought. (RPP2 660)

The inclination here may be to conclude that there is an interesting parallel—but nothing more—between the uncertainty that arises when reflecting philosophically on the problem of 'other minds' and the familiar uncertainty that is commonly experienced in such everyday situations. And if we assume that philosophical confusions arise *only* out of some compulsion to mangle our concepts, then it might remain an interesting parallel only.[49] But we have already argued that our instinctive, intersubjective relations—both to other persons *and* to animals— are integral to the formation and possession of psychological concepts. And so to the extent that these relations may be infected by the natural uncertainty described here by Wittgenstein, there is no reason why this uncertainty might not also infect the formation of our concepts, and so lie among the *sources* of the philosophical problem of other minds.

The uncertainty here is of the validity of projecting a concept into a novel situation different from the one in which it had been determined— which must have been 'certain' otherwise the concept will *not* have been determined. But it is not merely an example of the very familiar situation where a concept is not clearly determined *at its boundary*; for example, it is not to be compared with uncertainty over what we are prepared to call a 'heap' of sand, which we may say *is* arbitrary. Rather it is an uncertainty already lying in the patterns of behaviour—linguistic and non-linguistic—that *surround* the possession of the concept. It is something inherent in our form of life and which may vary naturally from one person to another. Hence, there may not be a 'solution' to the conceptual problems that grow from it, nor any way of reconciling the differences between people's attitudes towards animals.

CRATES: So there is an essential indeterminacy in our concept, which may resurface either as intractable confusion within philosophy or in insoluble failure to arrive at a common understanding in the employment of our concept.

LATO: Yes. Inasmuch as the determination of our concepts is dependent on instinctive linguistic and—especially—*extra*-linguistic reactions, and insofar as there is both enough common ground between people to determine a concept *and* a significant band of divergence, it is quite possible for irreconcilable conceptual differences to emerge. These differences are not philosophical differences, but they may give rise to intractable difficulties within philosophical argument.

So in this sort of case—and no doubt we could find many others where there is uncertainty at the very heart of a concept—it may be better to say that what philosophy has to offer is not a resolution to a particular difficulty but just a clearer view of the situation in the possession of the concepts that gave rise to the difficulty.

CRATES: Yes, we can agree on that.

11   A subjective source of confusion: the 'Experience of Meaning'

LATO: Finally, in this dialogue we would like to investigate a special situation that arises in the way we experience language and which we believe has been instrumental in the generation of certain specific conceptual difficulties. For the situations that create confusion in our understanding of our most fundamental concepts are not limited to outward features of our language-games, or to special situations in the way that concepts are seated in our lives. Familiar introspective states or impressions may also play a part. Such impressions undoubtedly have many roots—some of which we have already touched on—but among these must be counted the influence of certain experiences that attach themselves directly to the use of language. Principal among these, I believe, is the so-called 'experience of the meaning of a word'. Of the conceptual difficulties in which we believe this experience is implicated, the impression that one can give oneself a private ostensive definition of a psychological concept is perhaps the most notorious. So it is an important phenomenon.

Wittgenstein spoke of the experience of meaning and related experiences at length in the second part of his most oft-quoted discussions.[50] And so first we must make a distinction, because there are two possible experiences here, only one of which is directly troublesome— though I think we should probably treat the latter as a variation on the other.

The use of language is something that falls within our *perception*— whether it be spoken out loud or heard only 'in our heads'. And so it is normal that there should be characteristic ways in which we experience words and sentences. Indeed we should *expect* words to be experienced differently from other objects in virtue of the part they play in our lives. These experiences evidently belong within the general category of experiencing a thing *as* something,—which, we may say, are the experiences we have of things in virtue of our habitual ways of acting towards them. As this applies to language, we may say that at the most general level we just see them or hear them *as* words. However, at another level, we may also have characteristic experiences of them in virtue of our *understanding* of them. Hence, we should also expect *individual* words to be experienced as meaningful in their own unique way in virtue of the unique rôle that each has—as unique as Schubert's name fitting his face and works, for example.[51] Thus, we experience our words as meaningful and we experience particular words as uniquely meaningful.[52]

This is fine. But things go wrong if we interpret this experience as a *direct apprehension of the meaning*—as easily seems to occur when introspecting. For it remains the case that meaning, grammatically, is *not* an experience. Hence, the extension from the experience of words as meaningful to the thought that one can literally experience their meaning— the very essence of the concept to which the word corresponds—is an illusion. Moreover, it is an extension guaranteed to create havoc in philosophy. Indeed, it may well have been partly responsible for our own confusions over the reality of the Forms. For these reasons, talk of the 'experience of *meaning*' in this sense is at best a secondary use of language (we shall be examining the secondary use of language in more detail in the next dialogue), and at worst it is a pernicious illusion of the way that the corresponding concepts are seated in our lives. So when we speak of the 'experience of meaning' in the present discussion as a source of trouble in philosophy, we shall be speaking of it in this latter sense.

CRATES: This experience is especially dangerous in philosophy when it attaches itself to the words used to express psychological concepts, where it undermines our understanding of the nature of mental life and of the kind of reality possessed by subjective phenomena.

LATO: Yes, indeed. The belief that one can give oneself a private ostensive definition of a mental state is the case in point. For it is not difficult to see the connection between the experience of meaning and the subjective feeling that one can also experience the essence of the *object* to which the word refers,—the essence of a colour, for example. The perception of meaning and the perception of the essence of an object or item of experience are evidently sister experiences. And it is but a short step from this—from the thought that we can *see* the essence of the colour—to the thought that we can name it with assurance subjectively. For of course, the *essence* will always speak to us with certainty. It is the force of this experience of essence that persuades us to think that experience provides the very basis and justification for the use of language—and here we surely are reminded of the way that the objects of experience were supposed to partake of the Forms—rather than that this experience of essence is the *product* of the formation of the concept and the habitual use of language. Reality has been turned back to front.

CRATES: Perhaps we might look at another example to explore further this interaction between the experience of meaning, concept-formation and philosophical difficulties. Consider Wittgenstein's 'visual room':

> The 'visual room' seemed like a discovery, but what its discoverer really found was a new way of speaking, a new comparison; it might even be called a new sensation. (PI 400)

> You have a new conception and interpret it as seeing a new object. You interpret a grammatical movement made by yourself as a quasi-physical phenomenon which you are observing. (Think for example of the question: 'Are sense-data the material of which the universe is made?')

> But there is an objection to my saying that you have made a 'grammatical' movement. What you have primarily discovered is a new way of looking at things. As if you had invented a new way of painting; or, again, a new metre, or a new kind of song.—(PI 401)

Wittgenstein was describing here the muddling up of the formation of a new concept with the discovery of a new fact or object.[53] The subsequent wavering between speaking of a movement in grammar and of a new way of looking at things was really a fluctuation between two aspects of the same thing: *the formation of a new concept,*—understood either from the point of view of its being a new extension to our grammar, or from the point of view of its *content* (a way of looking at things). But the important point remains: we are not in the act of discovering some new object but a new *conception*.[54] What drives this confusion is that a change in the way we organize our experience—a 'seeing as'—has been interpreted as the seeing of a thing we had not seen before, *this* visual room. Again I believe this is related to the experience of meaning; for just as this experience provokes us into interpreting our *understanding* of a word as the *perception* of its meaning or essence, so it causes us to interpret the formation of the concept of the visual room as the seeing of an object, the visual room.

LATO: This matter of the confusion of concept and fact, which has pervaded our dialogues and raised its head in many forms, is pivotal to achieving an understanding of the barriers to philosophical reflection. So it must be worth emphasizing the probable influence of the experiences of meaning and of essence in this.

We have argued that the possession of our concepts lies essentially in our *practice,*—which in the case of our most fundamental concepts is distributed through our use of language. And yet this layer of practice goes unobserved in normal discourse, engrossed as we are in the actual content of our speech. As a result, our appreciation of the whole relation between language and reality is affected if, oblivious of this pragmatic context, we take what is immediately present to us—the proposition and the state of affairs it describes—as our *guide* to understanding the general nature of this relation. It is precisely this divorce in our thinking between the propositions considered in themselves and their pragmatic context that generates the 'view from the boundary', as we have called it, and keeps us from the 'view from the midst', which, as we have said, is essential to true reflection.

We believe that the experience of meaning may be implicated in this divorce because of the way it is inclined to present the sense of the proposition, or our understanding of the proposition, as if it were an *item* of experience. Consequently, not only do we *not* have to recognize how the sense of what we say depends on the entirety of our social interactions and our engagement with our environment—the 'hurly-burly of human actions'—we also seem to have a ready explanation for this.[55] The opportunity to appreciate the pragmatic context of language and its concepts has been short-circuited and the gate is left open for all the theories of mind and reality that have plagued philosophy for millennia.

LATO: A crucial point for us here is that this most fundamental misconception of our relation to the world is also an aspect of our misunderstanding of the nature of the philosophical enterprise. The acceptance of the view from the boundary is both an aspect of the failure to acknowledge that which can only be *shown* from the midst and the refusal to enter it; while an understanding of the nature of the life with language and concepts is also a realization of what we need to do to understand that nature.

CRATES: But of course to come to this realization, first you have to recognize that this is what you have to do.—And it is hard to recognize this just because it too is something that has to show itself.

LATO:—While our instincts tell us otherwise.

12   Conclusion

In this dialogue, our intention has been to explore the situation where the seating of a concept or class of concepts in our lives is inextricably bound up with the exercise of a fundamental aspect of our form of life, namely with our lives as subjects of experience—which we have called our 'subjectivity'. This subjectivity enters into the possession of these concepts not just in the case of the subjective linguistic reactions that are among the primitive components of language-games—for example, where the word 'pain' replaces crying. For it also is observed more broadly in the way that the language-games are an expression of subjective and intersubjective dispositions and attitudes. Hence, these language-games may also be seen as extensions of the pre-linguistic forms of these dispositions and attitudes. Our understanding of psychological concepts partakes of the subjective states of which their deployment is an expression, for this understanding is 'of the midst'.

The possession of any concept only obtains where a person can *speak*, and speaking is 'living a life and speaking out of it'. But this is largely a function of our lives as subjects. Hence, we are only speaking if there is at least a dimension of our use of words that is a function of our lives as subjects. This applies equally to what we have to say of psychological concepts in philosophy. For it follows from the fact that philosophy does not view grammar from a transcendental perspective beyond daily discourse, that philosophy's exploration of psychological concepts is itself 'from their midst' and where the *showing* cannot disengage from the subjective components.

We concluded with reflections on some related aspects of the seating of these concepts in our lives, and on the subjective impressions we have of language, which conspire to create difficulties in philosophy. The next dialogue will develop related themes to do with philosophical reflection.

Dialogue 6   Metaphysics, Instinct and Language-games

1   Introduction

CRATES: In the preceding dialogues, Lato, we have told of how intimately the possession of our concepts—and especially of those that are most pervasive of our thinking—is woven into the fabric of our lives. Along the way, and as a part of this, we have also tried to improve our understanding of how this intimacy qualifies philosophical reflection and may be implicated in the characteristic ways that difficulties with these concepts arise in philosophy. In the present dialogue, we shall extend the latter part of this discussion. In particular, we shall try to show how the genesis of these difficulties is not an exception to the nature of discourse but, in its own way, *partakes* of the processes of concept-formation and possession.

An examination of the form that these difficulties take will be helped from the outset by observing another aspect of the distinction between, on the one hand, how we construe the actions that are needed to solve these problems and, on the other, how we construe the responses or reactions that express the perplexity that gave rise to this need in the first place.

LATO: It has been a consistent theme of our dialogues that philosophical problems are conceptual in kind, and that this determines how they are to be solved. But it seems equally clear that a recognition of their conceptual nature does not have to *precede* the original, spontaneous generation of philosophical perplexity. Bafflement, conviction or uncertainty over the nature of mind, or truth, or reality may arise quite independently of any understanding we might have of the nature of such difficulties, still less that it reflects a confusion or uncertainty over the *concepts*, and so requires a specific analysis of how the concepts are embedded in language.

CRATES:—Unless, of course, we are already acquainted with philosophy as a subject and have arrived at a settled view of the nature of its subject matter.

LATO: Quite so.

It is because of this distinction that it is possible for such spontaneously arising convictions or attitudes to have a life of their own quite apart from any understanding of what is actually required to confirm or to settle them.

Let's suppose, for example, that I am looking at the people around me and wondering whether I can know the reality of their minds. In terms of the place that such a reaction has in my *life*, it is not consciously the same reaction as being baffled as to the correct analysis of the grammar of the concept *mind*. Similarly, if I wonder whether I can really know or be certain about anything then, within my immediate perspective, this is not the same as being puzzled by the grammars of the concepts of knowledge or certainty. What I experience in these cases has the form of an uncertainty over some phenomenon in the world or in my relations to the world such as might produce feelings of alienation from my fellows or an uncanny sense of ignorance.

CRATES: And in this—we must quickly add—we are not deviating in any sense from the view that philosophical difficulties are essentially conceptual in nature. We do not falter in our conviction that the individual experiencing the difficulty needs to come to see the conceptual nature of the problem and to master the appropriate methods of analysis before he or she can come to a solution. For what we are adverting to now is how the difficulties enter our *lives*,—the rôle that they occupy in our lives.

Our contention, then, is that philosophical perplexity need not first show its hand in puzzlement over the grammars of the concepts *mind*, *belief* and *knowledge*; rather, we wonder whether we can really know other minds, what our belief in the world is based on or whether we can really know anything. This is the form of our puzzlement in its most natural state; and it has the character of a reaction *by means of* our concepts to the respective *phenomena*.

LATO: Yes. In fact we might refine this thought a little further. For indeed, it is not that we are deluded into thinking we are puzzling over a phenomenon until we realize we are actually puzzling over a concept, as these are in any case the two sides of the same coin—which is the position we urged in the second dialogue. The observation that these primary reactions in philosophy are legitimately directed towards phenomena should be informed by the view that the concepts we have formed of the world, of ourselves, and of our relations to the world, form our understanding of the *nature* of these things *in their most general form*. This is why, when thinking in the most general way about the nature of a thing, our reflections really are reflections upon a *phenomenon* and not just upon the language in which the concept is articulated,—and it also clarifies further what is meant by saying that philosophical perplexity arises *within* our understanding of the world.

CRATES: So we have distinguished between, on the one hand, the pre-occupation with phenomena which characterizes the perplexity that is at the origin of philosophical thinking and, on the other, the overt reflection upon our concepts that is required as a response to this original perplexity; the continuity between these two processes lying in the fact that our reflections upon the grammars of our concepts, while outwardly being reflections on the governance of our concepts, are by the same token reflections on the nature of the phenomena to which the concepts correspond. The second process will engage with these original reactions, but it requires a further step: an immersion in the subject of philosophy and a recognition—or at least, the adoption of a *view*—of the nature of the difficulties encountered.

But let us now focus on these original reactions and explore further their status in our lives.

2   The instinct for metaphysics and metaphysical concepts

LATO: It might be of interest to start this discussion in a somewhat con-trary way by examining a very striking remark by Wittgenstein on the way that instinct drives philosophical thinking generally, both in respect of the origin of the difficulties but also in respect of what is required in response to them:

> /People are deeply embedded in philosophical, i.e., grammatical confusions. And to free them from these *presupposes* pulling them out of the immensely manifold connections they are caught up in. One must so to speak regroup their entire language.—But this language came about //developed// as it did because people had—and have—the inclination to think in this way. Therefore pulling them out only works with those who live in an instinctive rebellion against //dissat-isfaction *with*// language. Not with those who following all of their instincts live within the herd that has created this language as its *proper* expression/ (BT, p. 185)

Unless we experience this deep discomfort with our language and its forms, and a natural suspicion of where it would lead us, we are not going to be in a position to resist those other instincts that drive our grammatical confusions. The arduous intellectual activity that is required to work through these difficulties may well depend on other instinctive reactions going *against* those that are at the origin of the difficulties.

Indeed, on another occasion, Wittgenstein said that '[w]hen you are philosophizing you have to descend into primeval chaos and feel at home there'.[1] I think this must express the same thought. When we do philosophy, we descend into the nightmare of language; but we must keep our nerve and not be driven—like the herd—by its temptations. This can only be served by another instinct,—the instinct *'against* language'.

CRATES: It is also an interesting remark, Lato, because it contains a suggestion that is diametrically opposed to the view most frequently attributed to Wittgenstein, namely that it is just an unfortunate accident that our language is laced with irresistible false analogies and pictures— the 'mythology' embedded in the *surface* of language. On the contrary, we may not be such passive recipients of these myths; for we might just as well suppose that the forms of our language are the *product* of these deep-seated inclinations to think in certain ways and that the false analogies lying on the surface may only crystallize and perpetuate these tendencies. This is an important possibility; not the least of its merits being that it helps to account for the extraordinary grip that philosophical perplexity can have on our thinking—a grip that is otherwise difficult to explain.

LATO: Crates, there are no doubt many circumstances arising in connection with the way that concepts are seated in our lives that may explain, or help to explain, how specific philosophical perplexities take root. We have described many of these in the course of our discussions, especially towards the end of the previous dialogue, and it is not our intention to work our way through every possible combination. Suffice it to say that in most cases these are of the deep-seated kind, and so may belong with the instincts that 'live within the herd', as Wittgenstein put it. And yet, however we may account for these urges or wish to explain them, the fact remains that a great effort of will is required if we are to pull ourselves out of 'the immensely manifold connections [we] are caught up in' and recover to consciousness the instincts and the understanding that drive the proper employment of our concepts. Wittgenstein remarked:

....the very things that are most obvious can become the most difficult to understand. What has to be overcome is not a difficulty of the intellect, but of the will. (BT, p. 161)

This is the effort of will that is required to overcome our instinctive philosophical doubts and movements,—the courage to *see* what grammar *shows*. And it informs us also of the strength of these instincts. This is why it is of such interest to us that for Wittgenstein the concept of instinct played such a vital part in understanding both the general nature of language and the generation of philosophical difficulties. In so doing he forged a link between these two topics and invited comparisons. He once remarked, regarding the latter:

> We must not forget: even our more refined, more philosophical, scruples have a foundation in instinct. E.g. the 'We can never know ...' Remaining receptive to further arguments. People who couldn't be taught this would strike us as mentally inferior. *Still* incapable of forming a certain concept. (CV, p. 83e)

And again:

> I really want to say that scruples in thinking begin with (have their roots in) instinct. Or again: a language-game does not have its origin in *consideration*. Consideration is part of a language-game.
>   And that is why a concept is in its element within the language-game. (Z 391)

In a related context, he evidently also found a kinship between the origin of philosophical perplexity and the generation of the instinctive responses that are at the bottom of superstitious practices and beliefs—which is the one we shall now pursue. One could examine the evidence for this claim in detail, but for our purposes it should suffice to point out that he used the very same phrase—which you have just adverted to—on two separate occasions to comment on how both our magical and our metaphysical inclinations are rooted in us:

> An entire mythology is stored within our language. (RFGB, p. 133)[2]

The relationship between these two inclinations, their possible common origin and their operation within the foundations of philosophy, was explored by another of his later commentators, H. O. Mounce,[3] who observed that certain kinds of superstitious belief have their origins not in some faulty or mistaken reasoning but in certain *reactions*. These reactions are in themselves neither rational nor irrational,[4] but they may, if unchecked, develop into irrational beliefs. As an example, he cited the kind of disturbance we might feel at the loss of a wedding ring and how such a reaction might lead to the belief that the marriage is in jeopardy. In a similar vein, he described the revulsion we might experience at sticking a pin into the eye in a picture of our mother. This might produce the irrational belief that her sight will be affected.[5] The important feature here, for our present purposes at least, is that disturbance and revulsion are *primitive* reactions; they occur to us irresistibly and are not the *product* of reasoning—faulty or otherwise.[6] Indeed the attempt to appeal to reason to explain them away would constitute a failure to see the reactions for what they are. This is why the campaign of philosophers and anthropologists to dismiss these primitive responses as just stupid mistakes are misunderstandings of them and of how they are situated in our lives.

Mounce then compared such reactions—and the irrational beliefs that they can give rise to—with the genesis of philosophical problems. He found similarly that we can differentiate between the reactions that are often at the bottom of philosophical puzzlement and the genuinely confused metaphysical beliefs that they can generate.

The principle of this distinction may also be observed in the way we distinguish in philosophy between *what we are tempted to say* and what our critical faculties tell us is intelligible; the salient point here being that we may continue to feel the temptation to speak in a certain way *in spite of* our recognition that giving in to it would lead us into irrationality.

CRATES: You quoted earlier a typical example of such a temptation, namely the feeling that '[w]e can never know … [what another person is feeling, for example]'. Unchecked, the reaction will develop into scepticism about other minds. Could you perhaps develop this distinction between temptation and belief with an example more of this type?

LATO: Yes, indeed. Mounce also cited another example relating to the nature of mind, and which bridges the realms of the superstitious and the metaphysical, namely the belief that 'there are certain men who can see into other men's minds'.[7] This is a common enough belief among so-called 'primitive' peoples,—but it also has its analogue in 'civilized' society. For example, we may imagine a man who, noticing that someone about whom he had just been thinking is looking at him, feels instinctively that the man 'knows what [he] is thinking' and 'can see into [his] mind'.[8] In all these instances, and in many more besides, the pattern is repeated: an instinctive reaction—innocuous enough in itself—arises in a particular setting; it then leads *as a matter of course*—because there is as yet no critical intervention to stop it—to conceptually confused beliefs as soon as we enter a more philosophical train of thought.

So this is an example of how philosophical confusion might be initiated. We might also register the fact that, whereas it may be some particular circumstance or train of events that provokes or encourages a given superstitious or metaphysical reaction, it is also quite possible for such reactions to arise for no special reason, in which case there may be no further explanation. The reactions may be just a quirk of our psychology.

CRATES: Lato, we want to raise an issue here which may seem, at first sight, to go off on a tangent, but which we think is suggested by the comparison with superstitious beliefs. The transition from an instinctive reaction to a fully fledged language-game with its own system of concepts is typical of the growth and development of language—as we have discussed at length previously.[9] In the present discussion, we have described how a suite of instinctive reactions may give rise to the formation of ideas—and even form a *system* of ideas—which, we accept, are confused and indeed incoherent. We have seen this in the case of superstitious ideas and have suggested that it might also occur with more typical metaphysical ideas. Now this process certainly resembles normal concept-formation in some important respects, even though it parasitizes otherwise well-founded language-games and takes them off in a wrong direction. So we want to take this a step further and suggest that it might be fruitful to think of the development of a metaphysical belief as itself the formation of a *language-game*.

LATO: The alignment of the origins of philosophical perplexity with superstitious reactions has been helpful in conveying the deeply rooted nature of that perplexity and that it is not merely the result of intellectual error,—it is not a *foolish* 'entanglement in our own rules'.[10] One way of responding to the question '*How* deeply rooted?' will be to remind ourselves that philosophical talk arises *naturally* out of our lives; it is a response to our world. It has been an abiding theme of our discussions, Crates, that among the determinants of a language-game—and so of the formation of the concepts within the language-game—are the instinctive reactions (linguistic and non-linguistic) that are its cornerstones. So there may indeed be profit in conceiving of the instinctive reactions that are at the bottom of philosophical perplexity as if they were themselves determinants of a language-game,—what we might call the 'metaphysical language-game'.[11]

CRATES: We are very aware that in putting forward such a notion we are moving into dangerous territory. After all, it is axiomatic to the thrust of Wittgenstein's philosophy that 'metaphysics' refers to that species of conceptual confusion that philosophy aims to unravel and expose. And so, to speak of a 'metaphysical language-game' might seem a nonsense from the start.—Isn't this precisely what we would want to say is *not* a genuine language-game?

LATO: Yes, from one point of view what you say is absolutely correct. But we must remember that our concern here is with *how* these reactions form a part of human life,—with the *status* they have on our lives. This is of interest in its own right; but it is also essential to an understanding of their corrosive effect upon our understanding of our nature, the world and the nature of our relations to it. To this end, conceiving of these reactions as constitutive of a language-game may help us to see how the reactions insinuate themselves into our lives. To be sure, the reactions in question do represent a tendency towards the abuse of the concepts; but it does not follow from this that a comparison with concept-formation may not be fruitful from some other point of view. This is the context in which we will find it profitable to speak of a 'metaphysical language-game'. And it lies quite naturally with the idea that philosophy forms its own *ideas*, whether we think of these as ultimately confused or not.

A philosophically confused conception is perhaps most often thought of as a conception that has been arrived at by making wrong moves within an *analysis*. If so, the confusion is probably best regarded just as a problem within an existing language-game, rather than as being comparable with the establishment of a new one. But the principle we wish to establish here is that the deeper confusions in philosophy originate at a level that is *prior* to analysis, indeed at the level at which our other most fundamental concepts emerge. In other words, they arise in the establishment of a *practice* rather than in the description of a rule or in giving a definition. The sense of logical compulsion we experience with these reactions surely belongs with the compulsion of an established linguistic rule, rather than with the persuasiveness of an analysis. It is this that confers genuine properties of a language-game upon the talk that emerges from these primitive philosophical reactions.

CRATES: And it is—as you suggest—a commonplace to speak of philosophically confused *conceptions*; so it should hardly be regarded as exceptional to speak of philosophy as generating specifically metaphysical concepts. But how useful is this for our purposes?

LATO: Let's return for a moment to some of the essential features of what—following Wittgenstein—we have referred to in previous dialogues as 'secondary' uses of words, which I think will shed light on this matter.[12] This is where a concept is formed by means of a primitive linguistic reaction that parasitizes a previously established word use, whence it may become an important component in the determination of a subjective concept—the use of 'dull' in 'a dull pain', for example. Now, notwithstanding the fact that here too we may be *inclined* to say that the secondary use is a kind of abuse of the primary use, there remains an important difference between this and the reactions that are of interest in philosophy, inasmuch as the language-game that is subsequently erected upon the secondary use does not come into conflict with the primary use. This is because the secondary use occurs in a *new* context, while in philosophy difficulties arise precisely because the new conception—of 'truth' or 'knowledge' or whatever it may be—is returned to its original context, where it tries to occupy the same logical space as the established concept. This is characteristic of the major conflicts in philosophy. On the other hand, I see no essential difference *qua* reaction between secondary uses of words and the instinctive employments that can lie at the bottom of philosophical confusions. This is why I think we'll find this comparison fruitful.

CRATES: And yet, Lato, I think there may still be a question as to whether it is just accidental that some secondary word uses are innocuous while others are destined to compete with established primary uses, or whether there is some more essential difference between the two. For where there *is* competition with the primary use, the reaction is occurring in a context where we are *already* thinking about philosophical questions and ready to usurp an incumbent concept from its logical space. So, does this not mark a difference in kind from the start?

LATO: I don't disagree that in such cases the philosophical stage may already have been set—at the very least we are already likely to be worrying about the status of some concept. But remember that we have only just now distinguished between the spontaneous reactions that might arise apropos of nothing in particular and those that might be at least partly explained by their circumstances. The former might be more akin to the classic secondary uses with which we started this discussion, while the latter are more likely to be restricted to philosophy; and yet I see no reason why both might not occur in philosophy, nor that this need mark some *essential* underlying difference in kind between the two reactions in the way they function in our lives. Remember that either way our interest here is in the reactions that are at the *origins* of philosophical perplexity, rather than in those that arise out of developed philosophical thinking. The important feature that they share in common—their spontaneity—remains. This is their irreducibility.

The connection between the secondary uses that occur outside philosophy and the reactions that occur within it can perhaps be made clearer by considering an example which—depending on context— might count either as a secondary use of language or as the beginnings of a conceptual confusion. While working on his private language argument, Wittgenstein considered the spontaneous statement 'I know how the colour green looks to *me*.'[13] This is the kind of remark that might be uttered in the course of a philosophical argument by someone wishing to defend private ostensive definition. But I see no reason why it might not also be uttered outside the context of philosophical discussion, where the phrase may be used to express a particular 'sensation' of privacy—as we might call it.

Another example is the 'experience of meaning' that we discussed in the previous dialogue. Here we have an experience that we believe has been widely responsible for spreading confusion in philosophy but which in a non-philosophical context may be just another expression of this sensation of privacy. Indeed, far from being harmful, it may play an important part in the inward appreciation of meaning in poetry or music, for example.—We have an immediate sense of looking into the meaning of a thing. We assumed previously that it arose out of a misinterpretation of the 'experience as meaningful', but there is no reason in principle why it might not be a primitive experience in its own right.

And if one objects that sense cannot be made of such a conception of privacy, then of course the same might be said of any secondary use of language, such as '[f]or me the vowel *e* is yellow'.[14] A vowel can't be yellow! For it is of the essence of the secondary use of words that they do not 'make sense'—at least, not if that means being able to *derive* their secondary employment from their primary use. Either way, the facts remain, first, that we have the irresistible inclination to use these expressions in these ways and, second, that these uses are not the *product* of reasoning. Moreover, this inclination is *shared* among people. These are the very conditions that we find at the origin of a language-game. And it is sufficient to establish a legitimate language-game—to determine an intelligible *concept*—just as long as it is not treated as a *logical* extension of a primary use, and is not brought into conflict with its primary use. In this way it forms its own grammar.

CRATES: Can you clarify this, Lato? When you say that the reactions are *shared* and that this is one of the conditions of forming a language-game, can you say some more about how this works. Take, for example, the case of secondary uses of colour words as applied to the description of sounds. I ask because although there is clearly a shared reaction, I think it is not quite clear yet how a concept is established.

LATO: The first point I would make is simply that inasmuch as the reaction is shared—in the sense of being held in common, or at least in principle—then there is the possibility of a shared understanding. I think it would be quite natural to say that I *understand* what someone means when he says 'for me the vowel *e* is yellow', just because I react in the same way. But I know what you are driving at, for once the statement is made there are no obvious consequences; the reaction has no obvious further application, which we would also say is essential to the establishment of a concept. My answer to that would be that the strength of the application will apply differently in different cases. It may well be that the example of colours and vowel sounds is a weak one in this respect—though I don't think it would be that difficult to imagine, for example, a culture that attached importance on this reaction in its art. But we can easily find clearer examples. We have already referred to the use of 'dull' in a 'dull pain', which can have an application in diagnosing illness or injury. And in the field of the arts, we might consider the way we describe musical harmonies and harmonic progressions in emotional terms or as 'leading to a close', and so on. So there are plenty of ways in which secondary uses can have applications and which justify speaking of these reactions as determining concepts. Do you not agree?

CRATES: Indeed I do. I accept that this illustrates how these classic secondary uses can determine a concept; but I think we are still to establish conclusively how this might also be said of the reactions that arise within philosophy.

LATO: Wittgenstein noted for himself the potentially equivocal character of this class of reactions—as between harmless secondary use and metaphysical use—when he spoke a little later of our inclination, when reflecting on our perceptions in a particular way, to speak of '[t]he visual room':

> The 'visual room' seemed like a discovery, but what its discoverer really found was a new way of speaking, a new comparison; it might even be called a new sensation. (PI 400)

When the visual room seems like a discovery, it gives rise to a conception that is at the bottom of philosophical idealism and other subjectivist theories of perception. Left undeveloped, it is just a harmless sensation. But in both cases, we may say that a *concept* is determined.

Wittgenstein described the compelling and primitive nature of the subjective impressions that distort our perception of the layout of our concepts; and he described the kinship between these impressions and secondary uses of language,—or at least, the secondary 'experiences' which they express:

> Think here of a special kind of illusion which throws light on these matters.—I go for a walk in the environs of a city with a friend. As we talk, it comes out that I am imagining the city to lie on our right. Not only do I have *no* conscious reason for this idea, but some quite simple consideration was enough to make me realize that the city lies behind us. I can first give no answer to the question *why* I imagined the city in *this direction*. I had *no reason* to think it. But though I see no *reason* still I seem to see or surmise certain psychological causes for it. In particular, certain associations and memories. For example, we are walking along a canal, and once before I had followed a canal which lay in the direction I had imagined. I might as it were psycho-analytically investigate the causes of my conviction. (LW1 787)

> But how is a person who feels that the city is located in this direction to express his experience correctly? Is it correct, for example, to say that he feels it? Should he really coin a new word for it? But then how could anyone learn this word? The *primitive* expression of the experience couldn't include it. He would probably be inclined to say 'I feel as if I knew that the city lay over there'. Well, the very fact that he says this, or something like it, in these circumstances is itself the expression of this singular experience. (LW1 789)

> 'I feel as if I knew the city lay over there.'—'I feel as if the name Schubert fitted Schubert's works and his face.' (LW1 791)

It is important to observe here that the compulsion to speak in these ways does not arise only in connection with the use of individual expressions in specific situations. The use of the expression 'the visual room' is not isolated from the way we use other expressions and say other things—otherwise, it *would* amount to little more than a nervous tic or passing fancy. On the contrary, the use of the expression forms part of a whole network of related trains of thought.—This is a hallmark of a *concept*.

CRATES: Yes, Lato, it is the hallmark of a concept. But many will still feel reticent of calling the generation of these responses *concept-formation*, for the question will be raised again as to whether or not this new 'concept' is *applied*. Unlike the other cases we have just discussed, it does not appear to find its way into the way we engage with the world about us or into normal conversation.

LATO: Well, even if the new concept were confined to the realms of the imagination, this should not necessarily undermine its status as a concept; for this rôle too is a 'use', even if an incoherent one; just as a painting with false perspective still compels us and functions in many ways as a picture even if it cannot be interpreted or applied coherently to reality.

Remember that there are many uses of language that are not 'applied', if we mean by this something strictly pragmatic or as possessing utility in a coarse sense. Think, for example, of the rôle of stories and story-telling in our lives; these may be full of fantasy and absurdity. When someone tells a grammatical joke, we laugh; we don't just look bemused. Even that which we recognize as incoherent may nevertheless be given the *status* of a concept.—This is the position it occupies in our lives. We are not dealing here, as I have said, with isolated reactions, but with reactions linked together in our thoughts in all sorts of ways.

But in any case, we should not assume too hastily that these tendencies do *not* find expression in our outward lives. It is beyond the scope of our book to address this question; but we might reflect, for example, upon the influence that this notion of mental privacy has had upon the genesis of the idea of the soul as having an identity independent of the body—an idea that has had ramifications throughout human history!

3   Conclusion

LATO: Crates, throughout our dialogues we have been trying to steer away from the view that philosophy is concerned with superficial aspects of the grammar of our concepts and, in parallel with this, from the view that the problems are prompted just by outward features of our language and its use. We do not deny that both these influences play a part; however, we have, along the way, been trying to show how the mythology that is stored in the language is more deeply rooted, having to do with the very intimacy of the way that language and its concepts are possessed. In the present dialogue, we have tried to illustrate something more of the way that the responses that are at the bottom of philosophical perplexity are themselves seated in our lives. We have done this by making connections with two other kinds of reactions that also surely emanate from deep down in our natures: superstitious thoughts and secondary uses of language. These show how the metaphysical reactions may be regarded as forming language-games in their own right—language-games of *mis*-understanding, we might say.

Dialogue 7 Epilogue

LATO: We announced ourselves at the outset of this book by distinguishing the continuities in outline from the contrasts in content as between our earlier and Wittgenstein's later philosophies. What we shared in outline was a preoccupation with the nature of concepts, with the ways in which we possess them and with their relations to the world. We also shared with him the view that the aim of philosophy is to reflect upon our concepts and to remove, or at least to see through, the effects of contamination upon them. Thus we arrive at a clear view of the nature of things.

Divergences in content, on the other hand, arose from our diametrically opposing views of the status of concepts. Our earlier philosophy comprised an extreme version of rationalist thinking, in which concepts— existing prior to experience—were reified into independent intellectual objects or Forms, as we called them. It was rare to find anything quite as extreme as this in the intervening period, during which time concepts or ideas were treated in various ways. But most theorists construed them as private mental objects of one kind or another. The empiricists, for example, regarded them as mental processes derived directly *from* experience; while other less extreme rationalists thought of them as being brought *to* experience—though pulling back from attributing to them our kind of complete independence. The radical aspect of Wittgenstein's view of concepts, on the other hand, is that it understands them as a facet of the *whole* of life, so that all the components of the human form of life must be seen together for a proper understanding of them.—The concepts of action, language, concept, experience, perception, thought, and person are all *internally* related to one another in one degree or another. Language, of course, is central to this complex; hence a philosophical understanding of the nature of language remains the principal entry into seeing how our concepts are possessed. Language is, more-over, the point of formation and articulation of concepts; hence their elucidation is also referred to as a *grammatical* investigation.

A key to this understanding is to get into proper view the *participatory* nature of our relation to language. For we do not participate in it just in the way we participate in any skilful activity—to which our relations remain essentially external, and where we may distinguish between what we do and our understanding or knowledge of what we do. In the case of language, our understanding is *through* the doing and the doing lies 'at the bottom' of language. Moreover, this understanding is central to our lives as persons—to our lives both as actors and subjects. This is why it is important to emphasize *speaking*, which is to say that it emanates *from* our lives and is a manifestation of our lives as persons.

CRATES: This brings us to the constitutive function of concept-formation. For the possession of a concept is not merely the acquisition of an *understanding* of things, because, in the case of the many concepts that are of the nature of our selves as persons, their exercise is also con-stitutive of the phenomena into which their use is woven. Our prime example was the use of language to express intention, which extends the *phenomenon* of intention. The acquisition of such concepts is an extension of our selves as persons—and hence also of our consciousness.

LATO: Indeed.

We also discussed at length the bearing of these observations on our methods of reflection upon language and concepts in philosophy. Our understanding of language is 'of the midst', as we have put it. And when we reflect on our most fundamental concepts—which are without grounds or justification—our reflections must take these concepts for granted. There is no further court of appeal; there is no privileged con-ceptual vantage point from which to describe these concepts and their grammar. It is true that there are many concepts that *are* founded on observation or reference to fact rather than on practice. In these cases, we *do* have an external conceptual vantage point. But this mode of concept possession does not lie at the bottom of our language-games considered as a whole. Hence, our deepest philosophical reflections are always circu-lar in nature; and the understanding they impart is of something 'shown' not 'said'. The elucidations show the internal relations between con-cepts; and they do so by *eliciting* these relations. Moreover, the objective is complete *conceptual* clarity not theoretical completeness.[1]

So the participatory nature of concept possession is central both to the constitution of the human form of life and to the form of our reflection upon the nature of that constitution. The obstacles to this reflection—which are many—also stem from the very intimacy of this possession.

CRATES: Lato, we have summarized here what we have found both radical and of the greatest interest to us in Wittgenstein's philosophy. It is a philosophy that has forced an end not just to our own metaphysical prejudices and indulgences but to a whole tradition of opposing theories. At the same time, we hear across the centuries both a continuity of purpose and a shared feeling for the great obstacles to achieving that purpose.

Philosophy is, in one way or another, always about those principles that are at the foundations of our ways of thinking and conceiving. Hence, the situations that may elicit an interest in philosophy will reach into every aspect of life. The scientist who calls for greater clarity in his understanding of the nature of scientific explanation, or the politician pondering concepts of freedom and justice, or the theologian struggling with the nature of transcendence are all labouring with philosophical questions and have their own reasons for paying critical attention to the fundamental aspects of our system of concepts. For them, the purpose of philosophy will be to help them move forward in their principal preoccupations with a more lucid appreciation of the underlying principles of their subject. All of this is warranted as a contribution to human knowledge and understanding. But we agree in remaining steadfast to our own conception of philosophy as the purification of the soul and agree that this is not frustrated by Wittgenstein's insights into the nature of our conceptual form of our life. We are happy to admit that our idealized conception of the Forms was itself the product of these prejudices and a hindrance to self-knowledge and, moreover, that Wittgenstein's elucidatory and non-theoretical view of philosophy is indeed the better fitted to our own purpose. For a clear insight into our nature from the midst of the concepts that are both *of* and *constitutive of* our natures—which is at the same time an insight from the midst of our selves—is surely what we seek, not a knowledge set apart from this self-engagement.

And yet there is also a less optimistic message that I receive from your meetings with Wittgenstein. Our discussions of the difficulties in reflecting on these fundamental concepts, and of the great forces that exist in us to falsify their content, show that human kind continues to live in a profound state of misconception of its nature and its place in the world. For what now follows from the intimacy of our possession of our concepts is that this is a confusion *at the heart* of our selves, of our relations to each other and of our relations to the world.

Notes

Dialogue 1   Synopsis

1. Whitehead (1929), p. 63: 'The safest general characterization of the European philosophical tradition is that it consists of a series of footnotes to Plato. I do not mean the systematic scheme of thought which scholars have doubtfully extracted from his writings. I allude to the wealth of general ideas scattered through them.'
2. Nietzsche (1962), p. 32: 'Thus all of them together form what Schopenhauer in contrast to the republic of scholars has called the republic of creative minds: each giant calling to his brother through the desolate intervals of time. And undisturbed by the wanton noises of dwarfs that creep past beneath them, their high spirit-converse continues.'
3. Nietzsche (1968), p. 33.
4. Ibid., p. 34.
5. Nietzsche (1973), p. 96.
6. Ibid., p. 17.
7. Nietzsche (1968), p. 34.
8. Plato (1969), pp. 99–183. The references to the Theory of Forms, Recollection and the purification of the soul are based on Plato's account in *Phaedo*.
9. Waterfield (1987). See this essay also for an exposition of the view that Plato's adherence to his Theory of Forms ended with the *Parmenides* and for a criticism of Cornford's view of the continuity in Plato's conception of Forms (see below).
10. Cornford (1960), p. 4.
11. See also Plato (1996) and Whitaker's introduction (1996). Whitaker takes the view, I believe, that the fate of the Theory of Forms in Plato's philosophy, following Parmenides' devastating criticisms, is somewhat more equivocal than Waterfield (1987) is prepared to allow.
12. That is, not by mere sense experience.
13. TLP 6.54.
14. Rhees (1998), Chapter 1: 'Plato and the growth of understanding'.
15. The phrase 'logical significance of facts' is borrowed from Hertzberg (1992), where he employs it—I believe—in the course of making a similar point.

16. See, for example, Plato (1987), 146a–8d.
17. See TLP.
18. PI 373: 'Grammar tells us what kind of object anything is.'
19. Hacker (1972); Baker and Hacker (1985).
20. See, for example, Rhees (1998).
21. PI 1 ff.
22. Rhees (1970c), p. 82.
23. Ibid., p. 81.
24. Ibid., p. 83.
25. That is, PI and the later philosophy versus TLP.
26. I will use the phrase 'psychological concept' to refer to all concepts to do with mental life. This is consistent with Wittgenstein's use.
27. PI 23.
28. Ibid.
29. Cf. ibid. 7.
30. See especially PI 243–486.
31. See, for example, Winch (1993) for a discussion of Wittgenstein's views on how words refer to sensations.
32. PI 219.

Dialogue 2   Facts, Concepts and Philosophy

1. Z 567: 'How could human behaviour be described? Surely only by sketching the actions of a variety of humans, as they are all mixed up together. What determines our judgement, our concepts and reactions, is not what *one* man is doing *now*, an individual action, but **the whole hurly-burly of** human actions, the background against which we see any action.' (my emphasis)
2. PI, p. 195.
3. Ibid. 7.
4. Ibid. 123; see also BT, p. 179: 'Learning philosophy is really recollecting. We remember that we really use words in this way.'
5. PI 1 ff.
6. Ibid. 82.
7. See, for example, Plato (1987), 146a–8d.
8. ROC 119 and 120.
9. OC 501.
10. By 'global scepticism' I mean trying to doubt the nature of reality as such and in general.
11. For example, OC 612.
12. PI 217.
13. OC 559.
14. PI 217.
15. Cf. OC 139.
16. Ibid. 501.
17. Rhees (1998); see also Rhees (1970a) and (1970c).
18. Cf. PI 16.
19. Emmett (1990), pp. 213–31.

20. In particular she had in mind Bernard Williams (1981), Jonathan Lear (1982 and 1986) and Lynne Rudder-Baker (1984). Whereas I do not defend Emmett on this point, elsewhere I shall criticize the transcendentalist approach.
21. Emmett (1990), p. 215.
22. Ibid., p. 225.
23. This point will be developed at length in the dialogues that follow.
24. We shall be examining this in more detail in Dialogue 5.
25. Wolgast (1987), p. 151.
26. Cf. PI 120.
27. See, for example, OC 450 and 625 and CE, p. 383.
28. This may be said without having to deny that the limit of doubt is not fixed.
29. OC 56.
30. Phillips (1999), p. 53.
31. Cf. PI, p. 195.
32. See Dialogue 3 for an account of the concept *speaking* as it is used here.
33. CV, p. 51e: 'It will be hard to follow my portrayal: for it says something new, but still has egg-shells of the old material sticking to it.'
34. PI 217.
35. The limitations of thinking of the employment of a concept as the application of a rule will be discussed at length in Dialogue 3; the important point here is that the application of a rule is at least an *aspect* of the employment of a concept—and it is an *essential* aspect.
36. Hacker (1972), pp. 156–66; Baker and Hacker (1985).
37. Hacker (1972), pp. 160 and 163.
38. Baker and Hacker (1985), p. 333.
39. Ibid., p. 332.
40. Ibid., p. 330; Hacker (1972), p. 166.
41. Baker and Hacker (1985), p. 333.
42. Hacker (1972), p. 165.
43. Ibid., p. 164.
44. Baker and Hacker (1985), p. 333.
45. Hacker (1972), p. 165.
46. Ibid., p. 165.
47. Baker and Hacker (1985), p. 336.
48. PI, p. 195.
49. Baker and Hacker (1985), p. 336.
50. PI 16. It may be argued that often there are no or very often no such discrete reactions to samples in the formation or learning of a concept. This is not the point. Even if the use of samples is *implicit*, it remains an aspect of the use of language.
51. See RFM, p. 200.
52. See TLP.

Dialogue 3   Concepts, Speaking and Persons

1. Rhees (1970c), p. 74, and (1969a), p. 135.
2. Gaita (1991), pp. 101–15.
3. PI 2 ff.

4. CV, p. 51e.
5. Rhees (1970c), p. 82.
6. PI 1 ff.
7. Rhees (1970c), pp. 76–7.
8. Ibid., p. 77.
9. Ibid., p. 81.
10. Ibid., p. 77.
11. Gaita (1991), p. 103 ff.
12. Ibid., p. 103.
13. Ibid.
14. Rhees (1970c), p. 79.
15. Ibid., pp. 79 and 82.
16. Rhees (1969b), 'Preface' to BB, pp. v–xiv.
17. Rhees (1970b), p. 67.
18. Malcolm (1989), pp. 35–44.
19. Rhees (1970c), p. 83.
20. PI, p. 152.
21. Rhees (1970c), p. 80.
22. Ibid.
23. Gaita (1991), pp. 110–11. My emphasis.
24. Rhees (1969b).
25. BB, the *The Blue Book*.
26. Ibid., pp. 43–4.
27. Cf. PI 125.
28. BB, p. 17.
29. Ibid., p. 18.
30. Rhees (1969b), p. xi.
31. Rhees (1970c), p. 80.
32. See Dialogue 2 for a discussion of the scope of the concept of grammar in philosophy.
33. See also Rhees (1998), Chapter 13.
34. Rhees (1970c), p. 82.
35. Rhees (1970a), pp. 46 and 49.
36. Cf. PI, p. 162.
37. Rhees (1970c), p. 83.
38. PI 136.
39. Rhees (1970a), pp. 48–9; PI 156–71.
40. Rhees (1970a), p. 49.
41. Rhees (1998), p. 112; PI 125.
42. Rhees (1970c), p. 74.

Dialogue 4   An Instinct for Meaning

1. PI 1.
2. The passage does not contain *only* two points of departure for Wittgenstein. For a point of view on Wittgenstein's the reasons for choosing this passage—with which I am sympathetic—see Walker (1990), pp. 99–109.
3. PI 1, footnote.

4. Ibid. 2–32.
5. Ibid. 7.
6. Ibid. 19 and 20.
7. Ibid. 33.
8. Ibid. 56.
9. Ibid. 143.
10. Ibid. 145.
11. Ibid. 143.
12. Ibid. 146.
13. Ibid. 147.
14. Ibid. 146–9.
15. Ibid. 151.
16. Ibid. 152.
17. Ibid. 154.
18. Ibid. 177.
19. Gaita (1991), pp. 110–11.
20. PI 179.
21. Ibid. 180.
22. Ibid. 184.
23. Ibid. 187.
24. Ibid. 185.
25. Ibid. 188.
26. Ibid. 201.
27. One may argue that the plausibility of Wittgenstein's case here lies in the fact that he imagines his example series as being worked out in complete isolation—it has no companions. If one imagines the working out of the series interacting with the working out of others, or being used in calculations engaging with other assumptions, and so on, then it may seem less easy to present the behaviour of the pupil as being anything other that an aberration. The meaning of the formula +2 also lies in its relations to mathematics as a whole, not just to an isolated exercise. My own view is that whereas this does lead to complexities that Wittgenstein seems not to have anticipated, it does not return us to the position he is attacking—his argument being that we cannot form a general conception of formulae as having determinate sense independent of their working out in practice. Wittgenstein's argument still captures the essence of this—which in all probability was his only purpose.
28. PI 190.
29. Ibid. 202.
30. CE, p. 399.
31. See Dialogue 2, Section 3.
32. At this juncture in the *Philosophical Investigations*, Wittgenstein moves on to expound the so-called 'private language argument' (PI 243 ff.). This is no accident as the argument is an extension of the case against mentalism. Up to this point the argument has been that in essence the concept of following a rule is not the concept of an experience or mental state that accompanies a practice. However, the private language argument is more than just a corollary to this, for it argues that it makes *no sense* to speak of a rule (and hence of a language) as *founded* on subjective judgement. It is therefore a keystone

in the attack on mentalism. I do not intend to rehearse the argument here, though I shall refer to it from time to time and discuss it in more detail in Dialogue 5.

33. RPP1 630, footnote: ' *"Forms of life"* was a variant here. *Trans.*'
34. In LW1 365 the variant is: 'The signs of hope are modes of this complicated pattern of life.'
35. Quoted from unpublished notes here translated by G. P. Baker and P. M. S. Hacker in: Baker and Hacker (1985), p. 242.
36. 'Steady ways of living' here refers to the instinctive regularity that belongs to the notion of rule following as explained previously.
37. Baker and Hacker (1985), pp. 238–43.
38. See, for example, Newton Garver (1994).
39. Goethe, *Faust I*, opening scene in the Studierzimmer.
40. Wolgast (1994), pp. 587–603.
41. Rhees (1997).
42. PI 109.
43. See PI; I say 'apparently' for it is now known that Wittgenstein willed his literary editors to publish his writings 'as they think fit', which means that we are not in a position to dismiss any of his extant remarks see Rhees (1996), pp. 56–7.
44. Wolgast (1994), pp. 588, 601 and 603.
45. CE, p. 368 ff.
46. Ibid., pp. 373.
47. Ibid., pp. 387–9.
48. Wolgast (1994), p. 591.
49. Ibid., pp. 601–2.
50. See PI.
51. Wolgast (1994), p. 591.
52. Ibid., p. 593.
53. PI 244; Wolgast (1994), p. 600.
54. Ibid., p. 592, footnote.
55. Ibid., p. 599.
56. Wolgast does refer to one example that seems to be of this type, namely a suggestion by Cockburn that a baby has fundamentally different reactions to humans than to objects (ibid., p. 595). Her concerns about the apparent ambiguity of a baby's reactions seem to me to stem from her only being willing to consider the narrowest time-slice from the baby's reactions.
57. CE, p. 371.
58. Wittgenstein used the expression 'basic forms'. We might equally adopt Hertzberg's description of them as 'independent reactions' (Hertzberg (1992), p. 30). I shall be discussing his account of primitive reactions in Dialogue 5.
59. Z 541.
60. Wolgast (1994), p. 593.
61. See PI.
62. See Part II of PI.
63. See especially ibid., p. 166; and for a full discussion see Mulhall (1990).
64. Though not only in these notes.
65. The second remark does appear to speak inconsistently inasmuch as 'being sure that someone is in pain' and 'doubting whether he is' do not obviously

qualify as pre-linguistic behaviour, so that when he speaks of the language-game as an *extension* of primitive behaviour, a more consistent sense would have emerged if he had said that the *rest* of the language-game is an extension of primitive *linguistic* behaviour. On the other hand, one may still wish to retain the continuity with the first remark and explain away the inconsistency as merely an unfortunate choice of example. Rhees favours the former interpretation; however in the course of his argument he does not quote 'our language is merely an auxiliary to, and further extension of, this relation', which is precisely that part of Wittgenstein's remark that favours the alternative interpretation. Rhees does not comment at all on Wittgenstein's use of the term *'pre-linguistic'*—the significance of which I shall discuss later in this dialogue. I am less nervous than Rhees in adopting Wittgenstein's terminology here, and likewise with his speaking of language as an *extension* of primitive behaviour, because I do not think that these ways of speaking necessarily imply a *theory* of concept-formation. See Rhees (1997).

66. PI 7.
67. I do not think that a new-born child's progression from incoherent movement to increasingly coherent behaviour could be described as *learning* in the sense in which language is learned.
68. Z 545.
69. Ibid. 541.
70. Rhees (1997); Malcolm (1982), pp. 3–22.
71. Rhees (1997), p. 7.
72. Z 541.
73. Rhees (1997), p. 2.
74. Ibid.
75. See Zettel 651: 'Shrugging of shoulders, head-shakes, nods and so on we call signs first and foremost because they are embedded in the use of our *verbal language*'.
76. Ibid. 541.
77. Ibid.
78. Rhees (1997), pp. 2–3.
79. PI 244.
80. Rhees (1997), p. 2.
81. Z 541.
82. Wolgast (1994), p. 601.
83. Gaita (1991), pp. 110–11. My emphasis.
84. Wolgast may well be right that the spontaneous babbling of infants is as a matter of fact 'one source of language'.—Certainly this is how an adult treats them. This is not a point of contention.
85. CE, p. 397.
86. PI.

Dialogue 5   Concepts of the Subject

1. In philosophy 'experience' is frequently used on its own to mean something more like 'immediate experience' or 'sense perception', even though its use in common parlance is much wider in scope. I will also use it this way, depending on context.

2. PI 243–315.
3. See, for example, Winch (1993), pp. 122–3.
4. Nagel (1974), pp. 435–50.
5. Hanna (1990), pp. 350–6; see also Hanna (1992), pp. 185–90.
6. Mounce (1992), pp. 178–84.
7. See, for example, Hacker (1987).
8. See, for example, Stern (1994), pp. 552–65.
9. Nagel (1974), p. 441.
10. Ibid., p. 436.
11. Ibid., pp. 446–8.
12. Ibid., pp. 449–50.
13. Ibid., p. 442.
14. Cf. PI, p. 152.
15. Note that I do not doubt that in particular instances we do attribute experiences on the basis of evidence; only, this cannot be at the bottom of the exercise of these concepts.
16. Nagel (1974), p. 438.
17. Ibid., p. 441.
18. Ibid., p. 442, footnote.
19. Ibid.
20. Winch extended this same philosophical principle to failures of understanding even *within* our own society. See Winch (1997b), pp. 193–204.
21. See, for example, Winch (1972), pp. 8–49.
22. Nagel does not deny this in principle, and indeed does not have to deny it. See Nagel (1974), p. 443.
23. Mounce (1992), p. 178.
24. Malcolm (1985), pp. 45–66.
25. Ibid., p. 46.
26. Ibid., p. 53.
27. Ibid., p. 54.
28. Hacker (1972), p. 289.
29. Mounce (1992), p. 184.
30. Hacker (1972), p. 251 ff.
31. Cf. Mounce (1992), p. 182.
32. Ibid., p. 184.
33. PI 580.
34. PI 244.
35. Hacker (1972), p. 289.
36. Hertzberg (1992), pp. 24–39.
37. Ibid., pp. 31–32.
38. Ibid., p. 39, endnote 11.
39. Ibid., p. 32.
40. PI, p. 152.
41. Hertzberg (1992), p. 33.
42. Mounce (1992), p. 182.
43. Z 540.
44. See Z 532 ff.
45. It might be worth emphasizing here that normally when we speak of human or animal *behaviour* we are already *not* speaking of merely physical

movement. The concept of behaviour already takes for granted psychological concepts.

46. One may ask what makes the difference between the moral *attitude* and
moral *judgements*. I think this is shown in the fact that the attitude is manifested in ways of thinking, feeling and acting that are woven together and
pervade our lives. This differs from a mere system of judgements. The point,
then, is that these ways of thinking, feeling and acting are expressed
through moral concepts that are not reducible to concepts of any natural
phenomenon.
47. PI, p. 184.
48. Ibid.
49. One might wish to argue that the uncertainty of our behaviour towards the
fly is itself the product of philosophical uncertainty. But I see no reason to
assume this, and Wittgenstein is surely right that there is such uncertainty
that exists independently of thought.
50. Part II of PI.
51. LW1 791.
52. PI, p.155.
53. See Dialogue 2.
54. The assumption here is that we are dealing with a concept that does not
contain a fact.
55. Z 567.

Dialogue 6   Metaphysics, Instinct and Language-games

1. CV, p. 74e. This is quoted as in the original translation published in the 1980
edition (p. 64). In the revised translation of 1998, the phrase 'primeval
chaos' has been amended to 'the old chaos' (or alternatively 'the former
chaos'). If 'old chaos' does not mean something like 'primeval chaos', then
it is not clear to me what it is supposed to mean. For this reason I prefer to
retain the original translation, which is more vivid and serves my present
purpose better.
2. Cf. BT, p. 199, for a variant translation of the same sentence in German: 'An
entire mythology is laid down in our language'.
3. Mounce (1973), pp. 347–62.
4. Ibid., p. 359. One may wish to question whether or not the reactions themselves are irrational. However the important point is to distinguish between
the primitive reaction, on the one hand, and the belief that may or may not
arise from it, on the other. If I am subject to the spooky feeling that if I am
able to avoid stepping on the cracks between the paving stones then, in
some nebulous way, I will be 'all right', one might say that this is an absurd
and irrational reaction. But I think we would hesitate before saying that in
exhibiting this reaction *I* had fallen into irrationality, unless I took it seri-
ously and allowed it to enter into my beliefs about how I should promote my
well being. A similar example: 'touch wood'. We see the attraction of a
thought that we otherwise recognize could not found a rational belief.
5. Ibid., p. 353.
6. Ibid., p. 355.

7. Ibid., p. 360.
8. Ibid.
9. See especially Dialogue 4.
10. PI 125.
11. I use the word 'metaphysical' here to refer specifically to confused conceptions of the natures of things. Philosophy also has its own legitimate concepts—which we might also call a language-game—that have been forged to facilitate the application of its critical methods, that is, for the elucidation of the grammars of concepts. See also my comments on the use of 'metaphysics' in Dialogue 2.
12. See Dialogue 5 for an earlier discussion of secondary uses of words.
13. PI 278.
14. Ibid., p. 184.

Dialogue 7   Epilogue

1. See PI 133.

References

Baker, G. P. and Hacker, P. M. S. (1985) *Wittgenstein: Rules, Grammar and Necessity*, (Oxford: Blackwell).

Blyth, R. H. (1964) *Zen & Zen Classics, Volume II, History of Zen* (Tokyo: The Hokuseido Press).

Cornford, F. M. (1960) *Plato's Theory of Knowledge* (London: Routledge & Keegan Paul).

Emmett, K. (1990) 'Forms of Life', *Philosophical Investigations*, 13:3, 213–231.

Gaita, R. (1991) 'Language and Conversation: Wittgenstein's Builders', in *Wittgenstein Centenary Essays*, ed. A. Philips Griffiths (Cambridge: Cambridge University Press), pp. 101–115.

Garver, N. (1994) *This Complicated Form of Life* (Chicago and La Salle, Illinois: Open Court).

Hacker, P. M. S. (1972) *Insight and Illusion* (Oxford: Oxford University Press).

—— (1987) *Appearance and Reality* (Oxford: Blackwell).

Hanna, P. (1990) 'Must Thinking Bats be Conscious?', *Philosophical Investigations*, 13:4, 350–6.

—— (1992) 'If You Can't Talk About It, You Can't Talk About It—A response to H O Mounce', *Philosophical Investigations*, 15:2, 185–190.

Hertzberg, L. (1992) 'Primitive Reactions—Logic or Anthropology?', in *The Wittgenstein Legacy, Midwest Studies in Philosophy*, Vol. XVII, eds. P. A. French, T. E. Uehling, and H. K. Wettstein (Notre Dame: University of Notre Dame Press), pp. 24–39.

Lear, J. (1982) 'Leaving the World Alone', *Journal of Philosophy*, 79.

—— (1986) 'Transcendental Anthropology', in *Subject Thought and Context*, eds P. Pettit and J. McDowell, (Oxford: The Clarendon Press).

Malcolm, N. (1982) 'Wittgenstein: The Relation of Language to Instinctive Behaviour', *Philosophical Investigations*, 5:1, 3–22.

—— (1985) 'Consciousness and Causality', in D. M. Armstrong and Norman Malcolm, *Consciousness and Causality* (Oxford: Blackwell), pp. 45–66.

—— (1989) 'Language game (2), in *Wittgenstein: Attention to Particulars*, eds. D. Z. Phillips and P. Winch (New York: St Martin's Press), pp. 35–44.

—— (1993) *Wittgenstein: A Religious Point of View?*, ed. P. Winch (London: Routledge).

Mounce, H. O. (1973) 'Understanding a Primitive Society', *Philosophy*, 48, 347–62.

—— (1992) 'On Nagel and Consciousness', *Philosophical Investigations*, 15:2, 178–184.

Mulhall, S. (1990) *On Being in the World* (London: Routledge).

Nagel, T. (1974) 'What Is It Like to Be a Bat?', *Philosophical Review*, 83, 435–450.

Nietzsche, F. (1962) *Philosophy in the Tragic Age of the Greeks*, trans. M Cowen, (Washington: Regenery Publishing, Inc.).

—— (1968) *Twilight of the Idols* (London: Penguin Classics).

—— (1973) *Beyond Good and Evil* (London: Penguin Classics).

Phillips, D. Z. (1999) *Philosophy's Cool Place* (Ithaca and London: Cornell University Press).

Plato (1969) *Phaedo*, trans. H. Tredennick (London: Penguin Classics).

—— (1987) *Theaetetus*, trans. R. A. K. Waterfield (London: Penguin Classics).

—— (1996) *Parmenides*, trans. & ed. A. K. Whitaker (Newburyport: Focus Philosophical Library).

Rhees, R. (1969a) 'Art and Philosophy', in *Without Answers* (London: Routledge and Kegan Paul), pp. 133–154.

—— (1969b) 'Preface', in L. Wittgenstein, *The Blue and Brown Books* (Oxford: Blackwell) pp. v–xiv.

—— (1969c) 'The Study of Philosophy', in *Without Answers* (London: Routledge and Keegan Paul), pp. 169–172.

—— (1970a) 'The Philosophy of Wittgenstein', in *Discussions of Wittgenstein* (London: Routledge & Keegan Paul), pp. 37–54.

—— (1970b) 'Can there be a Private Language?', in *Discussions of Wittgenstein* (London: Routledge & Keegan Paul), pp. 55–70.

—— (1970c) 'Wittgenstein's Builders', in *Discussions of Wittgenstein* (London: Routledge & Keegan Paul), pp. 71–84.

—— (1984) *Recollections of Wittgenstein*, ed. R. Rhees (Oxford: Oxford University Press).

—— (1996) 'On Editing Wittgenstein', *Philosophical Investigations*, 19:1, 56–57.

—— (1997) 'Language as Emerging from Instinctive Behaviour', *Philosophical Investigations*, 20:1, 1–14.

—— (1998) *Wittgenstein and the Possibility of Discourse*, ed. D. Z. Phillips (Cambridge: Cambridge University Press).

Rudder-Baker, L. (1984) 'On the very Idea of a Form of Life', *Inquiry*, 27.

Stern, D. G. (1994) 'A New Exposition of the "private language argument": Wittgenstein's 'Notes for the "Philosophical Lecture"'', *Philosophical Investigations*, 17:3, 552–565.

Walker, M. U. (1990) 'Augustine's Pretence: Another Reading of Wittgenstein's *Philosophical Investigations* 1', *Philosophical Investigations*, 13:2, 99–109.

Waterfield, R. A. K. (1987) 'Essay', in Plato (1987), pp. 132–246.

Whitaker, A. K. (1996) 'Introduction', in Plato (1996), pp. 1–20.

Whitehead, A. N. (1929) *Process and Reality* (New York: Macmillan).

Williams, B. (1981) 'Wittgenstein and Idealism', in *Moral Luck* (Cambridge: Cambridge University Press).

Winch, P. (1972) 'Understanding a Primitive Society', in *Ethics and Action*, (London: Routledge & Keegan Paul), pp. 8–49.

—— (1993) 'Discussion of Malcolm's Essay', in Malcolm (1993), pp. 95–135.

—— (1997a) 'Norman Malcolm, *Wittgensteinian Themes Essays 1978–1989'*, *Philosophical Investigations*, 20:1, 51–64.

—— (1997b) 'Can We Understand Ourselves?', *Philosophical Investigations*, 20:3, 193–204.

Wolgast, E. (1987) 'Whether Certainty is a Form of Life', *Philosophical Quarterly*, 37: 147, 151–165.

—— (1994) 'Primitive Reactions', *Philosophical Investigations*, 17:4, 587–603.

Index

essence(s) – *continued*
  of a concept/grammar/
      language-game, 33, 115, 117,
      192, 217
  the experience of/perception of, 193–4
  of Forms, 4
  of the world, 80
European, 213
experience(s), 163, 169, 209, 217
  and animals/bats/creatures/robots,
      163–6
  of a cause, 123, 131, 133
  compare, 172
  and concept-formation, 76, 167
  concepts prior to, 3, 209
  of depression, 171
  description of, 114
  of essence/meaning/words as
      meaningful, 191–4, 205
  use of 'experience' in philosophy, 219
  expression of, 154
  form of/organisation of, 167, 194
  go together with/accompany
      language, 133
  knowledge of what it is like, 164,
      167–8
  mental processes, 209
  necessary feature of, 72
  of our selves/the mind, 155–6
  primitive/primitive expression of,
      205, 207
  and reading, 114
  reflect on, 169
  'secondary', 207
  sense, xiii, 3, 56, 213
  subject of/subjective/personal,
      21, 154, 156–8, 161–2, 164–7,
      187, 195
  subjective character of/quality, 154,
      162–4, 167–8, 170–2
  understanding, 4, 171
  visual, 60–2
  see also perception
explanation
  behaviourist, 24
  causal, 61
  of concepts(s)/language/meaning,
      44, 55, 103–4, 106, 111–12,
      117, 131, 149, 174

vs. description, 32
vs. elucidation, 10
of an expectation, 171
follow an, 99
learning by/teaching by, 99, 103
mentalist/mentalistic, 110, 113
metaphysical, 61
in philosophy, 29, 32, 53, 194
of a rule, 116
scientific, 211
theoretical, 80
see also description; theory

facts of living, 118
  see also form(s) of life; pattern
fallow deer, 44–6, 48, 50–2, 57
form(s) of life, xii–xiii, 6, 16–19, 23,
    25, 114, 118–20, 125, 136–7, 140,
    151, 161, 164–5, 176, 182–6, 189,
    191, 195, 209–10, 218
  see also facts of living; pattern
Forms, theory of, xii–xvi, 2–4, 29, 79,
    192–3, 209, 211, 213
foundation(s)/foundational
  of a concept(s), 127, 128
  concepts, 23
  of a form of life, 119
  of language/language-game, 52, 54,
      70, 119, 121, 128, 150, 180
  of philosophy, 200
  of a way of thinking, 211
  see also bedrock; ground; justify
foundationalism/foundationalist, 125,
    127, 135, 150
  anti-foundationalism, 74
  see also bedrock; ground; justify

Gaita, Raimond, 86, 89, 92–3, 114,
    149–50, 215–17, 219
game, 40–4, 55, 63, 95, 98, 101,
    114, 144
  see also language-game; prototype
Garver, Newton, 218
Goethe, 218
grammar, 8–11, 19–20, 30–40, 42,
    44–50, 54–7, 60, 62–3, 67, 71–2,
    74–6, 79–81, 83, 85–6, 90,
    93–102, 104–6, 108, 114, 120,
    122, 146, 150, 153, 155, 159, 161,